THE
FOCUS
PROJECT

The Not So Simple Art of Doing Less

EQUALMAN

THE FOCUS PROJECT by Erik Qualman

Equalman Studios
Cambridge, MA
www.equalman.com

Copyright © 2020 Erik Qualman

Cover design by Anthony Ortiz, Illustrations by Sahiti Rudravajhala

ISBN: 978-0-9911835-7-9 (paperback)
ISBN: 978-0-9911835-8-6 (ebook)

Printed in the United States of America

Whether you're a programmer, mother, executive, teacher, or an entrepreneur,

THIS BOOK IS FOR YOU IF...

1. You feel stretched too thin by trying to do too much.

2. There's no time for relaxation or deep thinking.

3. You're completing thousands of tasks without achieving your goals.

Welcome to The Focus Project, a book designed to provide answers and solutions to the challenge of focusing in an unfocused world. Combining street science and institutional research alongside his own personal focus project, Qualman delivers practical advice on doing the important things instead of a bunch of things.

The following is a guide to pursuing less in order to achieve more—both personally and professionally. We will realize that leading an overly busy life is a choice, but it's not a wise one. Being overscheduled isn't something to be proud of; it's something to avoid at all costs. Instead, we should choose to focus on what matters most.

This choice determines our success, happiness, health, and fulfillment. Successful and happy people understand it's not about getting more things done, it's about getting more of the big things done.

The pages within will help you learn the not so simple art of doing less.

If you're ready to start focusing on your best life, then please continue reading...

For my wife and two daughters.
You are my light.

MY FOOTPRINTS

As a youth with little a plan,
My dad oft-asked,
"What footprints are you going to
  leave in the sand?"

It meant little then,
But with time,
it became a motivating line.

If up to me,
What will be,
My ultimate legacy?

A legacy for me,
It would seem,
A far off, lofty dream.

After all, who am I?
I'm just average,
Somewhat shy.

Then I realized something, you see,
It is up to me,
My ultimate legacy.

My grandchildren and great-grandchildren,
What will they see and think of me?
What is my legacy?

Will they see that I pursued my dreams,
Or that I settled,
For something in-between?

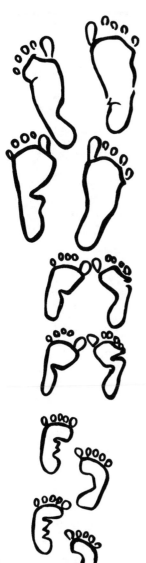

That I lived a life doing what I loved,
Or one filled with,
Should've, could've?

Footprints remain for all time,
So I can't commit,
The ultimate crime.

What is that crime, you say?
It is, of course,
Not seizing the day.

Yes, before I die,
I'd rather fail,
Than not even try.

I will reach for the sky,
Laugh,
And cry.

I'll cry from joy, not sorrow,
Because I lived for today,
And planned for tomorrow.

My legacy,
You see,
Is truly up to me.

That's my view,
But now I ask,
What will **you** do?

Poem by Erik Qualman

TABLE OF CONTENTS

First, Focus

Following my keynote on Digital Leadership at the National Confectioner's Conference, I found myself, as I often do, at the conference cocktail reception. However, this was not your average party. CEOs and business owners in the room had last names such as Mars and Cadbury. They lived in cities called Hershey. Intimidating. I decided my best plan was to grab a martini—shaken with three olives—speak very little, and ask many questions.

Bumping into a family founder whose name lands in every kid's Halloween basket, I asked her to explain the key to her family's sustained success. Her answer, without skipping a beat, was *focus*.

Fascinating. I then asked for her greatest challenge. Her answer? *Staying focused*. Others in the room nodded in agreement. The words seemed to linger in the air: Focus. Staying Focused.

The next day I boarded a flight to India to keynote a Google client event. Everyone there—from the interns to the executives—shared the same response to my question. *Focus* was the answer. This was also true as I visited with Facebook, IBM, Huawei, and Samsung. Trying to focus topped the list of challenges for tech companies. This issue wasn't limited to those in the Silicon Sisterhood. The same held true for school teachers, start-ups, parents, financial institutions, charities, stay-at-home dads, lawyers, health care professionals, consumers, government officials, and entrepreneurs. The same held true for me. I, too, was struggling with focus. That's when it dawned on me. Those who will win today and in the digital decades ahead will be those with the ability to focus in an increasingly unfocused world. Winners will be able to focus while everything around them is constantly changing.

Which begs the question: Can focus be learned? Can it be trained like a muscle? Can focus become a habit? I would devote the next twelve months to finding these answers. I would test, discover, and uncover.

In a sense, I would spend a year ardently pursuing less.

My hypothesis: Pursuing focus at all costs will lead to success and happiness. By sharing both the scientific and street research with you, together, we'll put ourselves on the path to a more fulfilled life—starting today.

Focus = Achievement = Fulfillment = Happiness

Whether you're a programmer, a grandmother, a school teacher, or an entrepreneur, this book is for you if...

- You feel stretched too thin by trying to do too much.
- You're in a constant state of emotional and physical exhaustion.
- You spend less and less time with your loved ones.
- There's no time for relaxation or deep thinking.
- Daily demands are disrupting your organization or company.

- Despite a high level of activity, you feel as if you're on a treadmill going nowhere fast.

- It seems impossible to get ahead of your email, tasks, competition...life.

- You always feel as if you're playing from behind.

- Your life seems to be one insurmountable to-do list.

- You feel extremely busy but also incredibly unproductive.

- You're completing thousands of tasks without achieving your goals.

Welcome to The Focus Project, a twelve-month journey designed to destroy an illness that is sweeping the world. It isn't Black Death, Spanish Flu, SARS, MERS, or a Coronavirus. But, it is a veritable virus.

It drains our energy and attitude. It negatively impacts our health, our work, our well-being, and our families. The illness is sneaky and unsuspecting. Millions suffer from it, yet it is not publicly recognized as a disease by doctors. If left unchecked, it can steal many years, sometimes decades, from one's life. The disease? Our inability to focus on what matters most.

This silent killer is similar to the fable of the frog in the pot. Recall that the frog happily sits in a pot of water, unaware of the slowly rising temperature. The premise is that if the frog is dropped into boiling water, it will immediately sense the danger and jump out. But if the water is at room temperature and slowly brought to a boil, the frog will not perceive the danger until it is too late.

Our goal is to ensure that we don't end up like the frog. Our goal is to leap out of the boiling water—immediately—and never look back.

How many times do we find ourselves thinking: Oh, tomorrow I'll start my exercise program, tomorrow I'll start spending more time with my kids, tomorrow I'll start writing my screenplay, tomorrow I'll start my fashion company, tomorrow I'll start spending less and saving more, tomorrow I'll ask for a raise, tomorrow I'll look for a new job, tomorrow I will finish that report, tomorrow will be better. This, my friends, is the slow boil! We are in danger of wasting our most precious commodity—our individual lives.

Most years, I'm fortunate to do what I love—speak around the world. By meeting and entertaining people from diverse backgrounds and cultures, I've learned that while we're each different in many ways, we share the challenge of focusing daily on what matters most. This daily lack of focus causes us immense frustration when we fail to find what we are seeking in life.

These pages don't offer an overnight cure, but with time, patience, and persistence, significant progress is possible. This book will help to provide answers and solutions to the challenges of:

1. Focusing on what matters most.
2. Focusing in an increasingly unfocused world.
3. Becoming a focus ninja.

I've consolidated these findings and advice into a digest format that allows you, the reader, to select passages as desired. While many will read this book cover to cover, others will enjoy jumping around the pages, skipping entire parts, and easily returning to sections and stories that resonate. Rather than a set of rules, consider this a playbook from which you can choose the plays that work best for you.

If you have seen me perform on stage, you have heard me exhort, *"Be firm in your destination but flexible in your path."* Life and its solutions aren't linear. Purposely, this book isn't linear, either. Instead, it's flexible for you, the individual.

The following is a guide to help lead us on our individual paths of personal development—pursuing less in order to achieve more. Leading an overly busy life is a choice, but it's not a wise one. Being over-scheduled isn't something to be proud of—it's something to avoid at all costs.

Instead, we should choose to focus on what matters most. This choice determines our success, happiness, and fulfillment.

Being Noble

In the late 1800s, a man in Sweden received an invaluable gift courtesy of a *grave* error made by his town's local newspaper. The lucky man was able to do the impossible. He was able to read his obituary while he was still alive.

There were two brothers: Ludwig and Alfred. When the eldest, Ludwig, passed away, the Swedish newspaper erroneously reported that it was the younger Alfred who had died.

Alfred was shocked to read of his own death, his shock turning to horror the more he continued reading, the words describing him and his legacy were terrifying.

At the time, Alfred was a successful entrepreneur. His ingenious invention had made him a very rich man. His invention? Dynamite. Unsurprisingly, the obituary headline read, "Dynamite King Dies." It later went on to call him the "merchant of death."

So dismayed about being tagged the "merchant of death," Alfred immediately set out to ensure that this was not how he would ultimately be remembered. Not wasting time, Alfred drafted his Last Will & Testament. In this four-page document, he donated the majority of his fortune to a very specific and new charitable cause.

When Alfred eventually did pass away, his obituary read differently. By changing his focus for his life before it was too late, Alfred successfully changed his legacy. He made such a positive impact on the world that, while many today may not immediately recognize his greatness, they certainly know of the prizes he established and left behind. One of these prizes, the first Peace Prize, was awarded in 1901 to Henry Dunant, the founder of the Red Cross.

Reading his obituary shocked Alfred into changing his life's focus. As a result, Alfred isn't known today as the "merchant of death," but rather as the man who established the prizes for chemistry, economics, literature, peace, physics, and medicine, all carrying his last name—The Nobel Prizes. Before passing away, Alfred Nobel learned the magical power of focusing on what matters most.

Thinking about our obituary can motivate us to consider how we're spending our 1,440 minutes or 86,400 seconds each day. I challenge you to find a single eulogy that praises someone for being a workaholic who traveled so much for work they never had time for their family, who answered every email in three seconds or was obsessed with their lavish homes.

Alfred Nobel changed his focus, changed his life, and changed his legacy. Don't wait to read your obituary before focusing on what matters most. Will you be missed? Who will miss you? How many people will be at your funeral? How many lives will you have touched deeply?

Greatness is often determined by what one decides not to do.

If you're ready to start focusing on your best life through the art of relentlessly pursuing what matters most—both personally and professionally—then please continue reading, because a life well-lived is one helping others live their lives well.

As you begin the journey of transforming into a focus ninja, I offer this executive summary of the top learnings from my own Focus Project.

For those of you who decide to embark upon your own Focus Project, this image and list should provide helpful resources. Feel free to share insights from your own personal Focus Project on your favorite social media outlet (I'm @equalman across the board) or simply drop me an email at equalman@equalman.com.

My Top Eureka Moments:

1. Focusing today is hard...really hard. But it can be learned. It can become a habit.

2. Systems, processes, and routines trump willpower.

3. Letting something go is sometimes the best way to complete it.

4. A not-to-do list is more important than your to-do list.

5. To attain knowledge add things every day; to obtain wisdom subtract things every day.

6. The difference between successful people and very successful people is very successful people say no to almost everything.

7. If you try to help everyone, you will end up helping no one.

8. Neil Armstrong got it right...small steps lead to giant leaps.

9. WWW: What am I doing right now? Why? What should I be doing?

10. Focus on the important, not the immediate.

11. Not my circus, not my monkeys.

12. Trying to be the best at everything is the surest path to being the best at nothing.

13. Start with simple.

14. Be persistent in the short term and patient in the long term.

15. How we spend our days is how we spend our lives.

99 Notes for a Focused Life:

1. Focus on living your dreams instead of living your fears.

2. Questions are the building blocks of great relationships.

3. "Whether you think you can, or think you can't...you're right." — Henry Ford

4. Hard work...works.

5. Be Flawsome.

6. Unless your name is Atlas, the world doesn't need to rest on your shoulders.

7. Nobody cares if you can't dance well. Just get up and dance.

8. Fail fast, fail forward, fail better.

9. Always keep your words soft and sweet, just in case you have to eat them.

10. Sleeping isn't for wimps. It's for warriors.

11. Spend time with who you love, doing what you love. Life is too short.

12. If what I'm doing doesn't eventually lead to producing smiles, then why am I doing it?

13. Show me your calendar and bank account, and I'll show you your priorities.

14. Despite what others say and despite what you say to yourself, you *are more* than enough.

15. "Everything seems impossible until it is done." — Nelson Mandela

16. The most important things we learn in life are learned in kindergarten.

17. You've got to know when to hold'em, know when to fold'em.

18. With great power comes great responsibility.

19. Serving others is the best medicine.

20. Our children might not listen to what we say, but they always watch what we do.

21. Innovation is simply a series of failures.

22. "When walking, walk. When eating, eat." — Zen Proverb

23. The exact opposite of a known truth is also often true.

24. A life well-lived is one lived on your own terms helping others to get to live on their own terms.

25. The days are long, but the years are short.

26. Being early is a sign of respect for the person you're meeting.

27. The more people you thank, the more you will have to be thankful for.

28. Embrace an attitude of gratitude.

29. Being organized has so many positive benefits.

30. The best things in life aren't things.

31. If you lend someone $100 and never see that person again, it was probably worth it.

32. Losers are overly busy.

33. Planning makes the difference between relaxing and rushing.

34. If it doesn't challenge you, it won't change you.

35. Real change is real hard.

36. Respect capacity, especially your own.

37. It's impossible to be grateful and upset at the same time.

38. If you say yes to everyone, you are saying no to everyone.

39. Giving is the real gift.

40. Less, but better.

41. We are the average of the five people we spend the most time with.

42. Regret in the future weighs tons, while focusing today only weighs ounces.

43. Act like the mirror in *Snow White*...make those around you feel the fairest of them all.

44. Traffic sucks, but being in the accident sucks even more. #perspective

45. Always read stuff that will make you look good if you die in the middle of it.

46. Run your race today, because nobody knows when the finish line will appear.

47. Above all else...balance.

48. We can learn a lot from crayons. Some are sharp, some are pretty, and some are dull. Some have weird names and all are different colors, but they all are able to live in the same box.

49. Failing to plan is planning to fail.

50. The best productivity tool is the word NO.

51. It's funny, but the gift you receive for answering all your email is more email.

52. Success is measured by the quality of people at your funeral.

53. Teachers are underpaid, yet they are the richest among us.

54. I once felt ashamed about my tattered shoes, then I met a man with no feet and I felt even more ashamed.

55. The band Journey got it right...*Don't Stop Believing!*

56. "Find a way." — Diana Nyad

57. Living doesn't cost much, but showing off does.

58. "I didn't have time to write you a short letter, so I wrote you a long one." — Mark Twain

59. Half of life is simply showing up.

60. T-I-M-E is how kids spell L-O-V-E.

61. A truly happy person is one who can enjoy the scenery on a detour.

62. You can never get back on track if you never go off it. Forge a new trail.

63. If you're trying to pull someone else down, that means you feel beneath them.

64. Leap, and the net will appear.

65. Being kind is allowing a person with a stutter to finish his or her own sentences.

66. It's healthy to remember that you will die, *Memento Mori*.

67. Today is a gift. That's why it's called the present. Make sure to unwrap it.

68. "Strive not to be a success, but rather to be of value." — Albert Einstein

69. Defaulting to *no* on the small things will allow you to say *yes* to the big things.

70. If you want to go fast, do it yourself. If you want to go far, do it together.

71. Success is a choice.

72. If you help people get what they want, you will get what you want.

73. Life is a journey, and sometimes it forces you to take a scary road to get to a better destination.

74. "If you can dream it, you can do it." — Walt Disney

75. Leaders know *let's get started* beats *let's get ready*.

76. The best view is always after a tough climb.

77. Accept the fact that some days you're the pigeon and some days you're the statue.

78. Pioneers get pushback. It's a sign you're actually pioneering.

79. Don't take yourself too seriously. Nobody else does.

80. Your brain is like a TV. There are good channels and bad channels; the key is remembering that you have the remote control.

81. Human-Kind...be both.

82. People don't care what you know until they know that you care.

83. Live for your eulogy more than your resume.

84. If it were easy, it would already be done.

85. Is the glass half-full or half-empty? YES. It's 100% full of good things: half oxygen and half water.

86. You can have it all, just not all at once.

87. Be quick to listen, slow to speak.

88. Perfect is the enemy of great.

89. When you teach someone, two people learn.

90. "Lack of direction, not lack of time, is the issue. We all have twenty-four-hour days." — Zig Ziglar

91. The sun's rays do not burn until brought into focus.

How would the person I wish to be... act today?

92. "The successful warrior is the average person, with laser-like focus." — Bruce Lee

93. Life is tough, but so are you.

94. When you can't find the sunshine, be the sunshine.

95. The most important thing is always doing the most important thing.

96. If you get tired, learn to rest, not to quit.

97. Successful people focus on goals, not obstacles.

98. Life is like a roll of toilet paper: the closer we get to the end, the faster it goes.

99. Have fun. Help people.

Making the Donuts

Dunkin' Donuts produced a television commercial so successful that the company decided to make over 100 slightly different versions. People would get up in the morning and humorously repeat its popular tagline to their roommate or spouse. Eventually, this catchphrase even became the title of the company founder's autobiography.

The star of the Dunkin' Donuts commercials was a character named "Fred the Baker," played by actor Michael Vale. Vale and his character Fred the Baker were so beloved that when Vale decided to retire, market research studies indicated the public didn't want Fred the Baker to go.

In response, the company hosted a retirement party and parade for Fred in Boston, giving away nearly six million donuts.[1]

The highly successful campaign led to an additionally accepted spelling of *doughnuts...donuts.*

In over 100 advertisements, the fatigued baker says the famous line, "Time to make the donuts." Sleepy Fred the Baker slowly rises and wills his body out of bed for another day of donut making. A popular spot features Fred shuffling out of his house, mumbling, "Time to make the donuts." Each time he exits his front door early in the morning, he moans, "Time to make the donuts," and each time he returns at night, he says, "I made the donuts." Every time the door opens, the weather or time is different: sunny, stormy, snowy, autumn, windy, dusk, dawn, midnight, but nothing stops Fred from making the donuts.

After Fred leaves and returns home numerous times, the ending sequence shows Fred leaving his house, then bumping into Fred returning, the words also colliding: "Time to Make the Donuts...I Made the Donuts." His world is literally upside down! He doesn't know if he is coming or going. Is he about to go make the donuts, or has he already made them?

Viewers could easily relate to Fred. In some form or fashion, viewers saw Fred the Baker in their own lives.

While we can identify with Fred's situation, we don't love this type of daily vertigo. It's unpleasant being so busy that we don't know up from down. Is it time to make our donuts or did we already make them? I answered 150 emails yesterday, so how can there possibly be 150 more to answer today? Didn't I answer them all!?

So many of us seem to be living this "Fred the Baker" life day after day, year after year. We're letting life happen to us. Instead, we should be protecting certain items as "non-negotiable." T-shirts with slogans like *seize the day...you only live once* seem trite, but they're right.

I, like many others, wasn't prioritizing my life. People such as Michelle Obama and Warren Buffett discovered this early on. If they didn't prioritize their time, others would be more than happy to gobble it up by prioritizing it for them.

> *Either you run the day, or the day runs you.*
> — Jim Rohn

My world was upside down just like Fred the Baker's life. I didn't know whether I was coming or going, and, as a result, my work, family, faith, health—everything, was suffering.

Your version of "making the donuts" might look something like this:

1. You get up late because you went to bed late—you just *had* to answer that last email.

2. Since you got up late, there's no time to go to the gym.

3. One of the kids makes a mess in the kitchen while the other can't find his shoes. You discover after ten minutes the shoes were left on the back porch and are drenched from last night's rain. You frantically dry them with your hairdryer while reaching to clean up the mess in the kitchen. You're out the door fifteen minutes later than expected, putting you into the heart of rush-hour traffic, taking you twice as long to get to the office.

4. You arrive later to work than you wanted.

5. You thought you'd have time to tackle what you needed to tackle before your first meeting, but by being late, your time has vanished.

6. Two unexpected meetings get added to your plate.

7. You're in meetings from 9 am until 3:45 pm.

8. At 3:46 pm, a co-worker drops by to chat, asking for your help.

9. You shoo him out of your office, finally, at 4:26, and you furiously start attacking all the emails that piled up.

10. You're exhausted, arriving late to your kid's soccer game.

11. You'll have to work after dinner before putting the kids to bed.

12. As your head hits the pillow, it's much later than you want it to be. You're surprised that your pillow doesn't catch on fire because your hair certainly has from your crazy, hectic, awful day.

13. Wash, rinse, repeat.

> Serving others is the rent that we pay to be here on earth.
> — Justin Timberlake

Like the donuts man or Bill Murray in the movie *Groundhog Day,* you may be falling into an un-enjoyable pattern. In *Groundhog Day,* Bill Murray's character finds himself in a parallel universe, living the exact day, day after day. Most of us find ourselves in this "Groundhog Day State" more than we would like. How do we break free from this spin cycle? The answer is FOCUS. It's that simple, but it's not that easy. To focus in this unfocused world seems impossible.

In the pages ahead, let's figure out how to do it. Let's figure out how to FOCUS.

Less, but Better

German designer Dieter Rams is considered one of the best industrial designers of the 20th century. He is credited with hundreds of iconic products—everything from the Oral-B toothbrush to home audio equipment, Braun coffee makers to calculators. He has inspired a generation of world-renowned designers, including Apple's famed designer, Jony Ive.

His secret? Rams firmly believes that "good design" involves as little design as possible. Rams described his approach with the German phrase *"Weniger, aber besser,"* less, but better. Rams's intention: to design an experience that was simple and effortless.[2]

Imagine taking this "Less, but Better" approach to our life design. Focus on its double meaning. By doing less, we can improve ourselves because we gain time and energy. By doing less, we will have more. When I feel overwhelmed, I remind myself of Rams' philosophy "Weniger, aber besser." Less, but better.

I have been blessed with what modern society would deem a successful career. Certainly part of this success is my ability to focus better than most. That being said, I would've given myself a Focus grade of a D-. Imagine how much more fulfilled and happy I could be if I increased my focus from a D- to a B+? A-? A+?

Ignorance wasn't the issue. I'd read numerous articles and books about the importance of being focused, so why wasn't I practicing it? Why wasn't I implementing it on a day-to-day basis? Why aren't you?

Focusing is similar to getting into better shape. Information isn't the issue. We know the simple formula: Eat Better + Exercise = A Healthier Life. We have the knowledge, but that doesn't mean we are executing on it. Most successful entrepreneurs and people believe success has much less to do with the idea and everything to do with the execution. This is so true. Success is about developing consistent daily routines and habits versus relying on willpower.

My mind raced around these thoughts until I hit something so captivating, I couldn't let it go. For weeks, the idea kept popping into my head, but the thought seemed like pure fantasy. An impossibility.

Regret weighs tons; while focusing only weighs ounces.

What would a year look like if I maniacally focused on one aspect of my life per month? Instead of having another year pass by, running around with my hair on fire while parallel processing a million things with very little to show for it, what would happen if I simply stopped the madness? What if I simply focused on one thing? It seemed simple yet impossible with my hectic schedule.

Picking up this book, you probably immediately thought, "I don't have time to read this." Ironically, you're exactly who this book is intended for—people who feel they don't have the time to read it!

Talking with thousands of people at my book signings confirmed that I was not alone in my focus quandary. Your path through the trees might be a different path from mine, but you're certainly weaving through the same forest.

While I believe we all struggle in our own way to focus, I also strongly believe this book isn't for everyone. It's for the person, like you, who is already working hard; in fact, you're probably working too hard, but on the wrong things. You're achieving success, yet you know there is more out there for you in terms of success and fulfillment. You're already motivated—this book will not be screaming about how you have to hustle and fill every waking moment of your day.

I already know you're hustling, side-hustling, and grinding it out. I also know you're exhausted after "making the donuts." And our donuts all look and taste differently, but they are donuts nonetheless.

Some of you are entrepreneurs at Fortune 500 companies with a side-hustle, burning the candle at both ends. Or, perhaps you're a small business owner with two toddlers at home wondering when sleep will come. Others of you are executives of billion-dollar companies who feel as if everyone needs a piece of your time, and you realize that being at the top of the corporate ladder may not be so glamorous after all. You discover that it is lonely at the top.

Many of you are running non-profits, erroneously thinking at first that a non-profit means fewer hours and less stress than a traditional 9-5 job. But boy, were you wrong! Stay-at-home moms and dads are wondering when they can squeeze in just a little "me time" to get back to center and happiness before the kids start lighting the sofa on fire.

Some of you are furthering your education at night while juggling work assignments during the day.

This book isn't a motivational book for the lazy or downtrodden. It's for you, the person who is successful but knows he or she can be happier, who knows that even though you might be hitting home runs, there are grand slams out there. You've already climbed many mountains, but you know there is that ONE special summit out there with the view you were destined to see.

This "summit" might be starting your own company, doing your dream job, writing your novel, or cruising down the Seine River under the cascading lights of Paris.

Whatever the particular summit, without focus, none of us will ever see it. Without consciously choosing to select only the essential, it will be a near impossibility to achieve the big wins. And, most importantly, it will be difficult to enjoy the journey itself and be fulfilled by it.

It's time to switch lanes in life. It's time to focus on what matters most.

Most of us overestimate what we can do in an hour but underestimate what we can do in a month, a year, or a lifetime, if we just stick to it, one small step at a time. Day after day we can become better at focusing and learning to WIN (What's Important Now). Writing for one minute per day eventually led me to write for five minutes, then fifteen, until I became disciplined enough to write this book from 8 am to 9:35 am each day and on many days was able to find other pockets to write.

This project was a series of steps. What small steps could I take every day to achieve my long-term moonshots and laughable goals, to help me feel happier and more fulfilled?

I wanted to be excited about waking up every morning, or at least most mornings, like a kid on Christmas Day. We all want each day to be our best day.

And, most importantly, I wanted the light of my happiness and fulfillment to reflect onto the people around me to make them happier and more fulfilled.

What if I were just to focus...

Christmas Eve. 2:36 am. Actually, not even Christmas Eve, but the beginning of Christmas Day. I was awake, but not because I was too excited to sleep. I was mentally and physically exhausted. It was likely that I would start hallucinating, seeing Santa's reindeer prancing through my living room. I'd already finished wrapping and assembling the impossible: toys and bikes for the children.

But, there I was, banging away on my keyboard, attempting to save a client.

Most of our clients are wonderful. This one was not. In fact, this client had just sent me "kill the contract" in the subject line of an email at 6 pm on Christmas Eve—no joke. The contract had four more months on it, so technically and legally it couldn't be "killed," but this is what I was dealing with. On Christmas Eve at nearly 3:00 a.m. My business sense said let the contract go. Even though it was written in stone that they could not break the contract early, just wish them well and head into the sunset.

Ironically, our team's efforts had taken their sales numbers to record levels. If they weren't happy now, then when would they be? This client was less than 3% of our business, yet they were causing 97% of our headaches. Funny how that works, isn't it?

Instead of settling down to a long winter's nap, there I sat in my stockings and cap, typing away late on Christmas Eve and well into Christmas Morning.

I, of all people, who get paid to speak on stage about being true to yourself, knew better. What is in our chemical makeup that compels us to behave so irrationally? Why couldn't I just move on and focus on a family Christmas rather than having this client gnaw at me? After pondering my email response for much longer than warranted, I pushed the send button.

That's when I heard my five-year-old daughter coming down the stairs. Fear overtook me as I glanced at the clock and then at the floor, where tatters of "Santa's wrapping paper" were conspicuous. It was my "'Twas the Night Before Christmas" moment...

> *I sprang from my bed to tend to the matter,*
> *Away to my daughter, I flew like a flash,*
> *Almost pulling my hamstring I was so rash,*
> *Toppling into the Christmas tree with a great crash.*
>
> *What a fool,*
> *When all along I had the right tool,*
> *And it didn't require St. Nick's magic or hocus-pocus,*
> *All I needed to do was focus.*

Focus on what matters most.

Fortunately, my daughter was moderately sleepwalking—the toilet paper caught onto her pajama bottoms was still attached to the roll in the bathroom, an umbilical cord of toilet paper a good 60 feet long!

My pecking away at the keyboard almost ruined Christmas for my daughter, and certainly damaged my well-being. And for what? To what end? This was my "wake-up" moment—the time for change had arrived. The time had come to focus on what would make me happier, healthier, and wiser.

I knew the antidote, but even if I prescribed it, would I be able to follow through on taking the medicine daily? I was also a bit skeptical— would the medicine actually work? Or were minimalism, essentialism, stoicism, pursuing less, and focus, all concepts that sounded great but didn't work in the real world? It was time to find out.

Later that afternoon I spent a few minutes sending an email and writing a handwritten note wishing the client a *Happy Holidays* and best of luck in the New Year. We would gladly let them out of the contract without penalty. Ironically, this felt like the best possible holiday gift for myself and my team.

Between Christmas and New Year's, I started having fun selecting what I would and would not focus on in the coming year.

Narrowing my list down to 12, for 12 months:

1.   Focusing on Growth
2.   Focusing on Time Management
3.   Focusing on Family & Friends
4.   Focusing on Health
5.   Focusing on Relationships
6.   Focusing on Learning
7.   Focusing on Creativity
8.   Focusing on Empathy
9.   Focusing on Mindfulness
10. Focusing on Giving
11. Focusing on Gratitude
12. Focusing on Your Story

Conducting a small test, I began focusing on sales for the month of December but failed miserably. I only dedicated nine minutes to sales...not nine minutes per day, a total of nine minutes for the month!

This focus project would not be easy. The plan was to focus on one thing per day for a sum of two hours.

Perform a search for "New Year's Resolutions," and you will discover that the top result is negative: *Top 10 Commonly Broken New Year's Resolutions.*[3]

Why the negativity? Because only 8% of us actually keep our resolutions.[4]

Top Failed Resolutions

1. Lose Weight and Get Fit
2. Quit Smoking
3. Learn Something New
4. Eat Healthier and Diet
5. Get Out of Debt and Save Money
6. Spend More Time with Family
7. Travel to New Places
8. Be Less Stressed
9. Volunteer
10. Drink Less

Also interesting—the top 10 failed resolutions were very similar to the top 10 most popular resolutions. Not one was easy to achieve.

Top 10 Most Popular Resolutions

1. Lose Weight
2. Get Organized
3. Spend Less, Save More
4. Enjoy Life to the Fullest
5. Staying Fit and Healthy
6. Learn Something Exciting

7. Quit Smoking

8. Help Others in their Dreams

9. Fall in Love

10. Spend More Time with Family

Comparing my list to this one, I had a crossover on 7 out of 10. I didn't have quit smoking, finances, or "Fall in Love" (I'm already married to the woman of my dreams, but I did decide to dedicate a month to love).

These resolution categories also have a crossover with some of the bestselling books of all time. Below is a list of the all-time, top-selling self-help books. You will notice crossover with the categories such as health, finance, sex, sales, productivity, and friends:[5]

1. *Chicken Soup for the Soul* by Jack Canfield and Mark Victor Hansen: Short, inspiring stories about real people's lives.

2. *Think and Grow Rich* by Napoleon Hill: Personal wealth and lasting success.

3. *Men are from Mars, Women Are from Venus* by John Gray: Men and women are so different, they seem to come from different planets. Understanding the fundamental differences in thinking between males and females is the key to healthy relationships.

4. *You Can Heal Your Life* by Louise L. Hay: How the body and mind are linked.

5. *Your Erroneous Zones* by Dr. Wayne W. Dyer: Published in 1976, including tips for a guilt-free life, positive thinking, and taking control of your life.

6. *Who Moved My Cheese?* by Spencer Johnson: The necessity of adapting to change at work.

7. *Rich Dad, Poor Dad* by Robert T. Kiyosaki: Stresses financial independence, entrepreneurial projects, and investments.

8. *The 7 Habits of Highly Effective People* by Stephen Covey: Habits to adopt to become more efficient and successful.

9. *The Secret* by Rhonda Byrne: The law of attraction—if you think about something hard enough, it will come to you.

10. *How to Win Friends and Influence People* by Dale Carnegie: Insights on how to make people like you.

For your own list, I suggest you do the following exercise: Formulate your list of what's important to you. Take a sheet of paper and form three columns.

ITEM	IMPORTANCE	PERFORMANCE
Family	10	3

1. Item: For example, "Family."

2. Rank: Rank the importance to you from 1-10 (10 being highest).

3. Performance: Score 1-10 how well you're performing that item.

Look at your sheet and identify the gaps. Where is there a big gap? If Family is a 10 in importance, but you feel you're performing at a 3 right now, that is a big gap. Consciously attack that gap and dedicate time to it to get it to a 8, 9, or 10. It works on the inverse as well, so if you have Faith ranked as a 2 (importance) and you're performing at a 4, well, you have some "give" there. Faith can slip to a 2 if it allows you to allocate time to improving the "Family" gap.

Throughout the day you should ask yourself where you are on a scale of 1-10? If you say you're at a 6, then why aren't you at a 7 or an 8? As you list out the reasons, ask yourself, is the issue solvable?

For example: *"Overall, I'm at a 5 out of 10 this afternoon. The reason it's low is because I wanted to go for a run this morning, but it was raining. Now, it's perfectly beautiful outside and I'm stuck inside here at work."* We need to ask ourselves if the problem can be solved and have an internal dialogue similar to this:

> "Now that it's beautiful outside, what's preventing me from going running right now?"

> "I have an important call scheduled, so a run doesn't seem feasible."

> "Can I find a quiet park and walk around while I take the call?"

While walking in the park isn't the same as running, at least we are now doing some exercise outside and this can help take us from a 5 to a 7. We need to control what we can control.

Spirit Animals

There are numerous reasons why we find focusing difficult, but most of us embody one of the following four spirit animals: Hedgehogs, Squirrels, Chameleons, or Army Ants. By identifying which spirit and characteristics we embody, we can better understand our focusing strengths and weaknesses.

Hedgehogs

When sensing a threat, Hedgehogs curl into a protective ball, their 5,000 to 10,000 spiny quills protruding for protection. Similarly, we curl up to protect ourselves from failure. Only wanting to enter battle when we are fully armed and ready, we often avoid doing what needs to be done. We become Hedgehogs. We are not lazy, rather our logic is playing tricks on us. If I never try something, I can never prove that I'm not any good at it. If I want to become the world's greatest singer, but I never sing publicly out of fear of not being a good singer, then my dream is still alive. I didn't prove to others, and most importantly to myself, that I'm not a talented singer. Unfortunately, if one never sings, becoming the world's greatest singer is impossible. This logic leaves us in the middle. We do *nothing* while telling ourselves that someday we will do *something*. We will do *something* when we have more time, when we are more prepared.

Hedgehogs often use procrastination as protection. For example, a student cleans his apartment to put off studying. Or someone binges on a TV series instead of designing the dress for her boutique. On the larger procrastination scale is the person who believes she will write her novel as soon as she gets her Ph.D. in English. In essence, we are always trying to build and make our armor stronger before going into the arena.

But what happens if we never actually step into the arena? The best armor in the world goes to waste. Keep in mind that the extra armor we feel we need can actually be detrimental—it is heavy and inflexible.

Or we tell ourselves that we will come out of our protective ball once all dangers and hurdles are gone. The truth is that this will never happen. There will always be dangers and hurdles. Fortune favors the bold. It's difficult for Hedgehogs to see this. It's difficult to understand that the best time for us to get into the arena is now.

> It is not the critic who counts; not the man who points out how the strong man stumbles, or where the doer of deeds could have done them better. The credit belongs to the man who is actually in the arena, whose face is marred by dust and sweat and blood; who strives valiantly; who errs, who comes short again and again, because there is no effort without error and shortcoming; but who does actually strive to do the deeds; who knows great enthusiasms, the great devotions;

who spends himself in a worthy cause; who at the best knows, in the end, the triumph of high achievement, and who at the worst, if he fails, at least fails while daring greatly, so that his place shall never be with those cold and timid souls who neither know victory nor defeat. —Teddy Roosevelt

There is a saying, "The best time to plant a tree was yesterday, the second-best time is today." The same applies to life. The best time to start focusing on your best life was yesterday, the second-best time is today. Amazon founder Jeff Bezos discovered this truth about himself: "In most cases, our biggest regrets turn out to be acts of omission. It's paths not taken and they haunt us. We wonder what would have happened," Bezos said. "I knew that when I'm 80, I would never regret trying this thing (starting Amazon) that I was super excited about and it failing. If it failed, fine. I would be very proud of the fact that when I'm 80 that I tried. I also knew that it would always haunt me if I didn't try."[6]

Squirrels

Squirrels struggle to stay on task. The next bright and shining object is just too good to pass up. Squirrels are great at trend-spotting and are aware of the hippest restaurants in town. Squirrels stay abreast of the news and can easily have conversations about pop culture. We Squirrels excel at starting and attacking projects, but before we can complete them, we move on to the next latest and greatest thing.

Many great visionaries and salespeople are Squirrels; they easily rally excitement around a new project. After the initial excitement wears off, they are best handing this off to an operations person to implement the project. Squirrels need to understand that they are easily distracted by the new and unusual. They must resist the temptation to jump from tree to tree, looking for the next sparkling acorn. FOMO (Fear Of Missing Out) is the best description for us mighty Squirrels. We struggle to focus on seeing a task through to completion.

A Chameleon changes colors to match his surroundings so that he's more difficult for predators
to see. This beautiful defense mechanism allows
him to hide his true self. Many of us are akin to
Chameleons. We adjust our behavior to blend in
with those around us. This skill can be particularly
helpful. However, when adjusting becomes our
norm rather than the exception, we are hiding our
true selves.

Chameleons

We all want to be outstanding. Yet, we do X instead of Y because society says X is the way to go. Like the Chameleon, we avoid stepping
into discomfort, thereby avoiding our unique stories and destinies.
Our intent as Chameleons is good—in choosing X, we often help or
appease others in the short term. Yet, the best way we can help others
long-term is by stepping into our own purposes and unique stories.

There are many ways we put off stepping into our stories. Some of
these examples you might be able to identify with:

- "As soon as the kids are done with high school and out of the
  house, I'll open my coffee shop."

- "If I didn't need to take care of my aging parents, I'd be going back
  to get my degree."

- "I'd love to write music, but my mother was a lawyer and I know
  she's so happy with me following in her footsteps."

- "I wanted to start my small business right away, but I know it
  makes my parents happy that I'm going to college instead."

- "I'd love to switch careers, but at this point, I'm just too old for
  that type of change."

- "I hate this job. It's killing me inside, but the pay is good and my
  family really needs the money right now. I can pursue my dreams
  once I get through this."

- "This job isn't so bad. While it doesn't stimulate or challenge me,
  it pays well with great benefits for me and my family."

Rather than trying to blend in, we need to blend out. In order to be outstanding, we first need to stand out.

Army Ants

We become Army Ants when we take on more than we should. We overload ourselves. Like an Army Ant, we can lift 5,000 times our weight, but that doesn't mean we should. We can handle the load, but when we get back to the anthill, we have a problem. All this stuff doesn't fit down the opening of the anthill! We would've been better off focusing on one thing at a time. This would've allowed us to take more back to the anthill and fit more inside. We would be better off saying "not yet" to most items and taking on one thing at a time instead of trying to parallel process hundreds of things at once.

While some fall squarely into one of these four spirit animals, most of us are probably a combination of two. Despite popular belief, I believe most people are both introverted and extroverted. For example, comedian Chris Rock is extroverted on stage, but his wife confirms he's introverted at a dinner party. Elton John, Abraham Lincoln, and Lady Gaga, by nature, skew more introverted than extroverted.[7]

My strongest focus tendencies were those of an Army Ant, taking on a ton at a time and carrying a heavy payload, which, for me, was parallel processing. This only resulted in all projects taking longer or not being completed at all. Even when projects were completed, the quality often suffered, along with my health. I needed to cut my project list from 10 items to 3. While I majored in Army Ant, I minored in Hedgehog.

I'd often procrastinate on major projects by:

1. Taking two hours to film a short social media video
2. Reading every single post on the Michigan State basketball team
3. Responding to emails

4. Reading for four hours instead of writing

5. Getting sucked into social media

Why This Book?

There is a saying that there are only two reasons to write a book:

1. *To Change Yourself*

    - or -

2. *To Change the World*

If executed properly, the reason I wrote this book is not only to help change me but to help others create positive change. Like all of us, I experience a lot of self-talk: that little voice rattling around inside our heads...constantly chatting and chirping at us. My self-talk for this book went something like this: "Hey Erik, is there even a need for this book? How is it different? Why should you be the one writing it? When you do write it, why not just give the facts of your research and findings? Why are you telling it through the lens of your personal journey?"

This last question harped at me the most: "Why are you making it personal?" The most common question and self-doubt circling in my mind was: "Who cares about my own personal insights and day-to-day triumphs and struggles with focus?"

Some people with whom I consulted about this book shared the same concern. However, the majority encouraged me to marry my own experiences and street science with rigorous institutional research and findings. They wanted to see someone *else* go through the actual struggle and experimentation. People love guinea pigs so long as they aren't the guinea pig.

I would serve as the guinea pig.

During this project my daughters and I finished reading a young adult fiction book I'd written. They wanted to start a new book and begged that I read this manuscript to them. That's right, my elementary-aged daughters helped edit this book, so be gentle in your criticism. After finishing the first chapter, my second-grade daughter innocently looked at me with wide eyes and said, "Daddy, that is what Ms. Hernandez is always telling our class. That we need to focus, people!"

Even though your journey and your particular focus project will be different from mine, having a Sherpa alongside pointing out pitfalls, inside secrets, and secret passages will ease your journey. Consider me your "focus sherpa." I'm hopeful that making this book personal will also make it more entertaining. So, for those who hate this marriage of personal anecdotes and findings alongside science and research, feel free to put this book down.

As for the rest of you crazy lot, please enjoy the pages ahead. Each month, I select one big item as my focus. However, the bulk of each chapter provides tips on how to develop the life-long habits necessary for focusing on the important versus the immediate—how we can start leading our best lives, starting today.

I've been fortunate to travel to 55 countries and reach over 35 million people this decade. While I speak on stage for a living, I spend my life offstage listening. One of my favorite questions to ask is: "What are you most excited about?" People's eyes open wide, and more often than not they can't give a straight answer.

To help them get to an answer, I often rephrase it to one of these:

1. What is the one thing you want out of life?
2. If in the next six weeks I can wave a magic wand and make your wildest dream happen, what would it be?
3. If you were to die tomorrow, what would be your one regret?

When a person realizes what they want—their eyes light up. A light bulb has turned on. I follow up with this question: "What is preventing you from getting what you want?" Interestingly, the answers are universally the same; people can't get what they want because they don't have the time, energy, or money right now. But, they all strongly believe they will have these resources in the future. Not today, but tomorrow will certainly be better. Guess what? Tomorrow never comes.

We all have the same number of hours in each day. Given this equality, why do leaders seem to be able to focus—even when they have 20,000 employees or teammates and a million to-dos and thousands of people reaching out to them for their attention? The answer? Through constant practice, they have become better at focusing. Their ability to focus is the reason they are in leadership positions. They are also sufficiently self-aware to understand that focus is a daily battle. Losing sight of this, they could easily topple from the mountain.

The most common response I receive from leaders when I ask how they maintain success and happiness is this: *"Understanding where I want to go and having the ability to focus on what matters to get there. It's a habit I will never perfect, but I practice it every day."*

Whatever reason compelled you to pick up this book, my hope is that it inspires you to take the next step.

Next Steps:

1. Determine what you want out of life and what makes you happy.
2. Intentionally focus on this each and every day.
3. Start your own focus project by picking one thing each month... each day...to hyper-focus on.

We can't go back in life to make a new beginning, but we certainly can begin today to make a new ending. Let's begin learning how to focus in this highly unfocused world.

Growth

There we stood. Toe-to-toe. My wife Ana Maria and I screaming at each other at the top of our lungs. Well, truth be told, Ana Maria was screaming, and I was calmly—perhaps one might objectively say annoyingly—repeating, "Relax, relax, relax." Which, one can imagine, was causing the exact opposite reaction. I might as well have lit a match in a nitroglycerin plant.

The stage setting of this dramatic scene? Our kids were running late for the school bus, resulting in us arguing about who was at fault. Who wasn't doing enough to get the kids ready on time? Which of us was not pulling her or his weight?

In reality, we were both pulling *more* than enough weight. We were pulling more and more. Yet, we weren't focusing on *pulling* the weight that specifically needed pulling. We were both equally guilty of trying to cut down a tree with a hammer when a chainsaw was easily within our reach. Or, more likely, we should have chosen a different path in the first place—one that didn't have a tree blocking the way. There had to be a better path.

The argument Ana Maria and I were having was silly. When we peeled back the layers of the onion, we weren't yelling at the other person, we were yelling at *ourselves.*

Interestingly, we all have the ability to change this scene, but we keep repeating it. We are no better than a hamster on a wheel. One might argue worse. At least the hamster is getting exercise.

Put simply, we should have put a mirror in front of us and started yelling at the reflection.

"Every day you're late or scrambling. How can this be?!"

"Why are you taking on so much stuff that you can't prioritize what is important, like being relaxed and enjoying time with the kids before school!"

"Get to bed earlier so you can get up earlier and be well rested and get the kids to the school bus early."

"Quit saying yes to everything that's small! Doing that won't allow you to say yes to the big things in life."

"The email can wait! Tie the kids' shoes for heaven's sake."

"I have to make the hard choices and select great opportunities while discarding the merely good ones!"

For you, it might be that another day slipped by when you didn't find time to practice yoga. Or maybe you've been saying you will take guitar lessons for five years, but, so far, you have yet to touch a guitar. Or, the book you're writing was to be completed 8 years ago, yet there it sits, half-finished and collecting dust.

After the kids were off to school, Ana Maria and I looked at each other, apologized, and then laughed at how ridiculous we had just been. It was January 3rd, and we both agreed this focus project couldn't begin soon enough.

My focus in January would be growth, growing our business. While it certainly wasn't the most important item on my focus project list, there were several reasons why choosing January made sense:

1. To focus properly in the months ahead, I couldn't be worried about our business staying afloat.

2. Starting with something easily measured is informative. I can ask myself: "Is my new focus helping sales increase?"

3. Lastly, I knew that focusing on growing sales would be difficult, with a high potential for failure.

As previously mentioned, I'd already tried focusing on sales and had failed miserably with my first four attempts! Yet, here I was, now spending two hours per day trying to focus on sales for an entire month—thirty-one straight days! Would this time be different?

Your particular growth can be about anything, but I recommend that your initial focus be centered on whatever you absolutely cannot allow to slip. Focusing first on sales gave me time to focus on other items in the months ahead.

This month, my critical priority had to be on growing the business. I would constantly ask myself the simple question, "Does this have anything to do with sales? And if not, why am I doing it?"

A key question to help determine your critical priority is, "If I get this one thing right, will everything else become doable?" Or, to put it in another context, there are ten important milestones in order to achieve your goal, but if this particular milestone was done really, really well, would the nine other items become irrelevant?

For example, if you're a parent volunteering to raise money for your kids' school, you likely have 50 to 100 small fundraisers throughout the year and you have one gigantic annual auction/gala. If the auction night is a booming success, all shortcomings of the other 50-100 efforts disappear. However, the opposite isn't true. If the auction fails, no matter how successful the other 100 events, they can't possibly make up for the shortfall of the auction.

This is similar to the Pareto principle, better known as the 80/20 rule. The principle being that 80% of our success is derived from 20% of our efforts. In short, focus on the stuff that matters as it drives the results. One way to ensure you are practicing the 80/20 rule is to do the following:

1. Make a list of the top 5 things that consume your time.

2. Circle the one that drives the most results.

3. Focus on spending more time doing the item you circled.

For me, the top priority was clear: To get booked for more keynote and motivational performances to large audiences. To go from 25 annual stage performances to 70. This was my "growth" and my way to help empower others from the stage.

The main source of our revenue is delivering entertaining and educational (i.e., edutainment) performances on stage for businesses, schools, governments, conferences, and others. In order to afford the luxury of embarking on this 12-month focus project, we first had to double the number of our performances.

Having a focus on sales was ironic for me. It took me a long time to realize that a large part of my role in our organization is sales. I thought my job was to *make*. To *make* the book. To *make* the podcast. But you see, whether we think it or not, we are all in sales. Whether trying to convince our spouse to fix a leaky faucet or attempting to ask our boss if we can work from home on Fridays, we are in sales. Or, perhaps you're a scientist trying to get additional funding for your research. Or someone trying to get a friend to attend church. The PTA volunteer trying to raise money for the school field trip is also selling. Or, maybe you're trying to convince your dad to stop smoking. The old adage that we are all in sales is an old adage because it's true.

And you know who's really good at sales? Kids. Your four-year-old daughter Bella asks for cotton candy and you say no initially and then proceed to say no twenty more times to her incessant prodding. Yet, guess what? Fifteen minutes later—after constant pleas and badgering—guess who's enjoying fluffy pink goodness? Good old Bella. Girl Scouts selling cookies are some of the world's greatest salespeople.

As you embark on your own focus project, my advice is to tackle the area that will have the most impact first. If you don't, you will find it nearly impossible to allocate the proper amount of focus to this project. Leaders always ensure that the most critical leg of the chair is always taken care of; otherwise, you will most certainly land on your ass.

> *What's the one thing I must do well to make everything else either easier or unnecessary?*

A serious hindrance to my personal growth and our growth as an organization was trying to focus on too many things at once (Army Ant). We were doing speaking deals, coaching, consulting, animation, videos, podcasts, newsletters, social media, partnerships, serving as expert witnesses, charitable works...You get the point. In fact, we left every meeting with three to five more to-dos. We quickly learned and implemented the mantra that adding three new items meant removing four existing ones from the to-do list.

This was game-changing.

I began asking myself consistently, "What's the one thing I must do well to make everything else either easier or unnecessary?" I've learned various forms of this question from many people, most notably fellow Austinites, Tim Ferris and Jay Papasan. Jay dives deeper into this concept in his book, *The One Thing*, co-written with Gary Keller; a book which I highly recommend reading. When I asked myself this question, the obvious answer was *speaking on stage*. If I rocked the stage—whether it was live or virtual—it would open a world of avenues and opportunities for our business. Making your goals as specific as possible is key to achieving success.

A study on accountability from the American Society of Training and Development calculated these statistics on the probability of completing a goal if:

- You have an idea or goal: 10%
- You decide you will do it: 25%
- You decide when you will do it: 50%
- You commit to someone you will do it: 65%
- You schedule accountability check-ins: 95%

I was introduced to the power of specificity early in my career when I was part of a little start-up called Yahoo! At the time, we could do no wrong at Yahoo! We were the darlings of Silicon Valley...of Wall Street...of the world. Looking at the long lines queueing up to get our Yahoo! giveaways (i.e., swag, tchotchke) during trade shows, my teammates used to jokingly say that if we "put the Yahoo! logo on a pile of purple poop, people would gladly line up to get a fresh scoop." We even had a purple cow in our lobby. Later, fellow Yahooligan Seth Godin titled his #1 bestseller *Purple Cow*.

One particular meeting at Yahoo! stands out in my mind to this day. It was a market research meeting conducted by Gartner. The research analysts and Gartner were shocked at the meteoric rise of the Yahoo! brand. After only a few years, we were the 6th most recognized brand in the world.

When survey-takers described Yahoo!, the majority of the respondents answered that we were a search engine. Most of us were elated to be the 6th most recognized brand in the world, and we boldly figured we would soon be #1. At the same time, many were deflated at being described as simply a search engine. Didn't people know we were much more than a search engine?

Oh, we were arrogantly soooo much more. We were a web portal, damn it! We were your irreplaceable window to the world: sports, weather, email, news, finance, music, movies, search, video, fantasy sports, restaurants, online dating...all tailored specifically for you. Everything all in one place. On one page. A good search engine was just one of the many amazing things we provided on your personalized My Yahoo! page.

To help our search engine performance, we were using new technology from a small company just down the road, founded by two Stanford Ph.D. students who had an algorithm called PageRank. The students wanted to resume their studies and were willing to sell their proprietary algorithm for $1 million dollars in 1998.

Yahoo! passed on this purchase.

Yahoo! instead bought Overture. Overture had discovered a way to charge people for clicks on search engine listings. Overture helped foster a new term called *paid search clicks*, which later would simply be called *paid clicks*. Before this, most search listings were simply organic listings (free) from the major search engines: Yahoo!, Ask Jeeves, AltaVista, Excite, Dogpile, etc. While we knew search was a key component of Yahoo!, we were most excited about being all things to all people, daily adding new widgets to our portal, ensuring that everyone had the ability to customize their portals. Providing such customization would make Yahoo! "sticky" and monopolize eyeballs, which could then be monetized.

The two Stanford Ph.D. students who had come up with PageRank got an inside view of Overture and began understanding how Yahoo!

was integrating the paid click model into advertising bundles sold to major companies such as General Motors, Pepsi, and Warner Brothers. These two students were fascinated by the concept and started testing items in foreign markets where the Yahoo!/Overture joint agreement wasn't in place.

Around the same time, Yahoo! had a changing of the guard when Terry Semel replaced CEO, Tim Koogle. Semel looked at the technology powering our Yahoo! search results and balked at PageRank's asking price of $5 billion. Yes, the offer had risen from $1 million to $5 billion in less than four years. Part of the reason Semel was hesitant to buy these students out related to our having been severely burned by a previous purchase of another start-up.

We'd acquired a company called Broadcast.com for $5.7 billion. The problem? We never properly integrated it. In fact, as our Yahoo! executives were debating whether to purchase this search engine company with PageRank, we were in the process of shutting down Broadcast.com. A $5.7 billion loss is a tough hit to any company's bottom line. It was, however, a big win for the owner of Broadcast.com, Mark Cuban.

As you might expect, Semel was hesitant to make the same mistake twice and decided to pass on buying the search technology with PageRank.

The two students who started the company were disappointed. However, when they successfully took their company public, they were soon arguing over what type of beds to have on their custom Boeing 767 jet—yes, arguing over bunk beds on their private jet.

Sergey Brin wanted to have a California King, but co-founder Larry Page thought it was ridiculous to have such a large bed in the plane. In the end, the newly appointed CEO, Eric Schmidt, stepped in: "Sergey, you can have whatever bed you want in your room. Larry, you can have whatever kind of bed you want in your bedroom. Let's move on," Schmidt told the pair, according to the Google court documents.

So, in terms of focus, consider that Yahoo! could have purchased Larry and Sergey's Google for $1 million dollars, but because of a focus on being *everything* versus being a search engine, they ended up being *nothing*.

Where in your life are you trying to be everything when simply being one thing, the best possible search engine, would be your best move? Ask yourself, "What's the one thing I must do well to make everything else either easier or unnecessary?" One needs to remember that the word "priority" only became plural in the modern age. Before the 1900's the word "priorities" didn't exist.

> *A brand for a company is like a reputation for a person. You earn a good reputation by trying to do hard things well.*
> —Jeff Bezos

Letting Go Before Going Nuts

Monkey-hunters use a simple box with a small opening big enough for the monkey to slide its hand inside and grab the nuts. The monkey smells the nuts, ranging from peanuts to Brazilian nuts, then reaches in and grabs them. As he does this, the monkey's hand becomes a fist. When the monkey tries to get its hand out with the nuts in its fist, the opening, wide enough for the hand to slide in and out, is much too small for the monkey's entire fist to exit.

Now the monkey has a choice: either let go of the nuts and be free forever or hang on to the nuts and get caught. Guess what the monkey picks every time? You guessed it. He hangs onto the nuts and gets caught!

It's literally *nuts* in this instance not to let go.

I had to ask myself, what was I holding on to so tightly? Where could I let go to help improve sales? The biggest nut I was holding on to was our branding presence online. Specifically, what we were posting on social media. A designer at heart, anything that wasn't beautiful drove me nuts (pun intended). To give you a sense of how nutty I was, let's look at my daughter's soccer team.

When coaching my daughter's first-grade soccer team—the Cotton Candy Cookie Rainbow Warriors—if a girl left her water bottle on the practice field (a daily occurrence) I would actually prop the water bottle in a nice setting and take a picture with a good aperture to blur out the background before sending a notice to the parents for anyone missing a water bottle...Crazy, I know! I was taking the time to scout, shoot, and send out a professional-level photograph of a lost Dora the Explorer water bottle. This is how obsessed I am with design.

I realized that if I wanted to go fast on social media, I should be doing it myself. But, if I wanted to go far, we needed to do it as a team. Trusting the team with our design and social media activities allowed me to spend more time deepening relationships with partners and prospects.

While it isn't easy retraining my monkey brain, I was beginning to learn the benefit of letting go of the nuts.

It All Started with Jam

One day, Mark Lepper and Sheena Lyengar carefully formed a large, twenty-four variety jam display in an upscale market. Every few hours, Mark and Sheena adjusted the large table display from twenty-four varieties of jam to only six options.

Their discovery? The larger display of twenty-four jams received 60% more attention than the showcase of only six jams.

However, what transpired was quite remarkable. While the large display garnered the most attention and had the most choices, the table with fewer choices available achieved significantly more sales. The results weren't even close!

People were ten times more likely to purchase from the table with fewer choices.[8] This Jam study, as well as many others like it, center around "Choice Overload" or the "Paradox of Choice." For example, several studies have shown that if employees are given more fund options for their 401K, fewer will actually participate. They experience choice overload. The lesson? Try to avoid choice overload in your life.[9]

Narrowing Consideration Sets

When I was on the Advisory Board at Bazaarvoice, the team embarked on an experiment. Bazaarvoice is a tool that captures online ratings and reviews for clients. As such, the team wanted to showcase how powerful online reviews can be in an offline retail environment.

Well-versed in the paradox of choice, the Bazaarvoice team felt that ratings dramatically help the shopper by narrowing the consideration set. In a well-known electronics store, they selected an aisle of similar products from various makes and models for customers to choose from. Then, they printed online reviews for a select number of these products that had similar online ratings (a 4-star rating on a 5-star scale).

They also printed the most helpful positive and negative online comments about that particular product and taped these on the shelf above the product.

After a few weeks of testing, what did they discover? Sales for every product with a review taped above it dramatically went up—the review helped narrow the shoppers' focus. The other surprise they discovered was that overall sales not only went up for those particular products, but total sales for the entire aisle went up compared to the rest of the store.

The takeaway here is to look at our list of projects and rate each project based on importance on a scale from 1 to 10. Rating them will help narrow our consideration set, thereby increasing the likelihood of us accomplishing our most important projects, first.

The One Question to Ask

One of the unforeseen benefits of focusing on growth is that I started becoming attuned to helpful advice on growth. Ironically, in sales, it's important to help our prospects to focus. Asking good questions is the best way to do this.

These questions help determine the root of their anxiety and how we can help remove pain points. *The New York Times'* bestselling author and organizational sales expert, Daniel Pink, uncovered a helpful tactic for getting prospects to focus. His approach is also helpful in motivating employees, friends, teenagers, and beyond.

I was fortunate to find myself sharing the stage with Daniel Pink at a conference, and we struck up a conversation in the green room. To explain this particular focusing tactic, he uses the scenario of a parent with a messy teenage daughter.

To paraphrase Pink from our conversation:

> Most parents will take the approach of, 'Cindy please go clean your room.'
>
> 'I don't feel like it, Dad, and why does it matter?'

At this point, the dad is most likely to respond in a manner such as, 'You should clean your room because I told you to clean it! The reason it's important is...'

And he will proceed down the path of listing out the benefits of cleaning: discipline, finding things more easily, accomplishment and pride, not being embarrassed when your friends visit, etc. These are all perfectly good reasons for cleaning her room. The problem? They aren't likely to change her behavior because the reasons are Dad's, not Cindy's. However, with the help of the two simple questions, everything can change.

'Good morning, Cindy, on a scale of 1-10, how ready are you to clean your room?'

'I'd say probably a 4. Yeah, a solid 4.'

'That's great, Cindy, but I'm curious as to why you didn't pick a lower number, something around a 2 or 3?'

'Oh, I don't know. I figure I should probably clean it today or tomorrow since Harley and Sarah are coming over on Friday. It would be a little embarrassing if my dirty bras and underwear are lying around. It will make things easier to find—like my favorite shirt, it will give me a sense of accomplishment, and I know it will make you and Mom happy. So, I guess that's why I answered a 4.'

The reasons she gives are almost exactly the same as Dad's reasons. The critical difference is that she is formulating them.

The key to this method is to use it sparingly with employees or teenage daughters. Otherwise, it becomes ineffective.

With clients or sales prospects, the interactions are less frequent, so it can be even more effective. I was hired by a very well-known jewelry company to help with its focus on the retail level. We were able to use this method effectively with their sales associates. Specifically, the scenario that most often played out in the store was this:

Sales Associate: Can I help you?

Customer: Yes, I'm looking for some earrings.

Sales Associate: Fantastic. Any special occasion?

Customer: Yes, it's for our five-year anniversary.

Sales Associate: Congratulations! That's wonderful news. When is the big day?

Customer: Next Saturday, so I'd really like to figure this out today.

Sales Associate: Great. Given the pressing timeline, on a scale of 1-10, how confident are you about knowing what she *doesn't* like?

Notice the salesperson purposely says "doesn't" to narrow the selection process. Most people feel confident in someone else's dislikes since that subset doesn't seem as open as what she *does* like. Also, the customer now views the world through a different lens. As long as he avoids picking the items she doesn't like, he can be confident in his selection.

Customer: I'd say I'm probably around an 8 on knowing what she doesn't like.

Sales Associate: Great, an 8 is pretty good. What doesn't she like?

Customer: She definitely doesn't like gold or copper. She also doesn't like anything too big since she has smaller ears.

Sales Associate: Well, you know quite a lot. On the opposite side, what earrings do you remember her wearing for a special occasion, like going out to a nice restaurant?

Customer: She wore some round double diamonds the other day. She wears those quite a lot.

Sales Associate: Perfect. If it's okay for you, I can show you our silver and platinum lines that have two or three diamonds—so they are similar to what you know she likes but also will be unique enough to be special.

This scenario is less about motivation and more about focusing on details to help suppress the anxiety and paralysis of making the wrong purchase. Notice that asking the right questions helps combat the paradox of choice. The question, *"What does she like?"* is too open, big, and overwhelming. Asking what she *doesn't like* is easier to answer and can often help the buyer focus.

> *Begin to weave and God will give the thread.*
> — German proverb

In a similar fashion, an emerging pattern with our sales emails showed that most were long and focused on us—what we do and why we are the best at it.

Holy hell, I thought...nobody is going to read all this. I received around fifty similar unsolicited emails myself from different companies each day and they always went into my trash folder.

After a few weeks with little success from these long emails, the team approached me for help and suggestions. I asked one of our team members, Shannon, a few questions, and I immediately saw the "aha" in her eyes.

Me: Do you like receiving long or short emails?

Shannon: Short.

Me: Would you consider this email you just sent to the prospect short?

Shannon: No. It's long, arguably obnoxiously long.

Me: If you received an email like this, would you read it or delete it?

Shannon: I would delete it. It's overwhelming.

Me: Are the most helpful emails you receive about you and your needs or are they about why the company emailing you is great?

Shannon: I like receiving emails about me and my needs.

Me: Do you like the emails to be serious/business-speak or fun and human?

Shannon: Fun and human.

Me: Do you think you have a possible solution?

Shannon: Yes, when you put it like that, it's a little easier to see that we should probably change our emails to be focused more on the recipient and less on us. We should make them shorter and ask a fun personal question that almost everyone will want to answer.

Shannon then changed her multi-paragraph email about our animation studio capabilities to focus on the recipient's specific needs.

I love your company's new electric toothbrush! If you ever need an animated video to help increase sales of your toothbrush on Amazon, we have done similar videos for Disney.

Speaking of Disney, what was your favorite Disney movie growing up? Mine was The Incredibles.

Best, Shannon

People will not only pause to think about their favorite Disney movie growing up, but they will also feel compelled to respond and share a little piece of themselves. It doesn't hurt to remind them of being a kid. Other questions that usually work include: *"What is your favorite Girl Scout cookie?"* or *"What is your favorite kid's cereal?"*

When we tell our prospects that our favorite movie is *The Incredibles* or our favorite Girl Scout cookie is Thin Mints, we do it with an image of *The Incredibles* DVD cover or an image of a Thin Mint cookie versus text. Most of us are visual learners and receive a sense of stimulation from images—hence the explosion of emojis.

A picture is indeed worth a thousand words. We found that by keeping our emails short and human, and by using images, that our success dramatically increased.

Lessening our customer consideration set can also have profound results. The CEO of a $3 billion dollar company told me that he kicked off the year by telling his board of directors, "We are doing too much," and then courageously asked the board for permission to focus only on their core competency—Banks and Credit Unions. Doing this meant they would be giving up potentially big clients in other industries such as airlines, food, real estate, etc. The board reluctantly approved the CEO's request, adding that if the plan failed, he would be held responsible. For the CEO to focus solely on the core vertical took guts, but the results were staggering: Over twelve months, they doubled revenue and tripled profits. All from one very difficult decision: Doing Less. This story resonated with me since it's exactly what we were trying to do by narrowing the focus and zoning in on U.S. performances versus all the other markets and opportunities.

> *Some people go through a forest and see no firewood.*
> — Anonymous

Good Questions are Bridges to Great Relationships

A beneficial and unexpected byproduct of improving my focus is my increased ability to help others improve theirs. This improvement resulted from my learning to ask better questions.

Focused questions are the building blocks of deep relationships. Think about it. When is the last time you said, *"Wow, I really love hanging out with Luke because he talks the whole time"*? Said by no one, ever.

The conversations we *actually* enjoy share a pattern: The other person spends the majority of the time listening, really listening. He hangs on our every word. Watch what he does. He leans in when we are speaking. He looks us in the eye and asks questions that he knows we will enjoy answering.

If focused questions are the bridge to great relationships, then the better our questions, the better we will be at building and maintaining relationships.

Relationships drive all transactions. Whether it's a sales transaction or a simple favor, we don't buy from companies—we buy from people. This statement applies not only to business but to life as well. If a daughter wants to sell her parents on the idea of getting a new social media account or staying out two hours past her curfew, her chances of getting to "yes" dramatically increase the stronger the relationship she has with her parents. Trust has been built over time.

Let's get back to the power of questions. An example of my questions becoming better—questions that helped others to focus—came when I was on a "prep" call with a partner.

This partner was bringing me in to deliver the keynote at their annual conference. They were nervous, as it was the first time in their history that the audience would be a mix of their top partners and clients. These were the CEOs and executive teams of the world's most visited restaurants.

Weeks before I took the stage, there were several prep calls leading up to the event.

When delivering a keynote, I always have three goals for the audience: entertain them, educate them, and empower them. My belief is that most people enjoy being entertained, and entertainment is the superhighway of opening one's mind to new ideas. It's as if one's head is physically pried open and we pour knowledge onto the sponge we call a brain. Education leads to empowerment.

Formulaically, it looks like this:

Entertain >> Educate >> Empower

A typical prep call would go like this:

Erik: I like to entertain, educate, and empower the audience. Knowing I will do all three, which is the most important?

Partner: Great question. I guess I'd say all 3 are equally important.

They are essentially saying *"Yes, I'd like it all."* It's analogous to asking a child if she could have only one scoop of ice cream, would she want vanilla, chocolate, or strawberry, and her replying with an ambiguous "Yes!"

Roughly 95% of the responses were similar to the above. This type of answer wasn't helping me tailor my performance for the audience. At first, I erroneously believed that the problem resided with the partner. I was blaming the other party: "It's not me, it's them! Why can't they just properly answer my question?"

I realized that if *all* the partners were giving unfocused answers, the problem was not their answers. The problem was my questions! This was a eureka moment.

A big part of focus is breaking problems down from a mountain into pebbles. To achieve a better answer, my question needed to help the partner focus. My question became more focused:

Erik:	My approach is to entertain, educate, and empower your audience. If I were to give you 10 unbreakable gold coins to put into the 3 buckets of entertain, educate, and empower, how would you allocate these coins?
Partner:	Well, my hunch is to lean more toward education, but that hunch is generally wrong with these conferences. Since you're kicking things off, we'd like them to be in a good mood. And since the day before they will have had tons of breakout sessions around technical education, I would allocate the coins as 5 for entertainment, 2 for education, and 3 for empowerment.

While this approach to questioning entailed a very small change, the answers and the results were dramatic. Everyone benefited—the partner, me, and the audience.

Occasionally, the events team says one thing and the CEO says the exact opposite. Better-focused questions give us a fighting chance to iron things out and get on the same page before performing on stage.

One of our partners paid us the highest compliment: "Wow. I've been doing this for twenty years and I've never heard such thought-provoking questions."

Another useful question, in any vocation, is one by Airbnb founder Brian Chesky. Most people are ecstatic with a 5-Star Airbnb Experience (out of 5 stars), but Brian wanted to know what an 11-star experience looks like.

Borrowing this idea, I will often ask, "A 5-Star Experience is great, but what does an 11-Star experience look like?" We eventually took this to my favorite number, 42—my college basketball number. What does a 42-Star experience look like? Research shows that people have a tendency to remember strange numbers—42 versus, say, 5 or 10.

The insights we've received from our 42-Star question have helped us deliver such an experience. The other surprising outcome? Now planted in our clients' minds was the expectation that I would deliver a 42-star performance. Following events, I'll often receive notes from the conference organizers along the lines of "Nice job, truly 42 stars!"

The best way to build relationships, the basis of both business and life, is to ask focused questions that help the respondent deliver focused answers.

We were closing in on January 31st and it was bittersweet. I was excited to begin next month's focus on organizing my life, yet sad that my dedicated focus on sales growth was coming to an end. I started this month nervously, thinking, "What if I focused on sales growth and didn't improve the results? What will I do then? Will I have to scrap the entire focus project? Scrap this book?"

Fortunately, the results exceeded my wildest dreams. A record sales month! Not only this, but (spoiler alert) this month propelled us to a record sales year. We also greatly increased the size and quality of the audiences and the circles I was running in. I met President Obama, was called to fill in for Apple co-founder Steve Wozniak as the opening speaker at a conference, spoke on stage with the Director of the FBI addressing 3,300 counterterrorism agents, coached the CEO of Godiva Chocolates, and then twice joined *Sex in the City*'s Sarah Jessica Parker on stage. I was even blessed to adopt a baby cheetah in Kenya.

Focus made it all possible. Keep Calm and Focus On...

CHAPTER SUMMARY

The One Big Thing

Ask yourself, "What's the one thing that I *must* do well?"

Grade: *A*

This month started with the question that had been rattling in my brain for years: Is it possible to focus in this unfocused world? Even if it's possible, will it drive dramatic change? Results? The preliminary answer from this month appears to be an emphatic YES!

Top Takeaways

1. Be intentional with your focus—what is my single focal point? Understanding this isn't easy to do. If it were easy, we'd already be doing it. Remember that I failed the first 4 times. After 19 months and on my fifth try, it finally clicked.

2. Dramatic focus drives dramatic results. This month propelled us to a record sales year!

3. Focused questions are the building blocks to great relationships.

Time Management

It was difficult to contain my excitement for this month's topic: time management. Specifically, I'm going to focus on getting organized and protecting my schedule! The payoff for cleaning and organizing is seeing the immediate results, the instant return on our most important investment: Time. A disheveled pile of books transforms into a neatly arranged bookshelf—voilà, instant gratification. A messy desk appears almost new after a few minutes of decluttering. A busy calendar can be modified in moments.

I was ready to attack, but I also wanted to avoid taking on too much. Most of us mistakenly set "more" as our time management goal. Managing our time better so we can do more. What I wanted to focus on was the opposite: Less. Do less of the little things so we can do more of the big things. Thinking about time encourages clockwatching, which has been repeatedly shown to undermine the quality of work. We need to focus on quality over quantity when it comes to our to-dos and physical stuff. We should treat our life more like the new hard luggage versus the old soft luggage. The soft luggage allows us to always cram just one more item in. Eventually this behavior causes the luggage to break or it no longer fits in the plane's overhead compartment. This was a metaphor for many of our overstuffed lives.

Everywhere I looked seemed like an opportunity—the entire world required organizing! To help limit my scope, I would focus this month on physical organization rather than digital organization. If time allowed for some digital organization, I'd sprinkle it in here and there (Here's looking at you, seven years of family photos still on my iPhone!).

Your list will differ, but here are my top 10 items for February:

1. Organize and reduce the number of items in my closet.
2. Clean the garage before it explodes from all the dangerous fumes.
3. Tackle the filing cabinets so I can actually find last year's tax return.
4. Clean the refrigerator—your time is up 2017 Christmas IPA!
5. Declutter my "electronic graveyard" drawers.
6. Update Last Will and Testament to include our youngest daughter... not joking.
7. Get a Texas Driver's License—Yes, I was going on 6 years using my Massachusetts one!
8. Adjust and organize the timing on the sprinklers to reduce our use of water.
9. Purchase all my airline flights for my speaking engagements and book signings at least three months out so I can stop being crammed into the middle seat while paying $950 for a 45-minute flight.
10. Get additional house keys made.

Getting the house keys made was a surprisingly fun activity and it only took five minutes. My daughters had a blast selecting from the key designs. Rainbows, narwhals, and princesses were the winners. While it is a little embarrassing giving my neighbor a sparkling rainbow key shaped like a unicorn, the memory with my daughters is one I cherish every time we use it.

Make Your Bed, Make Your Life

While I knew I would enjoy focusing on being organized, I questioned whether doing so was too indulgent. Would becoming more organized really help me achieve my bigger goals?

Has the right message ever found you at just the right time? This happened when I heard the University of Texas commencement address delivered by Naval Admiral William H. McRaven, the ninth commander of U.S. Special Operations Command.

Each morning, when I place my feet on the floor, I see them as my two choices for the day.

I have the choice to be enthusiastic or the choice to be very enthusiastic.

He stressed that little things matter, such as making your bed. If you can't do the small chore of making your bed, how do you expect to be able to achieve your big goals in life? Here's an excerpt of his speech:

> Every morning in basic SEAL training, my instructors, who at the time were all Vietnam veterans, would show up in my barracks room, and the first thing they would inspect was your bed. If you did it right, the corners would be square, the covers pulled tight, the pillow centered just under the head-board, and the extra blanket folded neatly at the foot of the rack—that's Navy talk for bed.
>
> It was a simple task—mundane at best. But every morning we were required to make our bed to perfection. It seemed a little ridiculous at the time, particularly in light of the fact that we're aspiring to be real warriors, tough battle-hardened SEALs, but the wisdom of this simple act has been proven to me many times over.
>
> If you make your bed every morning you will have accomplished the first task of the day. It will give you a small sense

of pride, and it will encourage you to do another task and another and another. By the end of the day, that one task completed will have turned into many tasks completed. Making your bed will also reinforce the fact that the little things in life matter. If you can't do the little things right, you will never do the big things right.

And, if by chance you have a miserable day, you will come home to a bed that is made—that you made—and a made bed gives you encouragement that tomorrow will be better.

If you want to change the world, start off by making your bed.[10]

Studies support McRaven's wisdom. People who make their beds are 19% more likely to get a better night's rest than those who don't. When we feel organized, we are more relaxed. Similarly, 75% of people who sleep in fresh, clean sheets report sleeping more peacefully and comfortably than those who did not.[11]

We can also learn from Olympic long jumpers. Next time you watch the Olympics, pay close attention. Notice that a long jumper's last stride, before her giant leap, is her shortest one—typically 25 cm shorter.[12]

The path to our own gold medal often starts with the smallest step right before our giant leap.

Make your bed.

Going Bananas

Returning from a trip to the supermarket, I realized, focusing was going to be difficult. My mind was a jungle of distractions.

I needed eggs, milk, and bananas.

Well, I ran into a neighbor, received a few text messages, and bought some items that caught my eye. From my list of eggs, milk, and bananas, I only remembered to buy the eggs.

Baby Steps Aren't Just for Babies

One reason I started writing *The Focus Project* is that, in some strange way, it will serve as an antidote for my book, *Socialnomics*®. It is an antivenom to the poisonous habits technology can manifest in us. For the purposes of this book, and in a similar vein to General McRaven's advice for making our beds, I'm most interested in BJ Fogg's research and philosophy about developing powerful habits via small steps.

Fogg, a Stanford psychologist and researcher, specializes in captology. A captologist studies the effect of computers and mobile devices on human behavior. Fogg first appeared on my radar when I was writing *Socialnomics*. Fogg's work was relevant to *Socialnomics* because many of us using social media are unknowing participants in the world's largest social science experiment—one being controlled by the data scientists at Instagram, YouTube, Weibo, Facebook, TikTok, Twitter, and others.

Fogg argues that we mistakenly try to *will* our way to habits around activities we don't enjoy. For example, we get up early and drag ourselves to the gym to ride a stationary bike for an hour. Eventually, since we don't like it, we stop doing it. We don't develop the habit.

Fogg believes this mistake is more detrimental to a major change in our lives than doing nothing at all.

Instead, Fogg explains that we need to start with small adjustments that lead to little victories and to celebrate these victories. A good example is that your car is notoriously untidy, but you want it to be clean and organized.

A small change? Every time you park, you remove a piece of trash from your car. As this trash lands in the trash bin, you yell "Yes!" and raise your arms as if you scored the winning shot in a basketball game.

Fogg's formula involves a trigger. In this instance, the trigger is parking your car. Another example of a trigger might be doing 25 sit-ups every time you wash your hands. Washing hands = sit-ups.

We normally associate triggers with a negative cause-and-effect relationship. In Fogg's formula, however, instead of negative triggers, the triggers are positive influences.

Here's the simple formula for identifying triggers.

"After I *Establish Habit*, I will *New Habit*."

Fogg's best-known example of this formula is:

"After I *Brush My Teeth*, I will *Floss One Tooth*."

This sounds preposterous—who would floss just one tooth? This is exactly the point! Once you put into motion the flossing of one tooth you might say, "What the heck, why not floss a couple more?"

Interestingly enough, research suggests this simple act of flossing can increase our life expectancy by six years. By starting to floss one tooth per day, we have the potential to add six years to our life—not a bad tradeoff.

We need to celebrate even the tiniest victory, Fogg explains, because we gain confidence from the success. A small change is easier to integrate into our busy lives, and the accompanying success helps us achieve a level of automaticity.

Despite popular belief, we don't rise to the level of our dreams; we fall to the level of our systems and habits.[13]

How to Schedule Like a Cowboy

My Chief of Staff and I began meeting daily at 9:35 am. The first order of business was reviewing my schedule for the day, week, and month. While monotonous, it was necessary to be forward-looking and forward-protecting.

> *For every minute spent organizing, an hour is earned.*
> — Benjamin Franklin

At first, my schedule was completely full. There weren't even realistic breaks to eat lunch or go to the bathroom between meetings. We then decided to fence off specific times for certain activities: 10-10:30 on Mondays, Wednesdays, and Friday were for coffee meetings. Most calls would be scheduled during my drive time. 12:45 to 1:45 was blocked for lunch meetings.

Most important was fencing off big untouchable patches of time on the calendar. Intentional fencing-off time:

1.   Helped maintain my sanity and health; and

2.   Allowed time for deeper thinking and writing.

Previously, I haphazardly ran my schedule. I'd get a pocket of 15 minutes here, 12 minutes there. It was sporadic, inconsistent, and stress-inducing. I was writing my books sometimes in the back of Ubers because it was my only "downtime" as I ran from place to place.

SUNDAY

We now have a method, a method we named *cowboy scheduling*: A calendar with wide-open spaces and fences. I still can't ride a horse to save my life, but I can now schedule like Annie Oakley or John Wayne. I just don't smoke six packs of cigarettes a day as Wayne did. This week give it a try—try scheduling like a cowgirl or cowboy by fencing off specific times for certain activities and leaving wide open spaces for creativity, relaxation, and deep thinking.

Killing Time Vampires

Cowboy scheduling also means that when a coffee meeting is scheduled for thirty minutes, we keep it to thirty minutes.

Previously, these coffee meetings could easily spill (no pun intended) into 60 to 90-minute affairs. Now, I'm being more intentional with my time. For example, if the line for coffee is 15 minutes long, I'll stand in line talking with the person I'm meeting with while they wait for their coffee.

We then sit down and chat for the remaining 15 minutes. This is a vast improvement over patiently waiting at the table, then feeling bad that there wasn't much time to chat. Before you know it, the meeting will have stretched to over an hour.

These unexpected fifteen minutes here and thirty minutes there begin to add up and vampire our time. They "suck" our time dry. They suck the life out of us.

Guess what? By being rigid with the time scheduled, we get to the heart of the conversation faster. Most people that we meet up with are also overscheduled, so it's a win-win when we collectively kill time-vampires.

Digitally Killing Time-Vampires:

1. Batch process our various inboxes (e.g., email). I prefer 10:00-10:30 am and 3-3:30 pm.

2. If you don't recognize the caller, let the call go to voicemail.

3. Don't read product manuals; these are often lengthy and poorly written. Do read online tips, hacks, and/or watch short product videos.

4. If you are financially able to order your groceries online, the incremental cost is often offset by the savings on your time, gas, stress, and physical transport (unloading the car, hauling a forty-pound bag of dog food up stairs, ice cream melting, etc.). Re-ordering is also easier than making a grocery list each week.

5. Treat digital conversations like a tennis match: quickly put the "ball" back in the other person's court by returning a short message (two sentences or less). When appropriate, hit the winning shot by politely ending the conversation. A messy desk makes you less efficient as does a cluttered email inbox. Remember the adage: a cluttered desk/inbox is a sign of a cluttered mind.

6. Most digital inboxes have tools helping you identify the important from the unimportant. Use these tools.

7. A keystroke in time saves nine. Learn the shortcut keys for the programs you use most.

8. The shower, car, gym, flights, or subway are excellent places to listen to recorded material like podcasts.

9. Purchase quality headphones or earbuds for your phone so you can perform minor, non-mental tasks while on the phone (e.g., empty the dishwasher, pack for your trip, fold laundry, take a walk).

10. Don't constantly monitor items. For example, unless you're a day-trader, the act of incessantly checking the fluctuation of stock prices throughout the day is a waste of time and energy.

11. Use artificial intelligence (AI) on your phone or computer. Use Siri, Alexa, Google Assistant, etc., to accomplish simple things to help save time and keystrokes.

12. Use the transcribe feature for your voice-mail; instead of listening to the voicemail, you can quickly skim the text version of it.

13. Instead of texting or typing emails, simply voice record and send the audio file.

The most important thing to do is always doing the most important thing.

Thomas Corley spent five years researching the daily habits of rich, successful people and discovered a common habit among them. Every day, they brainstorm on their own. Rich people block time to think.

He identified ten core topics the rich consider during these brainstorming sessions:

1. Careers
2. Finances
3. Family
4. Friends
5. Business relationships
6. Health
7. Dream-setting and goal-setting
8. Problems
9. Charity
10. Happiness

They ask themselves questions related to these topics and often journal both the question and the answer:

- What can I do to make more money?
- Does my job make me happy?
- Am I exercising enough?
- What charities can I get involved in?
- Do I have good friends?
- Which business relationships should I spend more time on? Which should I pull away from?

When we schedule like cowgirls and cowboys—creating wide-open spaces and fences—we allow ourselves time to think. To strategically organize our days, weeks, and months.[14]

Multitasking is Really Switch-Tasking

"Multitasking, the best way to screw up both jobs." T-shirt humor or truth? A study at The British Institute of Psychiatry shows that multitasking efforts like checking email while performing another creative task decrease your IQ in the moment by up to 10 points. Now, I'm not certain about you, but I can't afford to lose ten IQ points!

This decrease in IQ is the equivalent of the effects from not sleeping for 36 hours—and has more than twice the impact of smoking marijuana.

The reason? Multitasking is really switch-tasking. Researcher David Meyer, Ph.D., sheds light on this: "People in a work setting, who are on their computers while also having to answer phones and talk with co-workers are doing switches all the time. Not being able to concentrate for, say, tens of minutes at a time means a cost of as much as 20 to 40 percent in lost efficiency."

Instead of parallel processing tasks, our brains are actually switching tasks. Which task is more important—writing this book or listening to the conference call? As our brains switch back and forth between tasks, we lose efficiency. Jordan Grafman, chief of the cognitive neuroscience section at the National Institute of Neurological Disorders and Stroke, explains, "There's substantial literature on how the brain handles multitasking. And basically, it doesn't. What's really going on is a rapid toggling among tasks rather than simultaneous processing."[15]

A study by Stanford psychologists Anthony Wagner and Eval Ophir found college students who often juggle many flows of information, such as checking social media, texting, watching videos, studying, and chatting on the phone, perform significantly worse than college students who limit their multitasking.

Multitasking can also have negative long-term effects. People who regularly multitask have more difficulty with tasks requiring working memory and sustained attention than those who rarely multitask. Multitasking leads to attention lapses that, over time, make sustaining attention to any single task more difficult.[16]

So, could it be we've had it wrong all along? That the reason we multitask is to get more done, yet, ironically enough, multitasking is causing us to get less done? In a word, *yes*.

One way to help avoid switch-tasking is to eliminate the number of tasks we have on our to-do lists. Over 70% of us make to-do lists.[17] Canadians are most likely to have a list, Americans are most dependent on their lists, and the Japanese are least likely to have a list, but more than half of the country still makes them. Women across the globe are more likely to make a to-do list than men.[18]

The majority of us still prefer to list our tasks on paper.[19] One reason we do this is biological. Whenever we cross something off our list we get a free hit of dopamine from our body. Our brain releases dopamine when we accomplish something we desire, whether completing a home-improvement project or winning a game of chess. Dopamine makes us feel good.

By creating small, achievable goals for ourselves on our to-do lists, we can manipulate our dopamine levels into accomplishing goals.

For example, after Bob finishes organizing his desk at work, he feels a sense of accomplishment and joy as dopamine is released into his system. This feeling drives repeat behavior and encourages Bob to continue keeping his desk clean along with completing other projects on his to-do list.[20]

However, dopamine also contributes to all kinds of negative addictions. Different people need different pleasures and rewards to get enough dopamine. A food addict's neurons get activated with the bite of a juicy hamburger, or a sex addict's dopamine is released when viewing erotic images. Similarly, an alcoholic gets that same rush of dopamine when sipping that first drink. Programmers and Ph.D.s at social media companies are paid millions of dollars to program similar tactics to manipulate dopamine levels within teenagers to get them to stay for hours on their social media platform or application.

Understanding the biology behind it gives us a fighting chance in avoiding the major and minor addictions dopamine can cause.

For example, when writing this book, I found spending an entire day answering the hundreds of emails I often receive after giving a keynote performance to be easy. Watching my unread inbox count go from 300 to 0 gave me a dopamine hit. Knowing this email dopamine trap, I will set smaller goals around writing on the days I'm on stage (e.g., write for 20 minutes).

Most importantly, I started making a Not-To-Do List before making my To-Do List...[21]

Making a Not-To-Do List

To-do lists are great, but not-to-do lists are even better. Successful people understand it's not about getting more things done, it's about getting more of the big things done. Making a not-to-do list is one of the most helpful habits I learned from this project.

If you never finish all of your items on your to-do list, don't feel bad. Neither do the rest of us. In a LinkedIn survey of 6,000+ global professionals, only 11% said they regularly accomplish all of the tasks on their to-do lists. So, for the rest of the 89% of us, it's time to try a new approach. Why not start with a not-to-do list? We need to become cold-blooded killers with some of our tasks. Several times per day we need to ask ourselves what tasks can we murder (i.e, not do)?[22]

Almost everything should default to our not-to-do list. Or, if it makes you feel better, you can call it your not-yet list. The beauty of this list is that it helps declutter our to-do lists. The science shows that even though we might be working on item #1 from our list, our brain is unconsciously thinking about #37.

By coming up with a to-do-list, our brain subconsciously determines what information from the list to hold onto for later. This subconscious activity is referred to as the Zeigarnik effect. The Zeigarnik effect causes our minds to think about and plan for uncompleted tasks even when we don't know our brain is doing it.[23]

The Zeigarnik effect was named after Russian psychologist Bluma Wulfovna Zeigarnik. In the 1920s, Zeigarnik was eating at a restaurant when she observed waiters with the capability to memorize very complicated orders. Once the orders were completed and paid for, the waiters could no longer remember the detailed components of the orders as they were able to do just minutes before.

This got Zeigarnik thinking. How could the waiters remember such minuscule details about unfinished orders but recall little to nothing about the orders once completed? She organized a study to specifically test this phenomenon.

In one experiment, Zeigarnik gathered 138 children to complete arithmetic problems, puzzles, and other basic tasks. During half of the activities, the children were not interrupted. For the remaining tasks, the children were interrupted and distracted. The study found that when tested for recall an hour later, 110 of the 138 participants remembered more details from the interrupted tasks than from the completed tasks. In similar experiments testing recall of adults, research has found participants recall unfinished tasks 90% more than completed tasks.[24]

This effect often occurs to voracious readers. While they're engrossed in a book they know all the characters and the author's name. As soon as they finish reading the book, if someone asks them about the book they can recall very little. Many even accidentally reread a book they've already read years before. It happens to the best of us.

Essentially, our subconscious mind is encouraging our conscious mind to make a plan for eventually completing the task. This mind activity is designed to help us. Before we could write, it allowed us to remember to grab dry wood during the light of day to have fire at night. However, in our overwhelming modern world, our outdated brain software can sometimes be a detriment to our success. The more uncompleted tasks we have on our to-do lists, the more cluttered our minds. Our brain is trying subconsciously to complete tasks 37, 38, 39, and beyond, even when we aren't working on them.[25]

> There is no bigger waste of time than doing something really well that shouldn't be done at all.

To help free our minds to attack our smaller and more focused *to-do list*, we should place almost all items on our *not-yet list*.[26]

Warren Buffet's Circle of Competence

How did Warren Buffett, living in Omaha, become the richest man in the world? By keeping it simple.

Buffet learned from his mentor early on the two rules to focus on when investing:

1. Never lose money.
2. Don't forget rule number one.

In a televised documentary on HBO called "Becoming Warren Buffett," Buffett explains the secret to his success.

> There is a book by arguably the greatest baseball hitter to ever live—Ted Williams. The book is called the "Science of Hitting." In the book, Williams has the strike zone broken into 77 squares with a picture of him at-bat. If he waits for the pitch in his sweet spot he will bat .400 whereas if he has to swing at the lower corner he will bat .235. In investing there are no umpires to call strikes on me. So essentially I'm in a "no-called strike" business which is the best business to be in.
>
> I can look at a thousand different companies (think baseball pitches) and I don't have to be right on all of them or even fifty of them. I can simply pick the ball I want to hit. The trick to investing is to watch pitch after pitch go by and wait for the one right in your sweet spot and if people are yelling "swing you bum!"...you ignore them. Over the years you develop filters and set up a circle of competence. I stay within that circle of competence and I don't worry about things outside that circle. Defining what your game is, where you will have an edge, is enormously important.[27]

People weren't yelling "swing you bum," but they were urging Warren to invest in technology stocks during the .com boom of the late 90s. However, Warren knew that tech stocks were outside his circle of competence, and he would not have an advantage. When the .com crash occurred, Berkshire Hathaway was in a strong position because Warren had remained focused on waiting for the pitches that would be in his sweet spot.

Shortly after meeting Bill Gates, Gates's father asked Warren and Bill to write down the one word that would best describe what had helped them the most in their careers. Warren explains what happened:

Bill and I without any collaboration both wrote the word focus. Well, focus has always been a strong part of my personality. If I get interested in something I get really interested. If I get interested in a new subject I want to read about it, I want to talk about it and I want to meet people involved in it.

I can't tell you the color of the walls of my bedroom or living room. I don't have a mind that relates to the physical universe well. But, the business universe I believe I understand relatively well.

I do like to sit and think. While this can be unproductive, it's enjoyable.

Buffett has been famously quoted as saying, "Our investment philosophy borders on lethargy." Buffett knew early in his career the impossibility of making thousands of right investment decisions. He knew that he would be wrong. To stack the odds in his favor, he kept to his center of competence and, in baseball terms, swung for the fences on a few investment decisions that he was most certain about, then held them for the long term. Buffett owes roughly 90% of his wealth to ten investments. Part of this is also the result of Buffett's not-to-do list strategy, as Mike Flint, Buffett's long-time pilot, discovered.

Life is hard by the yard, but by the inch, it's a cinch.
— John Bytheway

Flint served four U.S. presidents. Flint and Buffett were discussing career goals, and Buffett asked Flint to perform a simple exercise, one Buffett had found helpful in achieving some of his greatest accomplishments. He kindly asked Flint to grab a pen and paper, then follow these instructions:

Step 1:   Write down your top 25 career goals on a single piece of paper.

Step 2:   Circle your top five.

Step 3:   Put the top five on one list and the remaining 20 on a second list.

Flint now had two lists in front of him, the Top 5 list and the remaining Top 20 list.

Buffett asked him what he planned to do with the items on the list. Flint said he would immediately start working on the top five items. "And what about the other list?" Buffett inquired. Flint responded that the other 20 items were still important to him so he would chip away at the other 20 items when time allowed.

This makes sense. While these were good options Flint wanted to accomplish, they just didn't make his top five. Buffett's response?

"No. You've got it wrong, Mike. Everything you didn't circle just became your *Avoid-At-All-Costs List*. No matter what, these things get no attention from you until you've succeeded with your top 5."

It comes down to this. Would you rather be carrying around twenty half-completed items or finish five major ones?[28]

This was a nice reminder to me, as this was essentially the reason I'd started this focus project. I was trying to parallel-process too many things and was never completing them.

Amazon Founder Jeff Bezos's 2 Pizza Rule for Meetings

Whether you work at a business, hospital, non-profit, or school, unfocused meetings can sap productivity. American companies have an estimated 11 million meetings every single day.[29]

Jeff Bezos believes that all it takes is one bad attitude in a meeting to "drain all of the energy out of the room."[30] To combat wasted time and energy in meetings, Bezos developed the "Two Pizza Rule," one that helps him schedule only worthwhile meetings. Despite the rule's name, there is no real pizza involved. The rule means that Bezos will not schedule or attend any meetings where two pizzas can't feed the entire group.[31] Essentially, the more people in a meeting, the higher the potential for a dramatic decrease in productivity. Reduce the size of your next meeting. Pizza is optional.

> *The key is choosing how we attack our days – not just letting the days happen to us.*

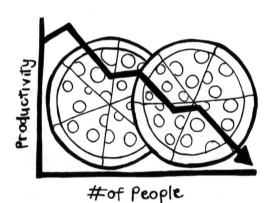

Dumping Grounds

In our homes, we all have a personal dumping ground for items we are not ready to discard, but don't know where they should go. My dumping ground is in our master closet. This is my dumping ground. My dad's dumping ground was always around his lounge chair. There were literally hundreds of magazines and other items towering near his chair.

It was time to tackle my dumping ground. Starting in the back of the closet, I began sifting through boxes of old mementos. It was very time-consuming, as each item brought up a specific memory, causing my mind to drift to faraway places. Without a system, the exercise of cleaning my closet would take months, if not years. Remembering that most successful people aren't smarter than we are, they just have better systems, I realized I needed a system. The system I came up with for memories and mementos was to ask two questions.

Memento Discarding System:

1. In twenty years, am I going to want this? Will I actually miss it if my wife accidentally discards it?
2. In forty years, if I give this to my daughters, will they want it?

95% of the time, the answer to these two questions is...no.

For clothing, the system was even simpler:

Clothing Discarding System:

1. Not worn in the past 11 months? Donate it. Can someone else benefit from this? Speedily donate it.
2. Is it useful for Halloween? Keep it.
3. Saving my clothing for a special occasion? Not doing it.

As it relates to #3 above, I had a pair of white shorts that I loved but rarely used since I didn't want to get them dirty. I'd only wear them on special occasions. Guess what? They went out of style. I should've worn them!

One can furnish a room very luxuriously by taking out furniture rather than putting it in.
— Francis Jourdain

My new motto became, *Wear your best every day.* Also, if we have a favorite shirt that fits perfectly, we are always going to wear that over the average shirt that fits so-so. We need to buy more of these same shirts and donate the clothes we aren't using to charity.

Staying organized positively influences our mental and physical health. A little tidying-up goes a long way. One study shows that people working in an organized space for just 10 minutes were twice as likely to choose an apple over a candy bar come snack time. Those working in an untidy space were more likely to reach for the candy bar. When our brain feels cluttered or stressed—a cluttered desk equals a cluttered mind—our body tends to crave comfort foods to help alleviate this stress.[32]

A study in *Personality and Social Psychology Bulletin* reported that women showed significantly higher levels of depression and fatigue when their "cluttered" homes were full of "unfinished projects."[33]

The Journal of Neuroscience indicates that a task as simple as decluttering our desks can significantly improve our work performance and health.[34]

The 3-Minute Rule

Any action that takes less than three minutes to declutter? Do it! It's liberating to embrace the phrase: "Less than *three* will set you *free*." Some have a one-minute rule or two-minute rule. In my case, there isn't much in my life that I can get done in this short amount of time.

Far too often, we postpone something that takes less than three minutes to complete. The 3-Minute Rule will help set you free. What happens when we don't perform these small tasks?

1. We forget it. It never pops back into mind, and it later causes problems. For example, turning off our water pipes so they don't freeze. Responding to an important email. Sending a quick "thank you" text. Dropping a Valentine's Day card into the mailbox.

2. We *can't* forget about it. It's there, nagging and draining mental capacity for the task at hand.

3. If it's a *quick win* and we don't do it, consider it a *long loss*. For example, if it will take me three minutes to remove a giant weed from the yard, that's my quick win. But if I don't do it, and see it day after day as it continues to grow and other weeds start to spawn, it becomes a long loss.

Many save items for their children or grandchildren, including china, desks, chairs, paintings, and the list goes on. When my grandparents moved from their house to the assisted living facility, they were shocked that our family didn't want any of their "things."

> *Out of clutter, find simplicity. From discord find harmony. In the middle of difficulty lies opportunity.*
>
> — Albert Einstein

Instead, everyone in my family wanted our grandparents' memories and mementos, photographs, family heirlooms. But nobody wanted their *stuff*. So, if you have been saving something for someone, ask them today if they actually want it. Consider a) if they do want it, give it to them now, and b) if they cannot see wanting it, immediately donate it to charity, sell it at a garage sale, or auction it online.

Examples of three-minute actions:

1. A photograph someone emailed you that you intend to print—print it!

2. Wash your smoothie glass out immediately—caked-on smoothy takes 3x as long to clean.

3. Pick up the shirt on the floor.

4. Put the timer in the electrical socket for the holiday lights.

5. Write that thank-you email.

6. Reorder your contact lenses or medical prescription before they run out.

7. Put new batteries into your garage door opener.

8. Wipe down the maple syrup outside the jar and unclog the sugar glut at the pour spout.

9. Unsubscribe from an email list instead of just deleting it. You can always re-subscribe (you won't).

10. Replace the light bulb.

One caveat to the 3-Minute Rule: Three-minute tasks are in abundance! Prepare yourself by combining the time-protecting and time-fencing techniques with the 3-Minute Rule.

The 3-Minute Rule works, and that's why it is one of my favorite parts of the day.

I'll put in my calendar 21 minutes for the 3-Minute Rule. It's exactly as it sounds. For that 21-minute block, I tackle only those tasks that take 3 minutes or less.

David Allen, in his bestselling book, *Getting Things Done*, suggests we can also apply the 3-Minute Rule concept to our goals and habits. Starting a new habit should take less than three minutes. Can all of your goals be accomplished in less than three minutes? Obviously not. But, every goal can be *started* in 3 minutes or less. And that's the purpose behind this little rule. Leaders don't say let's get *ready*, they say let's get *started*.

While this strategy may sound too basic for your grand life goals, I beg to differ. It works for any goal because of one simple reason: The physics of real life.

The Physics of Real Life

Sir Isaac Newton taught us that objects at rest tend to stay at rest and objects in motion tend to stay in motion. This is just as true for humans as it is for falling apples. People in motion tend to stay in motion.

The 3-Minute Rule works for big goals as well as small goals because of our inertia. Once you start doing something, it's easier to continue doing it. I love the 3-Minute Rule because it embraces the idea that all sorts of good things happen once we get started.

Want to become a better writer? Start by writing one sentence, and you'll often find yourself writing for an hour.

Want to eat healthier? Take one bite out of a carrot and you'll often find yourself inspired to make a healthy salad as well.

Want to make reading a habit? Read the first page of a new book, and, before you know it, the first three chapters have flown by.

That's been one of my mantras—focus and simplicity. Simple can be harder than complex: You have to work hard to get your thinking clean to make it simple. But it's worth it in the end because once you get there, you can move mountains.

— Steve Jobs

The Car Wash Experiment: Head Starts Help Create Finishers

As we covered in January, one of our top priorities as an organization, society, or individual is growth. As my parents always like to say, if we aren't growing, then we are shrinking. Seeing progress helps encourage us; it's the central reason why cleaning up the clutter around us can be so therapeutic. Marie Kondo's runaway bestseller on minimalism is entitled *The Life Changing Magic of Tidying Up*. When we hang up the towels in the bathroom or organize the desk drawers, we see progress.

In their 2006 study, Joseph Nunes and Xavier Dreze sought to discover the exact impact of progress. The study has become known as the "Car Wash Study."

Customers were given one of two loyalty cards. Both cards required the customer to have 8 car washes to receive a free car wash. Customers would receive a stamp on their loyalty card after every car wash.

Loyalty card ONE had eight blank circles. Loyalty card TWO had ten circles; however, two circles had already been stamped.

Loyalty cards ONE and TWO required exactly eight additional stamps to get the free car wash.

The essential question? Would people view the cards differently?

Yes, people did view them differently. 19% of customers with card ONE returned eight times in order to complete their card for the free wash. Yet, a whopping 34% of customers with card TWO returned eight times to receive their free wash. Almost twice as many![35]

The second group was coined the "Head Start" group. Although both loyalty card groups needed to return the same number of times (eight), the "Head Starters" felt they had already achieved progress—with their two "free" stamps—and were that much closer to getting their prize of a free car wash.[36]

As Nunes and Dreze discovered, seeing our progress encourages us to persist. How many times have we started a new diet and don't see any immediate results? If we notice small results at the beginning, we will be more likely to stick with the diet.

This study reminded me of when I was living in Cambridge and officing and assisting with the development of Harvard and MIT's edX. We saw a similar phenomenon. Students taking online courses at edx.org were more likely to stick it out if they saw progress in the first few weeks. If no indication of progress occurred by the third week, the drop-out rate was significant. As a result, the professors of the courses, within limits, managed for the students to see progress in those first few weeks. By helping show progress early in the course work, Harvard and MIT retained more online students, those who literally *stayed the course*!

So whatever the initiative, we should try giving recognizable wins early in the journey.

Show me your schedule, and I will tell you your priorities.

An Empty Drawer

My daughter's crayons were on the table, and I went to place them into their proper drawer. The drawer was stuffed and wouldn't budge. A little wiggling and finger fishing helped pry it open. Several items spilled over the sides. Cleaning up this mess, I opened the drawer next to it and was shocked to discover it was empty. Glory be to the highest!

The crayons fit easily into this drawer. My daughter entered the room and her eyes became as big as saucers:

Katia: Daddy! You can't put those crayons in that drawer!

[It's always great hearing your wife's voice through your child, btw]

Me: Um, and why can't I put these crayons in here?

Katia: That's Mommy's drawer. Nothing can go in there.

Me: But there's nothing in this drawer. It's completely empty.

[I placed the box of crayons in the empty drawer]

Katia: Ok, Daddy. But don't say I didn't warn you. You're going to be in BIG trouble.

Katia's warning turned out to have merit. I did get into trouble for using this sacred drawer.

Had I not been in the middle of this focus project, I may have admitted my wife to a mental institution. Instead, we sat down and discussed it. For her, the act of having at least one empty drawer in the kitchen

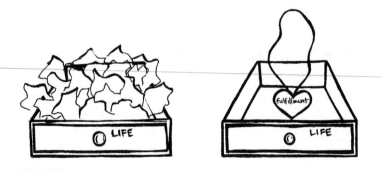

meant she wasn't just constantly adding stuff. Not just to the kitchen, but adding junk to her life. The empty drawer was symbolic for her.

Since I was deep into researching the power of less, this made sense to me (either that, or we were both crazy). She did compromise a little by switching the designated "empty drawer" from the largest to the smallest.

> *Simplicity is the ultimate sophistication.*
> — Leonardo da Vinci

While organizing, I stumbled upon a favorite proverb. A wise Indian chief, instructing the braves of his tribe on shooting an arrow, put a wooden bird in a tree and asked them to aim at the beak of the bird. The chief asked the first brave to describe what he saw. The first brave responded, "I see the branches, the mountains, the leaves, the sky, the bird, the bird's feathers, and its beak." The chief asked this brave to wait. He turned to the second brave and posed the same question. This brave replied, "I see the beak of the bird." The chief said, "Well done. You are ready to shoot." The arrow flew straight and hit the tiny beak target. Like the brave, unless we focus we cannot achieve what we want.[37]

CHAPTER SUMMARY

The One Big Thing

Successful people block out time to organize their items, minds, and schedules.

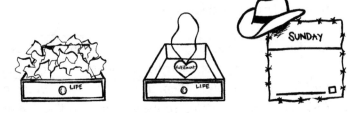

Grade: *B+*

I was happy with my progress this month and derived joy from seeing so many to-dos completed around me. Yet, despite my best efforts, I realize how much more could be organized and how much better I can manage my time! A great month, I will give it a B+.

Top Takeaways

1. Schedule like a cowboy—fence-off times and leave wide open spaces on the calendar.

2. Make a Not-To-Do List.

3. The 3-Minute Rule: If it takes less than 3 minutes, do it!

4. Rich and successful people aren't smarter than we are or have more time—they just have better systems and processes.

5. Stop multitasking and focus on your circle of competence.

6. It's ok, it's even healthy, to have a completely empty drawer in your house...your life.

Family + Friends

The year is 1930. World-renowned economist John Maynard Keynes begins to write an essay that will become widely read. He didn't know it then, but almost 100 years later, his essay still stirs controversy.

Despite Keynes's brilliance, his *Economic Possibilities For Our Grandchildren* is still discussed because it turned out to be wildly wrong.[38] In his essay, Keynes predicts, due to advances in technology, that his grandchildren, by the time they become fully grown, will be working roughly 15 hours a week.

How inaccurate was Keynes? He had neither children nor grandchildren. Keynes's sister did have grandchildren, including Nicholas Humphrey, a professor. Humphrey estimates that he worked closer to 15 hours per day; a whopping 75 hours per week—a far cry from 15 hours per week. Another sister's grandchild, Susannah Burn, a self-employed psychotherapist, estimates that she works around fifty hours per week and admits finding it difficult to take time off.

Most can relate to Nicholas and Susannah. Long working hours are so common that social media hashtags like #nevernotworking are often trending. Full-time American workers work an average of 47 hours per week, an hour and a half more than a decade ago. Alarmingly, nearly four in ten workers are working over fifty hours per week.[39]

These longer hours often result in less family time. The previous month taught me how to schedule like a cowboy. A big eureka moment this month was realizing I needed to schedule like a cowboy in both my professional *and* personal life. Author Tim Urban calculated that 80% of the time we spend with our family occurs before we are 18. This was a sharp reminder to me that the time I had with my daughters was right now.

If we don't prioritize quality time with our family and loved ones, then it will not exist. Our attitude of *wanting* to have more quality time with our family and friends is simply not good enough. We need to transform this into *must-have* time and appropriately fence it off. Specifically, when we say, "I must set aside time for my family," we are saying that we must ruthlessly protect time for our loved ones.

The Rule of 52

My hands were shaking as I boarded the plane. The flight attendant asked if I was ok. What I wanted to scream was "No! I'm not ok. I just want to sit down...The airport security machine broke and it took three hours...Ridiculous!...Who runs an airport like this?...I missed my first two flights because of this!...I don't think I'm going to arrive on time to be on stage!" Of course, I didn't scream such things. They simply were a wrecking ball inside my head.

I did feel as if I might collapse—a new experience for me. In college, I had endured Coach Tom Izzo's historically challenging practices. If I could make it through those, how could this be taking me down?

Yet, here I was at my wit's end. "May I please have some water?" I croaked. I could hear that my voice was off...It had a shaky quality to it—it was cracking. I was literally cracking up.

Making it to my seat, I was physically shaking and mentally shaken. It turns out, despite my superhero name, I'm not indestructible.

I'd performed in front of hundreds of thousands of people, and while I'd used adrenaline, stress, and nerves as tools for peak performance, I'd never been pushed to the edge—to the edge of a mental breakdown—until now.

Doing a 24-city book signing and speaking tour for a Fortune 500 company over a five-week period was taking its toll. We had two young daughters at home, it was the holidays, and we'd just started our animation company. On top of this, the publishing deadline for my next book was nearing. In sum, it was a classic case of me not respecting my capacity. Perhaps you can relate?

I was breaking down.

Yet, I realized this was an opportunity for a breakthrough, not a breakdown. How did I arrive in this land of overload? How can I prevent this in the future?

Being a big believer in the concept that things happen *for* you, not *to* you, this experience led to my *52 Night Rule,* a rule we track as our #1 KPI (Key Performance Indicator). From a short-term viewpoint, this rule costs the business revenue. Yes, it costs the company revenue in the short-term. But, from a long-term perspective, it is invaluable across all fronts, including revenue and, most importantly, fulfillment. In the short term we may lose a battle, but in the long run we are winning the war.

The Rule: A maximum of 52 nights per year away from my family, protecting at all costs what matters most.

> A man should
> never neglect his
> family for business.
> — Walt Disney

My hope is that you can learn from my experience by placing guardrails in your life to protect what is important. What is your equivalent of the 52 Night Rule?

Do What We Want, Not What We Think We Should

To avoid lines at Disney one has the ability to sign-up for 3 *Fast Passes*. These passes are the equivalent of the Willy Wonka Golden Ticket, allowing you to skip waiting 2-3 hours in line.

We found ourselves with one *Fast Pass* remaining. We checked the current ride wait times.

The Jungle Cruise wait was 70 minutes, whereas the *Barnstormer Roller Coaster* and *Winnie the Pooh* ride each had ten-minute waits. My kids highly prefer both the *Barnstormer* and *Winnie the Pooh* rides over *The Jungle Cruise*, but my wife and I were conflicted. It seemed like such a waste of our last *Fast Pass* if we didn't take the one with the most value in regards to waiting time (70 minutes for the *Jungle Cruise*), but when we asked our kids, their answer was resounding—"Barnstormer!"

It's enlightening how often kids make better decisions than adults. Even though the rest of the Disney attendees valued the *Jungle Cruise* enough to wait 70 minutes, it didn't matter. It wasn't something my daughters valued. If the lines were equally long, my kids would pick *Barnstormer* over *The Jungle Cruise*. In this case, the *Barnstormer* line was 7 times shorter. It was really a simple decision that we as parents had made complex, and if we hadn't asked the children, we would've made the wrong decision.

One key aspect of focus is doing what we really want to do, not what we think we should do or what others are doing or what others value. Often this is difficult—especially for us identifying as chameleons—because it might be the opinion of someone we respect, such as a parent, brother, or mentor. But, we need to remind ourselves that it's about what we value and what brings us joy.

> *If you can't live longer, live deeper.*
> — Italian proverb

Steve Jobs's Last Words

At the age of 56, Steve Jobs died a billionaire. Close family members say that his dying words were "Oh, wow. Oh, wow. Oh, wow." Whether he penned an essay during the days leading up to his death is probably unlikely, but it is still being debated. What we do know is that Jobs often sacrificed his family to achieve success in business. At one point he went so far as to deny that he was the legitimate father of his daughter, Lisa, surprising on many levels, especially given that Jobs was adopted as a child.

The following is thought to be the essay Jobs wrote in his last days. While its authenticity might be disputed, its profundity cannot be.

> *I reached the pinnacle of success in the business world. In others' eyes, my life is the epitome of success. However, aside from work, I have little joy. In the end, my wealth is only a fact of life that I am accustomed to. At this moment, lying on my bed and recalling my life, I realize that all the recognition and wealth that I took so much pride in have paled and become meaningless in the face of my death.*

> *You can employ someone to drive the car for you, make money for you, but you cannot have someone bear your sickness for you. Material things lost can be found or replaced. But there is one thing that can never be found when it's lost—Life. Whichever stage in life you're in right now, with time, you will face the day when the curtain falls.*

> *Treasure love for your family, love for your spouse, love for your friends. Treat yourself well and cherish others. As we grow older,*

and hopefully wiser, we realize that a $3000 or a $30 watch both tell the same time. You will realize that your true inner happiness does not come from the material things of this world. Whether you fly first class or economy, if the plane goes down—you go down with it.

Therefore, I hope you realize, when you have mates, buddies and old friends, brothers and sisters, who you chat with, laugh with, talk with, sing with, talk about north-south-east-west or heaven and earth, that is true happiness. Don't educate your children to be rich. Educate them to be happy. So when they grow up they will know the value of things and not the price.

Eat your food as your medicine, otherwise, you have to eat medicine as your food.

The One who loves you will never leave you for another because, even if there are 100 reasons to give up, he or she will find a reason to hold on. There is a big difference between a human being and being human. Only a few really understand it. You are loved when you are born. You will be loved when you die. In between, you have to manage.

The six best doctors in the world are sunlight, rest, exercise, diet, self-confidence, and friends. Maintain them in all stages and enjoy a healthy life.

Are You Hunting Mice or Antelope?

A lion's attentive golden eyes can help us focus. Not only literally, but metaphorically. A lion is powerful and fast enough to catch and eat field mice all day. However, the lion burns more energy catching a field mouse than the field mouse provides in sustenance. The lion is best served to let the field mouse be and to focus his attention on hunting antelope. While more difficult to catch than a field mouse, the antelope provides enough nutrients for the lion and its entire pride. A lion can't live on field mice, but it can live a long and happy life on a diet of antelope.

While it's tempting for us to do the little, easy tasks like cleaning out our email inbox, this is our version of chasing field mice. In the short run, it gives us a nice, rewarding feeling. But, in the long run, it will cause us to wither up and die. A lion that spent its day hunting and eating field mice will slowly starve to death.

As previously discussed, while we want to take small steps to achieve our goals, we need to ensure these steps lead to the right thing, that they lead to antelope, not field mice. That we are achieving items that bring us fulfillment rather than ones that leave us empty and mentally starving.

We need to spend this month ignoring field mice and focusing on antelope. Doing so starts with a powerful two-letter word: NO.

The Best Productivity Tool Is Saying No

Our mindset is that we can do it all. While this is a positive approach to life, it isn't a realistic one. While it's true we can have it all, we just can't have it all *at once.*

"Will you take my dog out while I'm at work today?" *Yes.*
"Will you pick up Sarah from school at 3:30 pm?" *Of course.*
"Can you sit in the meeting for me?" *Sure.*
"Can you pick up the cookies for tonight's parent-teacher conference meeting?" *On it.*

With these constant knee-jerk "yes" responses, we set ourselves up for stress or failure, or both.

As Steve Jobs famously quipped, "Focus is about saying no." While this sounds simple, it isn't easy. The truth is that most of us are terrible at saying no. We go to extremes to avoid uncomfortable situations. Think about the last time you had a subpar experience at a restaurant. When the waiter came over and asked how everything was, did you reply, "Not so great. The table was dirty when we sat down. We were missing silverware, so my eggs got cold waiting for a fork. You didn't refill my coffee when I politely asked for it." I'm guessing you didn't say anything remotely close to this. Instead, you replied, "Great, thanks." As people-pleasers, most of us steer clear of conflict. And, for the most part, doing this serves us well.

However, there is one glaring exception. This inability to say "no" is the primary reason we are not able to focus on what matters most. The equation is straightforward: Fewer commitments = more time for what really matters. The difference between successful people and very successful people is very successful people say no to almost everything. Being a novice at saying no is hurting you; become an expert at saying no.

Like many of you, I skew toward being a people-pleaser. And, like most people-pleasers, I find it difficult to say "no." Saying no will often trade popularity for respect. If I had to choose one I'd personally choose respect over popularity, so I'm constantly looking for tricks and hacks to help me say "no."

One hack I find particularly helpful, along with the six mentioned below, is to treat my time like a business. Specifically, I think of requests as an online order. Once the inventory of a particular item is depleted—that's it. Sorry, but this item is currently out of stock! In this case, the item is my time, specifically my ability to say "yes" to any new requests. Sorry, but we are all out of YES. All we have left on the shelf is NO. It's a classic supply and demand issue. We need to start treating it as such.

Avoid saying, "I'll get back with you." Delaying your response only adds anticipation and leads to increased disappointment.

6 Ways to No:

1. Just say it. Don't overthink it. Be confident and tell your friend or coworker "no." Be polite and brief in explaining why. Less is best. You don't owe anyone a full explanation. Just be honest: "Sorry, but I have too much on my plate right now."

2. Offer an alternative that does work for you. "I can't today, but tomorrow I will be heading that way and we can grab a coffee then."

3. Plan out your "no" ahead of time. Know your schedule. What do you have time for this week? If you're swamped, plan out a few things you might say if someone asks you for help. One of my favorites: "I'm heads down on my book, so I'll have to pass."

4. Be selfish. It's your schedule, not theirs. There's no way to reach your goals if you're taking on everyone else's challenges and forgetting about your own.

5. Start small. This week, try to say "no" to two things. They can be small things.

None of this will be easy at first, but with practice, just like in sports, you will improve.[40,41,42]

Economist Tim Harford states that "Every time we say yes to a request, we are also saying no to anything else we might accomplish with that time."[43] With this in mind, would you really want to work that extra shift and say "no" to going to your daughter's school musical? The greatest hockey player of all time, Wayne Gretzky, was famous for his focus and said, "I don't skate to where the puck is, I skate to where the puck is going to be."

Over time, we become more and more selective, transitioning from saying "yes" to good things to only saying "yes" to *exceptional* things.

We need to think about our level of excitement when deciding whether to say "yes" or "no." Using the "Hell Yeah or No" method from Derek Sivers, judge your reaction to the request. If the proposal isn't making you think, "Wow, this sounds *awesome*. I would love to do that!" then just say "no." "Hell No's" lead to emphatic "Yeses!"[44]

Surgically Saying No

The ability to say no, strongly and politely, is a must for achieving our goals. While we should certainly continue to help people, we don't need to, nor can we, help *everyone*. We need to respect capacity.

Let's take a look at how surgeons spend their time. Many surgeons fall in love with medical practice because they want to help and heal people. For them, turning away a patient is difficult. These are often life and death situations. Yet, we cannot reasonably expect our top surgeons to treat everyone.

Any intelligent fool can make things bigger, more complex, and more violent.
It takes a touch of genius—and a lot of courage—to move in the opposite direction.
— E.F. Schumacher

Research has shown that tired surgeons can make deadly mistakes. A study published in the *Journal of the American Medical Association* shows that patients of sleep-deprived surgeons face an 83% increased chance of complications. To help prevent this, laws limit the number of hours surgeons can operate.

As such, doctors aren't "on call" every night. Yet, many of us put ourselves on call every morning, day, and night. This isn't sustainable. Start acting like a surgeon. Don't operate on everyone. Instead, keep a set amount of hours, consistently separating the mundane from the emergency. Also remember that you're a human being, not human doing. We can't make more time but we can increase the amount of time doing things we love.

Number one bestselling author Seth Godin has a very polite but simple response for unsolicited requests/emails:

> Hi Seth!
>
> My friend, Kelly Kramer, is the CEO of Round Oranges Inc., and I think it will be great for you two to connect, so I'm introducing you here.
>
> Warmest, Terry

Seth's response to these types of communications and others is simple:

> Hello Kelly,
>
> It's nice to meet you. Because of my current projects, I don't currently:
>
> 1. Invest in companies
> 2. Promote products or services
> 3. Attend meetings
>
> How can I help?
>
> Seth

Similarly, while I was the Head of Marketing at Travelzoo, I wanted to showcase to the team how little email matters. That email is throughput versus output.

To help prove my point I went on vacation and had this as my out-of-office response:

Thank you for your email. We apologize, but the server is temporarily full. If your email is important please resend it on October 10 when we will have more capacity.

On October 10th I returned from my vacation to find 1,420 emails in my inbox. I deleted all of them. Nothing bad ever resulted from doing this; I wasn't fired and nothing of importance was missed. Only 8 people felt it was important enough to resend their email. This is how little throughput or "fake work" matters. Half of the hours we often invest don't produce any tangible output for the business. In 1970, Nobel Laureate, Herbet Simon, warned of the pending information age, "A wealth of information creates a poverty of attention."

Author Jim Collins, who has sold over 10 million books, including his flagship book *Good to Great*, recognized the pitfalls and attractions of fake work. To avoid this and to avoid falling into a rut, Collings tracks his days on a spreadsheet and the key item he watches for is to ensure for any twelve-month period that his creative thinking hours always exceed 1,000 hours.

We never lose the ability to choose what we are doing each day, but we sometimes forget that we have the ability to choose what we are doing.

Who's Your Priority?

Do you often find yourself staying at work an hour or two longer than anticipated trying to reply to all your messages? If this is a constant problem, you're most likely shortchanging your family. North Point Ministries Senior Pastor Andy Stanley recommends sitting down with your family, looking them in the eye, and saying:

> I just want to apologize upfront to all of you, because I'm going to be home a few hours late each night this week. I'm going to prioritize emails, phone messages, texts, and tweets from strangers. I also don't know the subject matter. But, when I receive these messages in the future, I'm going to prioritize them ahead of you. To be clear, what I'm saying is, answering these messages is more important to me than you are.

Sounds ridiculous? Of course it does. I'm guessing no one reading this book has ever sat their family down for such a discussion. Yet, this is exactly the message we send our loved ones every time we engage in this behavior. Our actions speak louder than words.

We also do it to ourselves. We often sabotage our goals and dreams. Try this exercise. Write your goals on pieces of paper and tape them to your mirror. Address your goals and yourself in the mirror and repeat the paragraph you wanted to say to your family, only this time you're saying it to yourself about your goals. Essentially, you will tell yourself that your goals will be secondary to future whims, messages, and unknown requests. It sounds like a silly exercise, but it's what most of us do. We are prioritizing future emails, texts, requests, tweets, and beyond over our passions and purpose in life.

Bottom line: If we say *yes* to everyone, we are essentially saying *no* to everyone.

The feeling of letting people down by saying "no" will decrease the more you practice, but it never truly goes away. To help in these moments, remind yourself that by saying "no" today I can say "yes" to someone or something in the future. It's a simple phrase: *By saying no today, I can say yes tomorrow.* The inverse is that by saying "yes" today, you have said "no" to something in the future. Make your yeses count.

Defaulting to Yes

For me, my "yeses" count the most with my family. By learning to say "no," I'm able to stockpile more yeses for important moments.

Oddly enough, before embarking on this project, I was defaulting to "no" with my family. For you, it could be your family, friends, charity work, your church, your quiet time, or something else. It's easy to fall into the

We can't accomplish big things if we are a slave to small things.

trap of defaulting to "no" with those around us. We take for granted that they can wait, but we feel that the important animation project or manuscript can't wait.

For at least a month, when it came to my family, I was going to default to YES! I was going to take this *family yes* mentality to extremes with my daughters:

Girls: Daddy, can we have ice cream for breakfast?

Me: Yes! While we will not have ice cream for breakfast every day, on this special day, why don't we have ice cream!

These moments created memories…"Daddy, remember the time that we had ice cream for breakfast?"

Following a huge rainstorm, my kids asked if they could ride their scooters through the water in the parking lot, then jump in the puddles on the way home. My mind defaulted to, "Absolutely not, look how dirty that water is." But, I paused and thought, *What harm can it do? They have their "roughhousing" shorts on, and we are going to shower as soon as we get home. They are going to outgrow these clothes in a few months, but they will not outgrow the memory. Just because jumping in the dirty puddles wasn't something I wanted to do at the moment, why prevent my kids from being kids? They grow up soon enough.* "YES!"

The first thing the kids told mommy the next day and then the grandparents on the phone was all the fun they had jumping and riding through the puddles. What a memory. I was definitely glad I'd said "YES!"

The next day, Sofia asked me, "Do you want to draw, Daddy?" At the time she asked, I was writing a note to an important client. The default answer in the past: "In a little while, pumpkin, let me just finish this." Invariably, in the past, this type of response would result in the moment passing, or Sofia would've moved onto another activity without me.

This time, when she asked me to draw, my response, without hesitation, was "YES!" I was saying "no" to everybody else.

At first, I felt guilty because I didn't feel like drawing. But, I realize by meeting her in their moment—rather than at my convenience—I can become a kid again. Sofia exclaimed, "Wow, Daddy, you're amazing. You're the best drawer in the entire world!" Trust me, I'm no Picasso, but he had nothing over me in terms of pride as a dad.

At the end, she blurted out of the blue, "Wow. That was really fun, Daddy. Thanks."

While the majority of the time we need to default to "no," there is one area in your life where you should default to "yes!" As Gretchen Rubin and others express, "The exact opposite of a known truth is also often true."

Saying "yes" to my kids more often allows me to be more instructional when my answer is "no." Before, if they asked me why they couldn't do something, I often lazily defaulted to: "Because I said so, that's why!" That's not a good way to lead in business, and it's not a good way to lead a family.

Visiting The Wizarding World of Harry Potter™, the kids fell in love with drinking Butterbeer. It's quite sugary—similar to a very sweet cream soda. The first lunch, they split one. The second lunch, they each begged for their own.

"You can have your own, but I think it's going to be too sweet for each of you to finish a full one. Are you sure you each want your own instead of splitting one?" I asked.

"We are sure, Daddy," they replied in unison.

Sure enough, halfway through, both were struggling. Like paying for most items at amusement parks, you almost had to take out a second mortgage to buy these Butterbeers. Ana Maria sternly told the girls, "You will finish those, every last drop."

But, by the bloated looks on the girls' faces, and the fact that we were going on rollercoasters later in the day, we decided it was best to consider the two Butterbeers a sunk cost and move on. I certainly didn't want to be wearing butterbeer for the rest of the day.

This episode allowed for a teaching moment, so I addressed the girls:

Me: As you can see, we would've been best off ordering just one Butterbeer to split. While you may not want to hear what your mom and I have to say, do you at least agree that we're often looking out for your best interests?

Girls: Yes, Daddy.

Me: So, the next time we have a situation like this, we might mention, "Remember the Butterbeer?" or we might just say "Butterbeer." This will help remind us, and we will learn from this moment. Make sense?

Girls: Yes, Daddy.

My wife and I will now often just say "Butterbeer" in moments when the girls are incessantly pleading for something, like making homemade rainbow slime in the living room or inhaling an entire jar of Nutella.

Moment of Truth

My 92-year-old grandma's health was declining. My grandfather was right by her side—as he had been ever since the day they met in high school. My grandma attended Wellesley and was an entrepreneur during the days when a woman doing such a thing was considered odd—very, very odd. She was smart, strong, and didn't tolerate any bull.

She would often tell people she met, "I wish we were meeting when I was more myself, but it's better than never meeting you at all."

In the final years, she suffered from dementia, and, near the end, this strong independent woman needed assistance getting out of bed. In an odd sense, her physical and mental decline was a paradox in that it was both rapid and gradual.

We knew it was only a matter of time before she ascended to a better place, yet we knew we would never really be ready to receive that phone call. My heart sank when I heard she was in hospice and only had a few days. I prayed.

Once these prayers subsided, the practical part of my brain cruelly took over—if she passed away tomorrow, I could catch a flight for the weekend for the funeral. If it were a few more days, however, I had some performances that I couldn't contractually cancel. This was another "eureka" moment for me. What kind of person thinks like this? Many of us do, and it's the result of the hyper-paced world we live in. It was a slap to my face. Moreover, it was as if my own soul were shaking me and saying, "Look at yourself! You need to focus on what's important!" And that was it—a nice reminder that focus is simply a word for prioritizing what's most important to us in life. It was a reminder that we are never guaranteed today, let alone tomorrow. Do the things that matter most, first.

After the funeral, I suggested to Ana Maria that we start taking the kids more on my speaking and book signing tours—even if it entailed taking them out of school. She was all for it.

Once, when I was speaking in Asia, we took Sofia and Katia to Singapore, Vietnam, and Thailand. They were even able to see me perform on stage for 11,000 people. We repeated this in Portugal, Spain, and France.

Taking the family lessened my guilt—in fact, being able to give my daughters these unique experiences thrilled me. While sometimes there were hiccups, such as the time I had to hold Katia all night before taking the stage in the morning, having them travel with us was well worth any downside.

Eureka Moment: Seeking work-life balance is difficult—seek work-life harmony.

What Would the #1 Dad in the World Do?

A eureka moment hit me in regard to comparative trading. When traveling, I need to be cognizant of every minute. When making it to my hotel room in the evening, if I start watching an NBA game or mindlessly scrolling through social media. I'm wasting time. Ultimately, this means less time for my wife and kids. I'm not simply watching an NBA game; rather, I'm burning valuable time in the future with my family.

I started asking myself, *"Is this something the #1 Dad in the World would be doing?"* When I found myself watching fail videos, I'd pause and ask myself, "Is this something the #1 Dad in the World would be doing?" It's a silly way to look at the world, but it works for me! This brief internal questioning reminds me that the days are long, but the years are short.

When I feel like criticizing someone—I often keep it to myself. At the cocktail party, I'll turn down that last drink to avoid being sluggish the next morning with the kids. This Jedi-mind trick doesn't work all the time—sometimes that second Martini is just too good to pass up. But, it's helping me make progress. My hope is it helps you as well: *What would the #1 Mom in the World do, #1 Friend, #1 Grandmother, #1 Writer, #1 Pianist, #1 Son, #1 Aunt, #1 Cousin, #1 Graphic Designer, and beyond.*

You're Gonna Miss Me When I'm Gone

In preparation for a triathlon, I started swimming. From past experience, I knew that on race day, to avoid getting kicked in the face and sucking salt water, I would be sprinting the first 200 meters. As such, I couldn't just "go through the motions" during practice.

My girls are good swimmers and the pool is narrow, so it works well for me to take them with me. I can keep an eye on them in the pool while I swim laps.

Then, I started seeing them *too* much! They were diving under me while I swam. Hence, I had to dodge errant kicks—to regions where you don't want to be kicked—or they were grabbing my ankles in an attempt to stop me and ask questions like, "Why do my goggles look like mirrors?" or "How long can mermaids hold their breath?"

In the past, these interruptions would've certainly bothered me. *Can't you see that I only have thirty minutes to train, girls? I need you to get out of MY lane!*

This time I shifted my focus. My focus wasn't about them being in the way but rather on how they wanted to wave at me and smile underwater, how they wanted to race me, to be near me. I realized the years would fly by and these special moments would be gone and I'd miss them.

A song from Anna Kendrick popped into my head:

"When I'm gone,
When I'm gone,
You're gonna miss me when I'm gone,
You're gonna miss me by my hair
You're gonna miss me everywhere, oh,
You're gonna miss me when I'm gone."

So true.

Rather than be annoyed, I relished the moment, in the moment. Focusing in the moment on being a better dad was a million times better than shaving a few silly seconds off my race time by yelling at my girls to get out of my lane. It wasn't lost on me, either, that metaphorically we often think of people getting *out of MY lane*. The truth is that success isn't singular. We need others to succeed in life. We need to embrace the fact that others will constantly be swimming in and out of our lanes.

The key is to recognize who's helping and who isn't. And understanding that, at any time, it's ok to switch lanes if someone in your life is dragging you down.

If someone in your family or some organization is trying to pull you into their drama, their negative vortex, simply repeat in your mind: *"Not my circus. Not my monkeys."* You have the power to change lanes. We have the power to change our focus.

If we think we are going to have wide-open beautiful swimming lanes, we are setting ourselves up for failure. The icebergs, waves, flotsam, and obstacles in our lives are there for a reason. They are there to make us better, and they're there to keep the competition out. A life well-lived isn't supposed to be easy.

I'm glad my kids still want to swim in my lane.

How Kids Spell Love

Understand that kids spell love T-I-M-E. When I travel for work, in their minds I'm gone for essentially two workdays. Hence, upon returning, it doesn't make sense to them why I will often go into the office the following day. They have a point. When I'm in town, I now pick "travel days" sans the suitcase. On these "staycation" travel days,

I don't go into the office, and I'm difficult to reach during certain hours—just as if I'm actually traveling.

These staycations allow me to drop into my kids' schools to grab lunch with them or to read to their classes. Because of my height (6'6"), their classmates always start chanting "Jump-Jump!" to get me to touch the ceiling. Or, they look all the way up at me and say, "Wow, you must be really old."

There are hundreds of pressing needs pulling us away from spending time with our loved ones. It's easy to take our loved ones for granted as we chase the next thing. Often, what we are chasing relates to fame or fortune. To ensure I'm focusing on the right things, I will often ask myself, "If my wife or daughter were to pass from this life today, how much would I pay for the ability to dance with her one more time?" The answer is easy for me. *All of it*. If I had amassed $10 billion dollars, I would pay all of it.

Kids spell *Love* T-I-M-E.

How About Them Pineapples?!

When I go to the supermarket, I'm always floored by the outrageous cost of a quartered fresh pineapple. Because of this high price, I've been "fooled," more than once, into buying an entire pineapple for $3. I'm paying $3 instead of $9.

Once at home, I start coring the pineapple. For anyone who has ever done this, you know it is no easy task:

1. A pineapple is big, tough, and spiny.
2. Remove the hard center core, a must.
3. Next, cut the skin, but barely. The sweetest part of the pineapple is found closest to the skin, so keep those brown ringlets on the first cut then v-cut them out.

4. Of course, the pineapple juice always seems to find some tiny cut on my hand that stings like the dickens.

5. It usually takes me 15-25 minutes to cut a pineapple properly.

6. In sum, it's a pain in the ass (PITA), so now I gladly pay the extra $6 to save 20 minutes of my time, avoid a huge headache, and have better pineapple. (My hand doesn't sting, either.)

The best things in life aren't things.

Unless I derive joy from cutting pineapples, I'm better off spending money on the fresh, store-sliced pineapple. One side of my brain says I'm wasting money because I can cut the pineapple myself, but the other side says that I'm rightfully buying more time with my loved ones. This shift in mindset brings me joy, allowing me to spend less time on items I don't enjoy and more time with people I do.

What is Our Time Worth?

If you make $150,000 dollars per year and work 45 hours a week for 52 weeks, minus 4 weeks vacation and holidays, this equals roughly $70 dollars per hour.

It is essential to know what an hour of your time is worth to the free market. Knowing this will help you make decisions more easily (e.g., buying sliced or whole pineapples), and, more importantly, will allow you to start buying the most precious commodity in the world...time.

Let's say you don't enjoy staining your outdoor deck. At your value of $70/ hour, what is the cost for you to stain the deck? If it takes you five hours, that's $350. Alternatively, you could hire someone to do it completely for $200. If you have the funds, it's an automatic decision—hire that person.

There is an opportunity cost whenever you devote your time to something. The time you would've spent staining your deck is now available, it can be redeployed to create $350. Any bid to stain your deck that is less than $349.99 should be an immediate "yes" to outsource it.

This formula seems pretty simple, but even when we are fortunate to have the funds available, it's difficult to execute. Many of us associate hiring a service to cut our lawn, trim our trees, or clean the house to being "lazy."

Yet, if I ask anyone if buying time were possible, would they make that purchase? Everyone emphatically answers "yes." What we just reviewed is exactly that. You're buying time! We live in an outsourced world. Just because you know how to drive a car doesn't mean you should always rent a car when you travel. It's often more economical to take an Uber, especially when you factor in the time that you could be working or sleeping to recharge while your driver takes you somewhere. Billionaires often employ drivers, not because they're privileged or lazy, but because they know they can make more money working in the back of the limousine than driving themselves.

Buying time is another way to focus. Outsource everything that isn't essential to what your main focus is as a person, business, or organization.

Blend over Balance

We need to strive for harmony instead of balance. We need to understand that pool parties, kids' pajama sleepovers, deadlines, meetings, soccer carpools, leaky pipes, delayed flights, PTA meetings, emails bouncing, and beyond are a reality, and reality isn't always neatly organized into airtight compartments.

Productivity expert, Joshua Zerkel, explains, "A lot of people try or claim that they have perfected balance. But in reality, they've just drastically deprioritized, so they really are just working on fewer things...The key is to accept reality and then come up with some strategies that prioritize within your blended lifestyle, knowing that's the playing field. The biggest challenge people run into with trying to have a balanced life is that they want to fit all of it in. It's like the game Tetris. You have to fit the pieces of your life in a way that makes sense to you. The key is to choose which blocks to fit in, instead of just having a big pile of blocks in the corner giving you anxiety."[45]

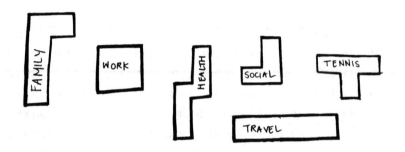

Zerkel indicates that instead of determining what to cram into your life, ask yourself what to *cram out*.

Part of my process when writing a speech, article, or book is to ask someone I trust to cut 25% out. I do this because I'm often too close to the content. It's my baby, and it's difficult for me to cut anything. It's a great exercise for life as well.

I had two close friends evaluate each other's lives. Where could the other trim 25% fat out of their life?

Their answers:

Todd could lessen or eliminate:

1. Watching sports
2. Playing video games
3. Watching people play video games
4. Watching fail videos on YouTube
5. Online poker

Caroline could lessen or eliminate:

1. Amount of time exercising at the gym
2. Binge-watching Netflix
3. Time watching HGTV
4. Time on Instagram
5. Excessive compulsive cleaning of the apartment

What does your list look like? Where can you trim 25% to gain 25% or 50%?

If our goal is to reach one of the big islands in our life, then why are we constantly picking up the oars and rowing furiously toward the small ones?

CHAPTER SUMMARY

The One Big Thing

The ability to say "yes" begins with the ability to say "no" to almost everything else. It starts with respecting our capacity.

Grade: *B*

This month was my favorite chapter to write, and it made me better at prioritizing family and friends. While saying "no" to friends was difficult at first, I became better at *how* I said "no," and I also started saying "no" more often. A "no" allowed me to say "yes" in the future to my friends and family. The reason I'm not receiving an A is that there is room for improvement. Specifically, I need consistency at blending my personal and business life. This month had a noticeable and positive impact on me and those around me. I'm excited at the possibilities of being better with the individuals who matter most to me.

Top Takeaways

1. If it's not an emphatic "yes," then it should be an emphatic "no." The best productivity tool is saying "no."

2. Establish protective guardrails, for example, my 52 Night Rule.

3. What would the World's #1 Dad, Sister, Grandmother, or Friend Do?

Health

There was no doubt that my health routine was officially in Rutsville. I wasn't alone. All of us are on a different fitness journey—some of us might be joining a gym for the first time with the desire to shed a few extra pounds, while others are trying to complete their first ultra-marathon.

With one's health, like most aspects of life, the key to progress is setting a goal and mapping to it. A tangible goal would help break my rut. I'd fallen into the bad habit of not setting goals for my workouts; I'd been going through the motions. It was just me and the weights or the hotel elliptical machine. Having played team sports most of my life, I missed the camaraderie and social interaction.

After much consternation, I landed on the following:

#1: Be able to do 100 push-ups straight—no stopping

I wanted a tangible challenge. At 6'6" with long arms (37" sleeve), my body is built for sports like basketball, rowing, and swimming. It's not built for snowboarding, being a jockey, or doing a lot of push-ups. On a good day, I could probably complete 40 half-assed push-ups in a row. So to get to 100 would be challenging.

#2: Play in a tennis league

While a volleyball league would be much more team-oriented, I knew with my travel schedule I could not be a reliable teammate. I played basketball in college, but in high school, I was on the tennis team and I wanted to pick the sport back up. A bonus—we could learn and play tennis together as a family. I decided to join a tennis league to meet and compete against other players. If time allowed, I could also team up with someone to compete in doubles matches.

Know Thyself—Know Thy Weaknesses

We all have a friend who's in the shape we want to be in. For me, this is my friend Bill. So I asked him how he moderates junk food. His response:

> Oh, I learned a long time ago there is no moderation. My weakness is anything salty, especially at night. I laugh when I read things like just take a portion about the size of your fist to satisfy a craving. Well, for me, that doesn't work. I either have none or finish the entire bag of chips.

This was fascinating to me, as I suffered from the same affliction with certain foods.

It turns out that most of us behave this way. Greg McKeown, the bestselling author of *Essentialism,* states: "...most of us aren't very good at moderation. When I cut out sugar from my diet, I had to completely cut it out, one hundred percent. Otherwise, I would always make an excuse on why it was okay to eat something with sugar: 'It's the holidays,' 'It's my wife's birthday,' etc.'"

#1 Bestselling author Brené Brown expresses the same conundrum: "I've learned I don't do well with moderation. I can't simply nibble from the breadbasket. So it just has to be a no."

My main weakness is dark chocolate-covered pretzels. Just like Bill, Greg, and Brené, I don't do moderation well. I can't just have three chocolate pretzels. It's either none or the entire bag.

Chocolate pretzels are now on my "Don't Have Anywhere Near the House List." The best system for me is to avoid purchasing them. The same holds true for Girl Scout Cookies—I cannot resist the Samoans/Caramel Delights. When I buy Girl Scout Cookies, I instantly gift them to friends...It's like an adult game of hot potato.

Eureka moment: Know thyself. Know thy weaknesses.

Poor Little Wilma

A girl entered the world in a poor part of Tennessee. From the beginning, the odds were stacked against poor little Wilma. At age four, she was paralyzed from polio.

A doctor gave her a special brace and mentioned she'd never put her feet on the ground.

Her mother told young Wilma that with persistence and faith, she could do anything she wanted. Wilma smiled and said, "I want to be the fastest woman on this earth."

Against the advice of her doctors, 9-year-old Wilma removed the brace. She took the first step—the step doctors said would be impossible. At the age of 13, she entered her first race and finished dead last.

She entered other races and continued to come in last. She wasn't giving up. She soon turned these last-place finishes into first-place finishes. At the age of 15, she met a track coach at Tennessee State University. She told him, "I want to be the fastest woman on this earth."

Wilma continued to work hard day and night. Eventually, she was racing against a woman named Jutta Heine. Heine had never lost a race.

The gun sounded in the 100-meter dash and Wilma crossed the tape first. The same thing happened in the 200-meter race. They were then the respective anchors of their teams in the 4x400 meter relay. They each received the baton to carry from the third runner. The only problem was that Wilma dropped the baton.

Wilma saw Jutta shoot out ahead. She picked up the fallen baton and raced her heart out, beating Jutta for the third time that day. That's the day, in 1960, that a paralytic girl named Wilma Rudolph made history by winning three Olympic gold medals and became the fastest woman on earth. Wilma didn't focus on what people said she couldn't do or the odds stacked against her. She focused on making her impossible dream a reality.

Comparative Trading & Triggers

Earlier, I briefly mentioned "comparative trading," which is applicable to most endeavors, including fitness and maintaining good health.

For example, on a flight to Paris, I asked myself, "Do I want to eat this airline's below-average gelatin dessert, or would I rather skip it so I can enjoy a chocolate croissant at a sidewalk cafe in Paris?" No brainer—chocolate croissant on the streets of Paris wins every time. It became almost as if I were channeling Einstein's theory of relativity but through the lens of food. It's all relative.

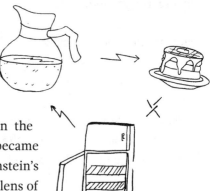

Negative Food Triggers

On the drive home from a family gathering, my wife made an observation, "I wish my cousin would avoid bringing up topics like politics that always trigger unpleasant conversations." The keyword in that sentence for me was "trigger." Yes, triggers.

If I could somehow limit the triggers to my bad eating habits or pitfalls in my health, that would be a huge win.

I asked friends to define their eating or health triggers and whether these are good triggers or bad. I was fascinated to learn most people know their triggers.

Drinking beer. With beer, I crave anything salty, especially corn chips. The bad part is too often this is late at night, which is one of the worst times to snack.

Being cold. If I'm at one of my son's football games and it's cold out, I start eating anything that is warm. And at a high school football game that means hot dogs, giant pretzels or nachos.

Stress. When I'm stressed, that's a trigger for me to easily eat an entire gallon of ice cream. It only provides short-term relief. In fact, I'm more stressed later about having inhaled a gallon of ice cream!

For me, like others, the triggers are easy to identify. If yours aren't easily identifiable, carefully journal what you eat, and you'll start to see a pattern.

My Negative Food Triggers:

1. Coffee
2. Red Wine
3. Watching Sports

I didn't start drinking coffee until I was in my mid-thirties. However, age doesn't lessen the fact that I absolutely *love* coffee. It's my favorite drug. I love everything about it—from the process of making it, to the smell of it, to the feel of the warm ceramic cup in my hands as I slowly sip and stare at the horizon as the sun rises. (Note: with two young children, this happens only a few times per year—but it's nice to fantasize that these Zen moments are regularly occurring.)

This month, I noticed that it was rare for me to simply have a cup of coffee. I wanted to nibble on something while enjoying my coffee. That's when I realized—eureka! Nothing healthy goes well with coffee. Here is my list of items that go well with coffee:

❑	Croissants	❑	Waffles
❑	Chocolate	❑	Pancakes
❑	Muffins	❑	Cake
❑	Scones	❑	Cinnamon Rolls
❑	Cookies	❑	Dessert

Did this mean I was going to get rid of coffee? Heck no! Coffee was worth it. But it did adjust my behavior around coffee.

At home, knowing these triggers, I had multi-grain waffles with my coffee instead of a decadent giant Belgian waffle. Instead of slathering on butter and processed syrup, I used almond butter and pure honey. The coffee and waffles are on my "Worth It" list. This is an example of replacing an existing habit with an improved habit.

Then there is my wine fix. I'm not a big wine drinker, but I do occasionally enjoy a glass of red wine. Red wine, for me, is similar to coffee. I never drink it without pairing it with food. Fortunately, not all foods that go with red wine are bad for you (e.g., grapes, nuts, apricots). My problem is always gravitating toward eating two pounds of cheese and crackers and a giant bar of dark chocolate.

This is where I reach for my handy-dandy "Is it worth it?" barometer. If the wine isn't that great, I don't finish it. A sunk cost is money that isn't coming back, so why double up the mistake by drinking something that doesn't taste good and comes with a headache in the morning?

> *If you chase two rabbits, you will not catch either one.*
> — Russian Proverb

Eureka moment: If it isn't worth it, it just isn't worth it.

Buddy Up

One of the most common New Year's resolutions is to lose weight, yet approximately two-thirds of adults are overweight or obese.[46]

The science shows that not achieving our weight loss goals often results from a lack of setting specific goals and recording our progress. While these seem easy to do, it's not so easy in practice.[47]

One way to increase our chances of success is finding a workout buddy, team, or group. Research backs up what we inherently know—that working out with others helps us stick to our goals, boosts performance and accountability, and is more enjoyable. You may have experienced a runners' high caused by the "feel good" hormones called endorphins, released when working out. When working out with friends, the body tends to release an even greater amount of endorphins, leading to improvements in our mood.[48] When we leave a workout feeling satisfied and joyful, we are more likely to incorporate it into our regular schedule.

One particular study found that 95% of participants who began a weight-loss program with a group of friends, completed the program and were 42% more likely to maintain their weight-loss goals following the program.[49]

The reason for this isn't based on support alone. We tend to imitate the behaviors of those around us. This is partially attributed to the Köhler Effect that states that no one wants to be perceived as the weakest link in a group setting.[50]

In the 1920s, a German psychologist, Otto Köhler, set out to test how working in groups affects the performance of individuals. He asked the Berlin rowing club to do standing curls with a 97-pound weight until they were too worn out to continue. Kohler then put them into various groups and tasked them with lifting one weighted bar cooperatively. The weight was twice as heavy for the two-person groups and three times as heavy for the three-person groups, so when one member of the group stopped lifting, the rest of the group could not continue long after. Köhler discovered that when in groups, the weakest athlete could withstand significantly more reps than he could individually. Additionally, the larger the variance in physical ability between the athletes, the higher the motivation to persevere for the weaker athletes.[51] Today, we recognize this discovery as the Köhler Effect.

We see the Köhler Effect all around us. For example, when paired up with a more physically fit exercising partner, participants increased their plank time by 24%.[52]

Even if you feel content working out individually, challenge yourself to a group exercise session periodically, preferably with people in better shape than you.

Bad Habits Need Good Replacements

Studies show that when we stop a bad habit, we need to replace that habit with something else—this helps explain why many people gain weight when they quit smoking. They replace smoking with eating. Or an alcoholic might become maniacal about running once he quits drinking. Replacing a bad habit with an equally damaging or worse habit is useless. If I broke my waffle-eating habit by eating chocolate cake or snorting cocaine, I would not be heading in the right direction.

Once I identified coffee as one of my triggers, I actively sought to replace it with something else, at least occasionally. A Japanese friend recommended replacing coffee with a warm cup of water. Definitely not as tasty, but it was a healthy substitute that at least gave me the same feeling and warmth as drinking coffee on my "no coffee days." Interestingly, research shows that women benefit more from this placebo effect (a warm cup of water as a replacement for coffee) than men.

I still drink coffee on most days and eat waffles, but I no longer do it every day. I wasn't striving for perfection; I was striving to get better. Perfect is the enemy of growth and greatness.

Sweet Dreams

In order to maintain our focus, we need to ensure we are well-rested. In Tim Ferris' book, *Tools of Titans*, he interviews 200 of the world's top performers, from intellectuals and financial wizards to elite athletes.

Ferris uncovered a surprising commonality among these top performers. Most make an intentional effort to get 8-10 hours of sleep.[53]

Most of us assume the exact opposite, that these overachievers never sleep, that they're able to get ahead, in part, by not sleeping when others are. No. One of their habits for maintaining focus is ensuring their minds and bodies are well-rested.

Below is a quick 1-2-3 pilots checklist from the American Sleep Association for better rest:[54]

1. Set and keep a sleep routine: try to go to bed and wake up at the same time each day. This is a little more challenging for many: parents with little kids; men and women in the military; business travelers, and many others. Do the best you can. Try to go to bed at the same time as your kids. For business travelers, try to stay in your own time zone.

2. Nap like a pro: make sure you nap for only twenty minutes at a time. Any longer than this depletes your sleepiness bank, increasing the difficulty of easing into sleep at night.

3. Exercise preferably before 2 pm. Try to avoid exercising right before bed. Exercise releases endorphins, making it difficult to initiate sleep.

If these three recommendations don't help, perhaps try a natural sleeping concoction that Tim Ferris recommends. Many have found this simple apple cider formula helps them sleep better.

Mix this before you go to bed:

1. 1 cup warm water
2. 2 tbsp organic apple cider vinegar
3. 1 tbsp organic honey

When needed, especially on international flights, I've found a tiny dose of natural melatonin works well for me.

Achievers understand the importance of sleep and the advantages of getting an early start. In his five-year study of 177 self-made millionaires, author Thomas Corley found that nearly 50% of those interviewed woke up at least three hours before their workday began. "These habits are like snowflakes—they build up, and then you have an avalanche of success," says Corley.

Richard Branson, the adventurous billionaire who founded the Virgin Group, wakes up at 5:45 am to exercise before starting his workday.[55] Square CEO and Twitter founder Jack Dorsey wakes up at 5:30 am to meditate and go for a 6-mile jog. While this chart is outdated the moment we include it, the key point is that many successful business people get up early.

> *Early to bed and early to rise makes a man healthy, wealthy and wise.*
> — Ben Franklin

Name	Title	Company	Wake-Up
Mary Barra	CEO	GM	6:00
Tim Armstrong	CEO	AOL	5:15
Ursula Burns	CEO	Xerox	5:15
Jeff Immelt	CEO	GE	5:30
Indra Nooyi	CEO	PepsiCo	4:00
Sergio Marchionne	CEO	Fiat Chrysler	3:30
Bill Gross	CoFounder	PIMCO	4:30
Richard Branson	Founder/Chairman	Virgin Group	5:45
David Cush	CEO	Virgin America	4:15
Jack Dorsey	CEO	Square	5:30
Tim Cook	CEO	Apple	3:45
Bob Iger	CEO	Disney	4:30
Michelle Obama	Former First Lady	U.S.	4:30
Howard Schultz	Founder	Starbucks	5:00
Frits Van Paasschen	CEO	Starwood hotels	5:50
Carl McMillon	CEO	Walmart	5:30

Lew Wallace's name is not on here. Not familiar with him? His is a name we should all curse when we wake up. Wallace is often cited and credited with inventing the snooze button. Lew Wallace also wrote *Ben Hur*, which, for some, is even more of a reason to curse him. GE introduced us to the snooze button in 1956.

Dr. Michael Breus, known as the Sleep Doctor, argues that the snooze button is the worst thing ever to happen to sleep. The main culprit and reason you want to hit the snooze button in the first place is that you haven't achieved 7-9 hours of restful sleep.[56]

When you aren't rested, you experience sleep inertia. The National Sleep Foundation defines this state as "the feeling of grogginess and disorientation."

Sleep inertia slows your decision-making abilities, impairs your memory, and hurts your general performance once you do get out of bed.[57]

"When you hit the snooze button, you're doing two negative things to yourself," says Robert S. Rosenberg, medical director of the Sleep Disorders Center.

First, "you're fragmenting what little extra sleep you're getting, so it's not the best quality." Basically, the extra minutes become meaningless. And second, "you're starting yourself on a new sleep cycle that you won't have time to complete." This "messes with your brain hormones" and disrupts your circadian rhythm, the body clock that regulates your awake and sleep time.[58]

The inventors of the first alarm clocks with snooze buttons understood the downside of such a button. The research indicated that any duration of "snoozing" for ten minutes or more would result in the sleeper falling back into a deep sleep. Hence the reason that most manufacturers set their snooze buttons to be under ten minutes.[59]

And, once we do lift ourselves from bed after a snooze button hit, we will be drowsier throughout the day. There is also something odd about setting an alarm for a time we don't plan to get up for in the first place. It helps to set the intention of not getting up when the alarm goes off.

Dr. Breus reveals that our natural circadian rhythm can adjust over time. For example, a nineteen-year-old will probably prefer to stay up until 4 am while your 90-year-old grandma is probably getting up at 4 am after having gone to bed at 8 pm. No matter what our age, if "you snooze, you lose."

Most of us are one of three birds. We are either a robin (morning), eagle (tweeners), or owl (night). Most of us are eagles—we are somewhere in the middle. Research by Jessica Rosenberg and her colleagues at RWTH Aachen University in Germany concluded that 10-15% of us are robins while 20-25% of us are owls.[60]

An oversimplified way to determine what type of bird you are is the following:

> If you were given 8 hours to sleep without any commitments or an alarm clock set, what time would you naturally wake up?

7 am or before = Robin   7 am – 10 am = Eagle

10 am or after = Owl

The type of bird we are can change over time to meet our lifestyle changes. For example, most kids and grandparents are robins while most teenagers are owls.

Throughout the day, we have three general flows—rhythm, wreck, and recovery. For example, a typical robin's day might look like this:

6 am - 1 pm [Rhythm]:   In the flow, we should work on harder cognizant tasks or ones that involve problem-solving.

1 pm - 5 pm [Wreck]:   As brain drain begins to kick-in we need to turn our efforts toward working on simple tasks like email, returning calls, and organizing.

5 pm - 9 pm [Recovery]:   Reading, meditation, journaling, dinner with friends/family, walking, etc.

The key is determining if we are a robin, eagle, or owl and testing out what is optimal for our mind, body, and daily demands.

"Life has a way of throwing wrenches into our day," Corley says in his book, *Change Your Habits, Change Your Life*. "How many of us raise our hands in frustration at the end of a workday because the three or four things we wanted to get done were somehow replaced by unanticipated disruptions?"

These disruptions wear on us, "eventually forming the belief that we have no control over our life," he writes. "This belief causes us to feel helpless." To avoid this helpless feeling, we should attack our most important items before the disruptions have a chance to disrupt.[61]

Now, if you aren't a morning person—a robin—don't fret.

The key is to get up before you need to—before you can become distracted by the "outside" world. Many adults become morning people when they start having kids. Parents train themselves to go to bed when their kids go to bed or, more often than not, they're just exhausted from chasing the kids all day. As we age, we naturally start going to bed earlier and waking up earlier. That's why a New Year's Eve party in my grandfather's retirement home drops the midnight ball not at midnight but at 9 pm!

Start small. Start by waking up a half-hour before you normally would, or, if you're lucky and you're near "Fall Back" daylight savings time, stay on your normal schedule and *voila!*—now you're up an hour earlier without doing a darn thing. If you desire to become more of a morning person, the following steps from *Business Insider* are a great place to start. I've included my personal testing notes with [brackets] around whether or not it worked for me [Yes/No].[62]

1.   Stop hitting snooze: Before we go to bed, we must envision not hitting the snooze button. [Yes. I disable the ability to snooze on my phone. Having my phone out of reach also forces me to get up.]

2.   Remind yourself of something you're grateful for in the morning. [Yes!]

3.   Dark and cold: The key to waking up early is ensuring you get a great night's rest. The darker the room, the better we sleep. If needed, buy a pair of comfortable eye covers to ensure darkness. Set your thermostat to automatically cool down at bedtime. [It took me a while to find a comfortable pair of eyeshades, but once I did, they helped. Cooling the room helps, but my wife doesn't like it as cold, so the temperature is a constant struggle. In my hotel rooms I cool it to 65 and find the benefits noticeable.]

4.   Turn off technology 30 minutes before you go to bed. [Easier said than done, but it helps when I do it!]

5.   Exercise: Get moving in the morning. Motion creates emotion, which creates energy. [Yes.]

6.   Chug cold water: When we wake up, we should hydrate by drinking extremely cold water. It's incredible how effective this is at waking us up. [I wasn't always great at doing this, and the ice maker can wake up the entire house, but it did help.]

7.   Fresh air: If you can sleep with the windows open, do it. One of the reasons we yawn is to draw in more oxygen. Oxygen can help wake us up in the morning. Many believe that Las Vegas casinos pump additional oxygen around the gaming tables so that players will have more energy to gamble longer. [Yes, when it's not allergy season.]

8. Set a routine: The best way to become a morning person is to have a night routine as well as a morning routine. [Yes. While tough to execute when traveling, it's a definite win when possible.]

My friend Mel Robbins has a unique method for avoiding the snooze button. She treats the morning like a rocket launch. When the alarm sounds, she counts down 5-4-3-2-1 and then launches herself out of bed. She's found this to be so effective that she's adopted the same concept for the rest of her life—stop hitting snooze on your life! She's the author of the bestselling book *The 5-Second Rule*.

Giving myself a rigid bedtime helped me tremendously this month. Similar to the importance of giving a child a set bedtime.

Sleep Your Way to the Top

Think of your brain as software and your sleep as rebooting your computer, deleting all junk files, and removing all viruses. Our brain consumes up to 25% of our energy. We must make proper rest a priority to recharge our central operating system.

Some studies conclude that our brain does its best job of rebooting when we sleep in a fetal position; this position is better than sleeping on our stomachs or backs. Going one step further, sleeping on one's left side appears optimal for maximizing blood circulation through our bodies because most of the venous return travels up the right side and those veins can compress when you lie on them.[63]

Once we lie down we experience four modes of sleep:

Awake:	Typically, we are awake 10-30 minutes each night. As we age, we are more likely to awaken during the night.
REM:	Rapid Eye Movement. This usually occurs late

in the evening and is important for memory and mood. During this time, the brain is cleaned of unnecessary things. Dreams are more vivid, the heart rate is elevated, and our breathing is faster.

Light Sleep: We are in this mode most of the night. Light Sleep promotes mental and physical restoration.

Deep Sleep: This mode helps with physical recovery and aspects of memory and learning. Feeling extra refreshed? You likely spent some solid time in deep sleep. Thinking is largely offline during this stage, while your body secretes a growth hormone associated with cellular rebuilding. Deep sleep also helps strengthen the immune system.

Sleep cycles vary, but the general flow is usually:

AWAKE → LIGHT SLEEP → DEEP SLEEP → LIGHT SLEEP → REM

Here is a typical sleep allocation:

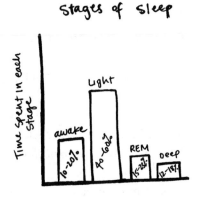

15% Awake 20% REM
50% Light 15% Deep

Affordable fitness trackers help monitor our sleep patterns, so when someone asks, "How did you sleep last night?" we can reply, "Let me check."

Just like tracking our progress at the gym, we should track what helps and hurts our sleep—our brains depend on it. If you're already sleeping well, go with what's working.

Mind or Matter?

I'd eat for three reasons:

1. Habit
2. My brain wanted it more than my stomach
3. I was actually hungry

How many of us eat just because it's a certain time of day? It's a habit. Oh, it's noon, so I better have lunch. Many of us have hardwired habits of eating at certain times—even though we aren't actually hungry! Or we eat and drink around events. If we watch soccer/futbol, we always grab a bowl of chips. At home for the holidays? It's time to drink wine with our relatives.

Other times, we eat simply because we are bored.

The eureka moment for me was: Eat when I'm hungry. So simple, yet so hard.

To help fight these ingrained habits, I'd always ask the question: *"Does my mind want this food/drink, or does my stomach want it?"*

More often than not, it was mind over matter. My mind wanted it, but my body didn't need it.

A simple example of this is taking my morning coffee accompanied by mini waffles with almond butter. After my breakfast, I was satisfied and had enough energy, but I envisioned sitting peacefully with my coffee and warm waffle while writing my next book before heading to the airport. I'm sure you have a similar ritual around something peaceful. The trouble is that it's *so* rare that these idyllic moments transpire as envisioned.

What actually occurs, more often than not, is that an unexpected distraction pops up, causing me to be pressed for time. This results in me chugging my coffee and cramming the burnt waffle into my mouth as I race out the door. In situations like this, the ritual isn't even enjoyable—it isn't "worth it."

Better to save this ritual for a day when I have time to relish it. The result is that a) I'm better at planning and ensuring I have the time, and b) when I do indulge, I see it as a special treat, because I'm not doing it every day.

Many of my colleagues have done a few days of fasting and rave about it. Going a few days without food wasn't for me, but then I discovered intermittent fasting...

Fasting to Focus

Exercise is proven to provide long-term benefits such as preventing memory disorders like Alzheimer's disease. People who exercise regularly have a 50% less chance of experiencing any form of dementia in their lifetime.

For our ancestors, most physical activity was a result of emergencies, such as fleeing a predator or hunting an animal to ward off starvation. During these moments, blood flow increased to the brain. This helped improve reaction times and heightened our instincts. So, the next time you're having a mental block and cannot focus, try hitting the gym or walking outside.[64]

Another productivity and focus method that's linked to our evolution is intermittent fasting. Our ancestors primarily lived as hunter-gatherers. There were many periods of food scarcity and famines. During these periods, their bodies became accustomed to going through cycles without food. This transferred into intermittent fasting intervals. During these times without food, focus was often heightened so they were more likely to sense prey or food in the area, like hunting a saber tooth tiger.[65]

For those of you who are unfamiliar with the term, intermittent fasting is defined as limiting our caloric intake for set periods of time. This process can be done in many different ways, including restricting calories two to three days a week, fasting once a week for 24 to 36 hours, or, the most popular practice is limiting your body to 8-hour eating periods every day, widely known as 16/8 (16 hours of fasting and 8 hours of eating).

Intermittent fasting can contribute to weight loss, lowered blood pressure, reduced heart rate, and improved brain health.[66]

Recent studies have shown that this method increases synaptic plasticity, which is attributed to learning and memory. Intermittent fasting provides an anti-inflammatory effect on the body, which can reduce the aging effects on the brain.[67]

It can also positively manipulate our cognitive function, helping improve our performance on memory tests and helping decrease the risk of Alzheimer's and Parkinson's disease.[68]

This month I tried intermittent fasting for two weeks. It seemed to work well with my limited experience. An unexpected benefit was the time it helped free up not having to prepare and eat breakfast. Feel free to test it yourself. It's the closest we can get to crouching down and stalking a saber tooth tiger.

Tight Swedish Suits

I love Sweden, and if I didn't live in the United States, you would find me living on the water in Malmö or Stockholm.

Sweden, and Europe in general, has a sense of style that permeates across borders. Wearing clothes much tighter than Americans prefer, the Italians and Swedes admittedly look better. When I say tight, I mean *tight*. To avoid splitting my tight "European" pants I had to be very careful getting into and out of cars. The only other pair of pants I had on this one trip was a pair of jeans. To use a circus term, I was essentially flying "without a net." These pants *had* to last the trip.

I wasn't alone in the "tight pants club." Two Swedish agents on the tour split their pants on separate occasions—and these were supposedly trained Europeans! When the audience posted some pictures of me on social media, my dad rightfully commented: "Don't grab that extra muffin; otherwise you will not be able to fit into those pants you're wearing."

When traveling abroad, I often get questions from the press and attendees during a book signing. Q&A sessions in other countries are particularly invigorating, as the questions often surprise me and I learn from them.

Here are some of my favorite audience questions: How old are you? Why do you wear those green glasses? Is your mother or father tall? Are there even lenses in your glasses?

On the last day of a weeklong speaking tour in Sweden, a member of the audience asked a question that surprised me. The question: How do you stay in such great shape?

The travel was tough on my body and I hardly felt that I was in peak physical condition—especially gorging on Swedish chocolate for a few days. But, I noticed a shift in my behavior following this question. The rest of that trip, I avoided anything unhealthy. All of a sudden, staying in shape became "my thing" in Sweden. Throughout the rest of the trip, people backstage started asking me questions like: Do you like sugar? Do you eat sugar? Are you Vegan? How many hours a day do you exercise?

Research shows that believing you're a particular type of person can dramatically change your behavior. For example, if you're trying to quit smoking, instead of believing "I'm a smoker who needs to quit," you say and believe "I'm no longer a smoker." While nuanced, it can lead to dramatic changes.

Or, in my case, during the trip to Sweden, the thought process looked like this:

I'm a person who is in good shape.

A person in good shape exercises. A person in good shape doesn't eat a bagel with cream cheese after finishing a full breakfast. A person in good shape doesn't eat the stale chocolate chip cookies backstage.

Your reframed mindset helps shift your behavior.

The self-concept theory explains that you become who you perceive yourself to be. Our self-concept, defined as our attitudes, beliefs, and opinions toward our personal existence, ultimately drives how we behave, think, and act. It is our opinion of who we are.[69]

Studies show we seek to be consistent. Most successful athletes use consistent routines.[70]

Routines help ensure athletes are prepared for most circumstances. The act of creating and sticking to a consistent schedule is beneficial for everyone, not just athletes. A boost in mental health and cognitive function can be attributed to routines.[71]

How others perceive us also helps to encourage certain behavioral choices. Think about it. If some of your friends say you're always the healthiest eater of the group, you're more likely to order the grilled salmon over the chicken fried steak. Or, if you're the funny one in the group, the fashionista, or whatever it may be, you will adjust your behavior to support the story those around you believe. You're striving for a consistent narrative.

If you have not yet developed a certain routine or habit, work for it. Although it was previously believed that 21 days of consistency was all it took to acquire a new habit, research shows it's probably closer to 66 days.[72]

We often form habits when pursuing our goals. We can have a push or a pull force around our goals. Push is based on willpower, but willpower isn't reliable. It looks like this: *I should go to the gym, therefore, I will force myself to go to the gym.* While pull is based on an outcome: *I must lose 10 pounds to fit into my tuxedo for the wedding.* As Tony Robbins is fond of saying, "We don't always achieve our wants but we do achieve our musts."

For me, the pull part of my goal of performing 100 push-ups at the end of the month looked like this: My first initial and last name form a superhero-like name in Equalman. Part of what I do in my books and on stage is to help unlock and unleash an individual's unique superpower. My mindset for the next thirty days? I must transform my body to appear superhero-esque. Most superheroes aren't wearing baggy trousers or bulky coats. Nope, thigh-hugging tights appear to be the popular choice. Hence, if I ever were tempted to skip a workout in the morning, I would just ask myself, "Would a superhero skip this workout?"

It also dawned on me that staying fit was part of my vocation. I had to be on stage. So, like an actor, I had to fit the part. I had to stay in shape for the videos and photographs that would be taken. My stage wardrobe wouldn't fit if I added too many pounds. Besides, the camera was already adding ten pounds. It reminded me of a funny line from the TV show *Friends*, "How many cameras are on that guy?!"

If I didn't stay in shape, I might lose speaking opportunities. I'd lose money, which might impact my daughters' college fund. This was silly reasoning, but it was reasoning that worked for me. I was using my brain to motivate my body.

It didn't always work, but it did occasionally stop me from grabbing the cookie in the hotel lobby or skipping the gym.

> *Don't think about the start of the race, think about the ending.*
> — Usain Bolt

Studies show that we are more likely to achieve our goals if we understand the *why* behind them. The more specific, the better. It might be that you want to fit into your favorite dress for a wedding or look good for your high school reunion.

For me, it was the ability to fit into my tight pants the next time I had to speak in Sweden.

Rush to Brush

Here's a quick trick that has worked for me and many others. If you feel as if you're about to eat something on your "Not Worth It List," immediately brush your teeth. The fluoride taste and thought of having to brush your teeth again often squelches the desire. I travel with a toothbrush in my backpack since I don't ever want to be caught with food in my teeth while I'm performing on stage. After I finish my main course, I quickly go to the washroom to brush my teeth before they bring out the dessert menu. It gives me a fighting chance to say "no" to dessert.

Does Coffee Help or Hurt Focus & Productivity?

Not being properly rested decreases our attention span, alertness, motivation, and performance. Many people, myself included, try to get a jolt throughout the day from coffee. But is the caffeine from coffee helping or hurting?

Studies show that, compared to other drugs, caffeine's power is relatively weak. Researchers agree that caffeine has three common effects:

1. Postpones sleep
2. Combats fatigue & boredom
3. Causes our hands to shake

Caffeine can also reduce audio and visual reaction times.[73] However, other studies show caffeine can boost your mood for up to three hours. It can also produce different physiological effects on users depending on whether the user is an occasional caffeine user or a regular user.[74]

In sum, although caffeine's effects vary from person to person, the common theme is that it can affect mood and performance even when taken at a low dose. Which is one of the reasons why regular coffee drinkers, like me, seem to believe that we can't be productive without that morning fix. But is this in our head, or is this actually true?

We do know that caffeine is extremely addictive. Regular ingestion of caffeine affects our brain's chemical makeup, which is why users experience fatigue, headaches, and nausea when deprived of the drug. Make no mistake about it, caffeine is a drug. Within 24 hours without it, our body begins to feel withdrawal symptoms.

These start small: a feeling of mental fogginess and a lack of alertness. Later, a throbbing headache may kick in, making it nearly impossible to focus. Muscle pains or flu-like symptoms can occur. Many people don't realize that caffeine is chemically addictive, which is the reason many coffee addicts feel as if they can't function without it.[75]

While difficult, distancing yourself from your coffee addiction can be extremely beneficial for improving focus. Caffeine increases the levels of stress hormones in your body. Without this added stress, we can devote our efforts to important tasks. Determine how much sleep you need to feel well-rested and this will help lessen the chance of you reaching for your caffeine fix.

A study conducted by the University of Barcelona[76] shows that women and men are affected differently by coffee. Men start to feel the impact of coffee 10 minutes after consumption. Women take 35-40 minutes to get their "alertness" kick, and it's less powerful than in men. The effects of coffee generally occur in the two-three hour range after consumption but can be longer or shorter based primarily on age and metabolism.

Women also experienced more of a placebo effect. Simply anticipating the warmth of holding a cup of coffee and the resulting stimulating effects of caffeine may be enough to feel these effects. When researchers had participants drink decaf, women reported feeling significantly more alert than men, who reported just a slight boost.[77]

An American term for coffee is a *Cup of Joe*. This slang dates back to 1914. Josephus Daniels, Secretary of the Navy, banned U.S. Navy ships from serving alcoholic beverages. The next best drug to alcohol was coffee. Playing off Daniels's first name of Josephus, *Cup of Joe* stuck in American culture. Little did everyone know at the time how addictive this little brown liquid could become.

Determine what works best for you and your own *Cup of Joe*. Many studies show a cup of coffee per day is healthy for you, but we also know that too much of a good thing is still too much. Find the proper balance.

My take on this? I decided to pick one day a week to go coffee free. Wow, was this difficult.

The day I normally pick to avoid coffee is either a busy morning or when I'm traveling. If it's a busy morning I won't have time to savor it, and when I travel coffee isn't quite as good away from home. Plus, I like my coffee the consistency of motor oil—the darker and stronger the better. This style of coffee is difficult to find away from home. Drinking coffee out of a paper cup is also on my "Not Worth It" list. Bad for the environment, bad for the taste, and bad for the Zen experience.[78]

Focus Foods

The old saying "garbage in, garbage out" is especially true when it comes to our minds. While most of us focus on our food for athletic performance, appearance, and well-being, very few of us pay attention to what foods are best for our minds.

Think of focus foods like wax for our snowboard or skis. It makes everything so much smoother. The best focus foods are:

Avocados have the highest protein and lowest sugar concentration of any fruit. Yep, it's a fruit.[79] Just like every part of the body, the brain depends on blood flow, and avocados enhance blood flow.[80] These green wonders are also packed with folate and Vitamin K, which help improve cognitive abilities such as focus and memory.

Avocados

Blueberries

Blueberries have antioxidants in spades, enhancing the flow of blood to the brain. Blueberries are also beneficial in protecting against cancer, heart disease, and dementia.[81] Studies further suggest blueberries may improve memory[82] and top the list for antioxidant health benefits.[83]

Green Tea

We already know that caffeine, in the right dosage, can help improve focus, speed, accuracy, and alertness. Green tea is naturally infused with mild doses of caffeine. A cup of green tea contains around 24-40 mg of caffeine, whereas a cup of coffee is generally in the 100-200 mg range.[84]

Green tea contains L-theanine, causing a slower release of its caffeine than coffee. This slower infusion of caffeine into the body helps prevent the crashing experience when we over-stimulate with caffeine. Green tea can also help our metabolism—naturally burning fat.[85]

Leafy Greens

A *Neurology* study showed that people who ate two or more daily servings of vegetables, especially leafy greens, had the mental focus of people five years their junior.[86] Leafy greens are loaded with carotenoids, B-vitamins, and antioxidants, which help to boost brainpower. The inherent folic acid also improves mental clarity.[87]

Quick Tip: The darker shade of green, the better.

Fatty Fish

Fatty/oily fish contain omega-3 fatty acids, aiding memory, mental performance, and behavioral function. People deficient in omega-3s are more likely to have poor memory, mood swings, depression, and fatigue. Fish improves our concentration and mood. The main sources of fatty fish are salmon, trout, mackerel, herring, sardines, and kipper. And, bonus points, salmon may also protect our skin from the damaging effects of the sun's UV rays.

Water is the elixir of life. Water gives the brain the electrical energy for thought and memory processes. Water has been proven to help us think faster, be more focused, and experience greater clarity and creativity. Every single function of our body depends on water, so it is critically important to get enough water. Start each day by drinking a glass of water.

Water

Yes! We have been given the green light to eat dark chocolate. However, this "go ahead" doesn't refer to most of the popular chocolates, often packed with sugar, corn syrup, and milk. So don't start binging on Hershey's Kisses.

Dark Chocolate

The magnesium in dark chocolate stimulates healthy chemicals in our bodies like endorphins and serotonin, helping reduce stress and heightening our moods—overall making us feel good.

Look for dark chocolate that has at least a 70% cocoa count. While bitter at first, over time, I've become accustomed to the taste. Looking for two superfoods in one? Melt dark chocolate, sprinkle in some flaxseed, and cover with fresh blueberries. Put onto waxed paper and freeze.

Regarding dark chocolate, adhere to the old saying that *all good things come in small packages.*

Flax Seeds

Flax seeds are high in magnesium, B-vitamins, omega-3 fatty acids, and fiber, all of which aid mental clarity, weight loss, and, ultimately, focus. Flax seeds are also rich in alpha-linolenic acid (ALA), a healthy fat that stimulates the cerebral cortex. In turn, this stimulation helps increase brain function.[88] Flax seeds are easy to sprinkle on cereal, yogurt, oatmeal, and salads.

Nuts

Nuts are loaded with the antioxidant vitamin E, which is associated with limiting cognitive decline as we age. We just need an ounce of vitamin E a day to get this benefit. It's also rich in essential oils and amino acids that aid our focus.

Sprinkle some almonds into your day. They increase attention, awareness, and memory. Walnuts improve cognitive functions and maximize our memory. Eating less than a handful achieves the best results.

Coffee

One of the top-selling t-shirts says *"But first, coffee."* Some of us just aren't "fully there" until we have our coffee. Coffee is loaded with caffeine, which can improve alertness and focus. However, results might vary.

Eggs

Incorporating eggs into our meals is beneficial as they're a high source of B-vitamins, antioxidants, and omega-3 fatty acids, which all stimulate cognitive functioning. Two eggs a day can drive significant improvement. Eggs are rich in tyrosine, which stimulates dopamine production in the body. Dopamine, coined as the "motivation molecule," heightens our productivity by increasing focus, motivation, and energy levels.[89]

Let's not beat around the bush here. Beets tend to inspire a love-it or hate-it reaction but have been proven to be a strong driver of focus. Beets increase blood flow and oxygen to the brain, in turn increasing brain function. Beets can also stimulate our athletic performance by preventing fatigue.[90]

Beets

The good news is that many of the *focus foods* are also *superfoods*—they help improve our overall health and wellness.[91]

Eat Decision Fatigue for Breakfast

Every day, we encounter decision fatigue. The reason Steve Jobs wore the same black shirt every day was because it was one less decision he had to make.

During this year of focus, I tested eating the same foods at home for breakfast every day to eliminate one decision. This healthy breakfast would help ensure I consumed the nutrients to start my day right:

- Egg white frittata: pour 100% egg whites into a small pan and flip over once when needed
- Green smoothie (banana, honey, baby spinach, mint, edamame, pineapple, plant-based protein powder, chia seeds, water, ice)
- Small avocado
- 5 cherry tomatoes
- A few slices of 0% salt turkey

I was at the deli so often that the wonderful folks started slicing no-salt turkey when they saw me approaching.

One day, Ana Maria was with me and we were wearing the same church volunteer shirts. Mariam at the deli asked, "Did you know that there is another girl in the store who has the same shirt on?"

"Oh, yeah, that's my wife," I replied.

"I told you that was No-Salt's wife!" Miriam shouted to her colleagues.

I'd ordered the same deli turkey so often that my nickname was *No-Salt*. Even more hilarious was now Ana Maria's nickname was *No-Salt's Wife*.

Take Recess Like a First Grader

The next time you're hitting a lull in the afternoon, instead of reaching for a soda, energy drink, coffee, or tea, go for a brisk walk or go up and down the stairs. Derek Randolph and Patrick O'Connor from the University of Georgia discovered that 10 minutes of moderate exercise is more stimulating than 50 mg of caffeine, which is the equivalent of a can of soda or a shot of espresso.

Taking an exercise recess improves our psychological and physical well-being—especially if performed outdoors. It also helps us sleep better. An exercise recess helps break the pattern of becoming tired, then reaching for the afternoon caffeine, but then not sleeping enough that night, only to be tired the next afternoon, and then once again reaching for the afternoon caffeine. It's a vicious cycle.

Consider *sitting* as the new *smoking*, so any chance we have to get off of our bottoms during the day, the better off we are. Walking meetings are an excellent choice. Replace your next scheduled meeting with a walking meeting. Not only will we get a break from the monotony of sitting at our desks, but small doses of physical activity can be more powerful than coffee.[92]

Morning Workouts

Only one-fifth of all Americans get the recommended amount of exercise.[93] This is largely due to 69 percent of us choosing to schedule our workouts in the afternoon rather than in the morning.[94] Few people follow through with their workouts in the afternoon.

Preparing our workout schedules for early in the morning will increase the likeliness of its occurrence.[95] Working out early and returning home before anyone else wakes helps you avoid cutting into precious family or friend time.

Other benefits of completing your workout first thing in the morning include:

1. It can burn fat more efficiently as fat oxidation occurs during exercise before breakfast.[96] This process breaks down lipid (fat) molecules, increasing weight loss and reducing type 2 diabetes.
2. In most regions of the world, morning weather is more conducive to exercising.
3. A feeling of accomplishment early in the morning gives us momentum for the day.
4. You only have to shower once.
5. It's done!

Unsure if you will be able to avoid the snooze button? Try laying out your clothes and running shoes the night before. Studies show you will be more likely to exercise by doing this simple act. After finishing your workout, you will feel energized and motivated to conquer the rest of the day's tasks.

Do what works best for your schedule and body, but if you haven't tried working out first thing in the morning give it a try this month.

Can You Dress for Focus Success?

On busy days, we are often so rushed that we don't give much time or thought to what we wear. In fact, we consider it a silent victory to have pants on as we rush from the house. But, we need to understand that what we wear impacts our focus and effectiveness.[97]

Some of our most successful leaders prefer dressing comfortably. For example, Mark Zuckerberg enjoys wearing his casual clothes— the same grey t-shirt and jeans—to the office because he believes it allows him to think about more crucial matters. Steve Jobs wearing black shirts and jeans all the time didn't stop him from being one of the most influential business leaders. Richard Branson, founder of the Virgin Group, refuses to wear a necktie.[98]

While these leaders swear by their casual choices of clothing, other successful people take a different approach. Bespoke Tailor Roberto Revilla states this opinion: "Generally speaking, what you wear to the office has some impact on productivity. As one of my CEO clients so eloquently puts it: 'When I'm at the office, I'm here to conduct business and look like I mean business. When I'm at home with the kids or at a rugby match, it's a different matter, but I never mix the two, and, therefore, my business and casual wardrobes don't mix, either.'"[99]

While opinions on the matter differ, research reveals that what we wear does have a correlation with how we think and process information. As you may know, I'm big on superheroes. Want to think like a superhero? A study at the University of Hertfordshire discovered that those who wore a Superman or Wonder Woman t-shirt automatically felt stronger and more confident in themselves.[100]

In another study, scientists set out to test the phenomenon coined "enclothed cognition," or the effects of clothing on our thinking and focus. White doctor or lab coats are widely seen as symbols of knowledgeable men and women who are also diligent and precise. The study gave participants white lab coats to wear while completing incongru-ent trials. Meanwhile, other participants conducted the trial in their regular clothes. The result? Those wearing white doctor or lab coats immediately became more focused and attentive to detail, committing only half as many errors as participants not wearing the coats.[101]

I mostly wear the same thing on stage: green glasses, black shirt, white belt, dark grey pants, and fashion sneakers. This consistency allows me to *focus* less on what I'm wearing and more on my audience and performance.

So, try it out, or try it on. Clothing not only impacts how other people perceive us but also how we perceive ourselves and how we focus. This month, test to see what works best for you. Power suit, white lab coat, jeans, or Wonder Woman shirt?

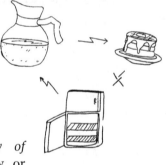

CHAPTER SUMMARY

The One Big Thing

Small steps are better than no steps: ten minutes of exercise at the hotel is better than zero.

Grade: *B-*

While I made improvements in many areas there is still room for consistency with my sleep, workouts, and diet.

Top Takeaways

1. Identify your negative triggers and try to avoid them (beer = corn chips).

2. Identify your positive triggers and pull them close (wearing your running shorts to bed = more likely to run in the morning).

3. All things in moderation.

4. *Comparative Trading* and *Food Theory of Relativity*—would I rather have this now or something better later?

5. Enjoy an occasional slice of chocolate cake—live life! However, the key is making sure our indulgences are worth it. Don't "waste" an indulgence on something that's so-so (e.g., random Halloween candy). Before indulging, ask yourself: "Is it worth it?" "Am I actually hungry?"

6. Eat brain foods to improve your focus.

Relationships

The president of a large university sent me a note stating that he, his faculty, and students enjoy my books. The books were positively influencing the students and faculty. Because of the books' impact, the university wanted to award me an honorary doctorate.

I was beyond flattered. What an honor. Never in my wildest dreams did I imagine this. This was a joyous day for me and a celebration for everyone who helped me along the way—those who had believed in me at times when there was little to believe in.

The university scheduled the ceremony during spring graduation.

The commencement speaker that day was only a few years my senior, but she was already on the state's supreme court. She was impressive. Her speech was captivating.

Addressing the recent graduates in attendance, she was also speaking to the thousands of parents and family members packing the large arena. Having previously given a commencement address at the University of Texas, I knew firsthand the difficulty of trying to resonate with such a diverse audience...from teenagers to grandparents. Plus, the honest reality is that a majority of the audience is just waiting for you to finish.

The honorable judge continued her address: "You see, in life, the older you get, the more time accelerates...when you're six years old, the night before Christmas seems like an eternity...yet when you're forty-five years old, it seems like you had just cleaned up the holiday decorations and dumped the eggnog when in what seems like a blink-of-the-eye, you're starting to hear those familiar holiday jingles on the radio again..."

This is so true. Major holidays such as birthdays, anniversaries, and religious occasions help mark time. We often measure our lives with these occasions—a twenty-first birthday, your tenth anniversary. They allow us to pause. Wow, has it really been another year? What have I been doing? What have I accomplished? Am I happier than I was a year ago? Feel more fulfilled? Have I helped make other people feel more fulfilled? What have I done in the past year? What did I do with those half a million minutes?

While the days are often harried and long, the years are short. Often in these reflections, we ask ourselves, did I focus on the things that matter?

None of us knows when the end will be. Sadly, this hit home just weeks after receiving my honorary doctorate. The incredible person who had so kindly bestowed upon me the honor, President Thomas Pleger, passed away unexpectedly at 48 years young. One morning he woke up perfectly healthy. Later that day, he wasn't feeling well and decided to go to the doctor. They discovered a brain mass requiring emergency surgery. A few days later, he passed away, a tragic loss to his family and the community.

In all likelihood, someone special in your life has left this world too soon. Experiencing such a loss is a jolting reminder to run our race today, because nobody knows when the finish line will come.

For centuries, people have carried the Latin phrase "Memento Mori" with them in their heads. Some, like Marcus Aurelius, carry it imprinted on a coin, wanting a physical reminder to always be with them. Translated to *You Will Die*, Memento Mori is a positive reminder not to get stressed by the little things but to live life to the fullest. It's the understanding that, yes, we want to be productive, but we also want to pause and focus on the beauty around us. While it may seem odd to remind ourselves that we will die, meditating on our mortality is only depressing if we miss the point. Memento Mori is a tool to create priority, urgency, and meaning, reminding us that time is a gift not to be wasted on trivial items. Death reminds us that life isn't pointless but rather purposeful.

I have been blessed in my career to have one-on-one conversations with some of the world's most successful people, from Dr. Thomas Phlegar to incredible stay-at-home moms, Fortune 500 CEOs, school teachers, founders of start-ups, chairpersons of non-profit organizations and presidents of countries. One common thread among them is their focus on the important versus the immediate. They focus on what matters most—relationships. Relationships with family, friends, neighbors, partners, teammates, and co-workers. Are you focusing on what matters most? Memento Mori.

This month was dedicated to focusing on deepening relationships. Deepening any relationship requires one essential: intentional time... quality time. For example, if I'm eating breakfast with my daughters but the entire time I'm scrolling my social media feed, I'm spending exactly zero quality time.

The Rule of 3

As Jim Collins penned in his bestseller *Good to Great*, if you have more than three priorities, you have none. The Latin phrase *"omne trium perfectum"* roughly translates to "everything that comes in threes is perfect," or, "every set of three is complete."

As a writer and speaker, I do my best to adhere to the rule of three. The rule of three in communication is a writing and speaking principle that suggests that a series of three events or characters is more humorous, satisfying, and effective than other numbers in engaging the audience.[102]

Hence, when information is bundled into threes, the audience is more likely to remember it. Part of the reasoning is that three bits of information are the smallest amount to create a pattern. The rule of three helps create a rhythm and is often used in advertising. *Snap, Crackle, Pop,* and *Just Do It* are examples. The rule of three helps us easily finish these patterns just by reading the first word:

- Life, liberty and the pursuit of happiness (Declaration of Independence)
- Stop, drop, and roll (fire safety)
- Veni, Vidi, Vici (Latin: "I came, I saw, I conquered" often attributed to Julius Caesar)
- Ho! Ho! Ho! (Santa Claus)
- Father, Son, and Holy Spirit (Bible)
- Blood, sweat, and tears (General Patton)
- The good, the bad, and the ugly (Film)
- Bacon, lettuce, and tomato (Sandwich)

Amazon founder and CEO Jeff Bezos applied the rule of three when he sent a letter to his board in the late '90s, outlining the vision for the company. In that letter, Bezos stated what he deemed the "single most important element" to ensure that Amazon continued to excel.

What was this element? It was setting the bar high in recruiting. Bezos knew that in an environment as dynamic as the Internet, succeeding without extraordinary people would be impossible. The relationships of team members would determine the ultimate trajectory of Amazon.

To help identify the right candidates that would make outstanding future teammates, Bezos applied the rule of three. He asked all of his hiring managers to ask themselves three questions during the hiring process before extending a job offer. These three questions would help ensure they have "smart, hard-working, passionate folks who put customers first."[103]

1. Will you admire this person?

If you think about the people you've admired in your life, they are probably people you've been able to learn from or take an example from. For myself, I've always tried hard to work only with people I admire, and I encourage folks here to be just as demanding. Life is short; surround yourself with people you admire.

2. Will this person raise the average level of effectiveness?

Our bar has to continuously go up. I ask people to visualize the company 5 years from now. At that point, each of us should look around and say, "The standards are so high now—boy, I'm glad I got in when I did!"

3. Might this person be a superstar?

Many people have unique skills, interests, and perspectives that enrich the work environment for all of us. It's often something that's not even related to their jobs. One person here is a former National Spelling Bee champion. I suspect it doesn't help her in her everyday work, but it does make working here more fun if you can occasionally run into her in the hall with a quick challenge: "onomatopoeia!"

Bezos knew it wouldn't be easy to find these people. He knew these were three demanding questions. But, he also knew that "creating a little bit of history" isn't supposed to be easy.

Whenever you're writing, speaking, selling, or facing a complex challenge in your life, try to use the rule of three.

Share Your Gifts with the World

The *meaning* of life is discovering our gifts, and our *purpose* in life is giving them away.

Actor Jim Carey summed it up well in his commencement speech to Maharishi University:

> My father could've been a great comedian, but he didn't believe that was possible for him, and so he made a conservative choice. Instead, he got a safe job as an accountant, and when I was 12 years old, he was let go from that safe job and our family had to do whatever we could to survive.

> I learned many great lessons from my father, not the least of which was that you can fail at what you don't want, so you might as well take a chance on doing what you love.

> That's not the only thing he taught me, though: I watched the effect my father's love and humor had on the world around me, and I thought, that's something to do, that's something worthy of my time.

My father used to brag that I wasn't a ham—I was the whole pig. And he treated my talent as if it was his second chance. When I was about 28, after a decade as a professional comedian, I realized one night in LA that the purpose of my life has always been to free people from concern, like my dad. When I realized this, I dubbed my new devotion, The Church of Freedom From Concern—The Church of FFC—and I dedicated myself to that ministry.

What's yours? How will you serve the world? What do they need that your talent can provide? That's all you have to figure out. As someone who has done what you're about to go do, I can tell you from experience, the effect you have on others is the most valuable currency there is.

Second Impressions

First impressions matter. Research shows that seven seconds is all it takes for a person to make a first impression.[104] While many understand this concept, most don't understand this important distinction: life is a series of first impressions. Even when you interact with someone you have known for twenty years, each time you engage with that person, the first few moments are a first impression. You will have thousands of first impressions with the same person over your lifetime. Second impressions matter. Seven-hundredth impressions matter. When I need to ask Ana Maria a favor, I read her mood and steer clear if the weather appears stormy.

> *Cheese, wine, and friends must be old to be good.*
> — Cuban proverb

These five simple actions below can help us deepen the impressions we make on others:

1. Let the other person do the majority of the talking.

This month, listen more than you talk. Be quick to listen, slow to speak. When you meet a new person, ask them questions about themselves, and make them feel important. Studies confirm that people love talking about themselves. About 40% of all conversations are spent on people talking about how they feel or what they think.[105] Or, as Dale Carnegie preached, "Remember that a person's name is, to that person, the sweetest and most important sound in any language."

The other benefit of listening is learning. Listening = learning.

The gravitational pull is for us to talk about ourselves. One way to help shift our focus to the other person is to give a short answer to anyone who asks us a question, then ask them the same question in return.

2. Smile.

Smiling is the easiest way to be more approachable and likable. Studies have shown that people find us more attractive and sincere when we smile.[106]

> If you see a friend without a smile; give him one of yours.
> — Proverb

Erroneously believing that smiling made me appear goofy, I tried suppressing my natural inclination to smile constantly. Gary Vaynerchuk described me as the person with "all the teeth." Admittedly, I even have a hard time suppressing my smile when someone is telling me a dark story or delivering bad news. In my head, I'm literally saying to myself, *"Oh no, I think I'm still smiling. Stop smiling, stop smiling."*

I now consider my ubiquitous smile a gift rather than a curse, and I try to give this gift away.

3. Be vulnerable.

People appreciate authenticity, even if that means admitting our weaknesses. Being humble about our failures is more impressive than listing out our successes. Owning up to our flaws takes strength, so communicating our faults and asking for advice to better ourselves can be one of our most attractive attributes.[107]

People don't love us or our organizations because we are perfect. They love us because we are perfectly flawed, so embrace being Flawsome. Being Flawsome means we are willing to:

1. Admit we made a mistake.
2. Give a plan for fixing it.
3. Follow through with fixing it.

4. Give a sincere compliment.

Who doesn't love a good boost? Genuinely giving someone a compliment will provide them with a sense of joy and appreciation that they will unconsciously attribute to you, causing them to perceive you favorably. It's also mutually beneficial. Studies show that giving compliments improves the mood and health of everyone involved.[108]

5. Tell a story.

When it is our turn to speak, communicate through storytelling. When possible, come prepared with a few stories that really showcase who you are as a person and what you stand for. Jot down stories, experiences, and funny jokes when they happen. Later you can review your notes, and when the moment strikes, you can more readily recall these stories and wow your listeners. But, the easiest way to wow an audience is always to listen first.[109]

I Will NOT Come Down From This Wall

Whether you're a religious or non-religious person, there is a story dating back to 444 B.C. that can help us.

At the time, the king of Persia was Artaxerxes. To ensure the king wasn't poisoned, a designated wine taster called a cupbearer was on hand. Artaxerxes' cupbearer was Nehemiah. Nehemiah was much more than the standard cupbearer. He was also a friend and an official—very similar to a president's Chief of Staff today.

Nehemiah was painfully aware that the city of Jerusalem was in a rough state. The walls had been destroyed and the gates burned. Any strong warlord who wanted to enter and steal could do so at will. Nehemiah watched this state of affairs from afar, and on the day he couldn't take it any longer, he took a big risk.

While Nehemiah and the king were indeed close confidants, Nehemiah was still a slave who could neither take time off nor approach the king for a favor. Nehemiah prayed long and hard for the courage to ask King Artaxerxes if he could take some time off to go help his people in the city of Jerusalem.

Artaxerxes benevolently replied that he would not only grant Nehemiah the time off, but he would make him the mayor of Jerusalem (called governor of Judea at the time) on the condition that once Nehemiah completed his work in Jerusalem, he would return to the side of Artaxerxes.

When he arrived in the city, Nehemiah's heart sank. The city was in worse shape than he thought, not only physically, but psychologically. He concluded that they needed to rebuild the wall around the city to give the people protection and a sense of pride.

Rebuilding Jerusalem was a huge undertaking. Nehemiah gathered everyone in the city, invited people from surrounding cities, and laid out the plan for a singular focus. The focus was to rebuild the wall. There are no miracles in this story, it's just an incredible story of one man with one unrelenting focus—rebuilding the wall.

Nehemiah pulled everyone together and said:

1.   here's the problem
2.   here's the solution (i.e., a wall)
3.   here's why we need to do it now (i.e., build the wall)

He rallied the city around these three simple statements.

Although this was a huge job, everyone was excited about it and they began making progress. Those outside the city walls weren't excited about it; many viewed a strong Jerusalem as a potential threat.

The person with the loudest voice against the rebuilding of the wall was Sanballat. He sent in spies to start rumors and actively discourage people from building the wall. When that didn't work, he sent armies to attack the people working on the wall. While Sanballat's actions were causing problems and slowing progress, Nehemiah stayed steadfast on the wall. The wall continued to grow higher and higher.

Sanballat then planned to kill Nehemiah. Without Nehemiah, the rest of the workers would become discouraged.

Sanballat's forces sent Nehemiah a letter asking him to join them at the village, Chephirim. Nehemiah realized Sanballat and his men planned to harm him and responded pointedly to Sanballat. *"I'm doing a great work and cannot come down."*

This sentence is so extraordinarily powerful.

Think about the most important position/responsibility entrusted to you—the one that keeps pulling at you whenever you have a quiet moment of reflection. Perhaps you've dabbled in it, and then put it aside. Imagine if you simply echoed Nehemiah's words, "I'm doing a great work and cannot come down."

The thought of being as focused and dedicated as Nehemiah should flush us with excitement. For example, if an email requested something from me, the response could be immediate: *I'm heads down on finishing my latest book. I apologize, but I can't take on anything outside of this right now. I hope you understand.* This is my version of Nehemiah's "I'm doing a great work and cannot come down." Think about what your version would be and pay attention to how good the prospect of doing this makes you feel.

Nehemiah continued with his response: "I'm doing a great work and cannot come down. Why should the work stop while I leave it and come down to you?"

Sanballat's group sent four different types of messages attempting to convince Nehemiah to come down, but each time Nehemiah sent a similar response, not so far removed from what we deal with daily in our barrage of emails. While people today aren't trying to kill us, they are trying to kill our time.

Had Nehemiah not remained focused on rebuilding the wall and instead come down to meet with Sanballat's men, they would've taken his life. What's important for us to consider is that not focusing on and not caring for our goals can potentially ruin our happiness, and in some instances, ruin our lives.

So yes, there is more golf you could play, more movies you could watch, more money you could chase, more fame you could pursue, more times you could go out late with your girlfriends and buddies, but you need to understand you're doing a great work. For many of us, this starts with our friends and family. So when you see your boy-friend, girlfriend, kids, or spouse, say to yourself: *I'm doing a great work here.*

Nehemiah's enemies didn't give up. They started a rumor that Nehemiah was building the wall with the intent of becoming king of Judea and starting his own empire against King Artaxerxes. The rumor mongers thought this would trick Nehemiah into leaving the wall to defend himself. But Nehemiah did not do this. Instead, he simply said, "I'm not coming down from this wall."

Next, his friend Shemaiah, or at least he thought he was his friend, came to him and said, "Nehemiah, you know you have enemies in the city itself. Many merchants here make their living trading with people outside of the city walls, and they're afraid that the rebuilt wall might discourage trade. There is a plan to murder you in your sleep. Nehemiah, we must go to the altar for your safety."

Nehemiah simply said, "I don't believe you. I'm not coming down from this wall for rumors of murder in my sleep, other opportunities, for fear of the King, nothing is going to take me from this wall. I'm doing a great work here and will remain."

Because of Nehemiah's focus, he and his forces completed the wall in 52 days. To rebuild a wall of this size so quickly after it had been lying in rubble for hundreds of years astounded nations and Nehemiah's enemies alike. When they saw the completed wall, they lost their confidence.

We already know what our walls are and the forces that take us down from our walls. For some of us, it's too much TV; for others, the overuse of social media. Some of us drink too much, are addicted to video games or watching people play video games, poker, fantasy sports, gossiping. Some of us chase too many opportunities at once, and some get pulled into the family drama. Whatever the pull to come down from our wall, staying on it is our challenge. Your great work can be:

- Focusing on your family
- Finishing your screenplay
- Going back to school
- Starting your company
- Getting out of a bad relationship
- Paying down your debt and getting your finances in order
- Finishing the project that will take your business to the next level
- Volunteering more time at your favorite non-profit
- Learning a language
- Living a healthier lifestyle so that you will be around to see your great-grandchildren
- Training for a marathon
- Etc.

Whatever it might be, this is the time to stop pretending. This is the time to climb the ladder and stay on your wall in the full knowledge that staying on the wall is never easy.

The book in your hands is a guide to help keep us on our wall. Like you, I'm tempted every day to come down from my wall. For example, my goal for this book was to write every day—this was my wall for the past year, but invariably, life happened, and I would go days without writing a single word or even thinking about this book. Think about that. I was knee-deep in focus, but I kept getting pulled down from my wall.

As the months progressed, I got better and better at focusing, for I was training my mind, body, and soul to stay on my wall. When you climb the ladder and get on your wall, nothing outside has changed. You don't have more time, you don't have more money, and you don't have more resources. But what you *do* have is a changed mindset. Lack of time or resources has never been our main issue; it's a lack of priority. Everyday distractions beckon us, but, like Nehemiah, we need simply to say: *"I'm doing a great work here and I will not come down from this wall."*

Seeing Your Goals Matters

On July 4, 1952, Florence Chadwick was on her way to becoming the first woman to swim the Catalina Channel. As the world watched, Chadwick fought the dense fog, bone-chilling cold, and sharks.

Those who wish to sing always find a song.

— Swedish proverb

She was exhausted, but if she could just see the shore, she would be able to push through. Every time she looked through her goggles, all she could see was dense fog. Unable to see the shore, she gave up. She was only half a mile from the coast but had no idea. She quit not because she was a quitter but because she couldn't see her goal anymore.

"If only I had seen the land, I could have made it." Two months later, she went back and swam the Catalina Channel. This time, in spite of the numerous challenges, there was no fog—she could see the shore, she could see her goal. As she strode ashore, someone informed her that she'd beaten the men's record by two hours.

It's important to make our goals and desired destinations visible.

Our Focus Map

Mind maps are visual aids that help us organize and process information. As a visual learner, I'm a big fan of them. Colors, images, symbols, and words are incorporated into these maps to help our brains make connections. Or, as mindmapping.com puts it:

> Mind mapping is a highly effective way of getting information in and out of your brain. Mind mapping literally "maps out" your ideas.

Mind mapping converts a long list of information into a memorable and highly organized diagram that works with your brain's natural way of visualizing things.

One simple way to understand a Mind Map is by comparing it to a map of a city. The city center represents the main idea; the roads leading from the center represent the key thoughts in your process; the secondary roads or branches represent your secondary thoughts, and so on.

You can put your ideas down in any order and worry about reorganizing them later.

We can see the effectiveness of mind maps in the research of Nobel Prize winner, Dr. Roger Sperry, who proved that the cerebral cortex in the brain is divided into two hemispheres: right and left.[110]

Mind maps bring together the left hemisphere of the brain, responsible for words, logic, and numbers, and the right hemisphere, responsible for images, color, space, and rhythm. The more our right and left brain work together, the more our brain can work at optimum efficiency.[111]

One particular study found that mind mapping enhances information processing, helping to improve memory formation. In one specific example, the recall of facts by medical students improved by 10% when they used mind maps.[112] Mind mapping is also beneficial in childhood development. Mind mapping boosts word recall for children more successfully than using lists—improvements can be as high as 32%.[113]

In short, mind maps are fun and effective whether you're 8 or 80.

Standing Firm

One of my favorite activities is volunteering at my church's Sunday school. Selfishly, I truly believe I get more out of it than the kids do. If you ever find yourself figuring out what to do next, consider this:

1.   Give yourself a break. You aren't alone. We all experience this limbo in certain seasons of our lives.

2.   Donate your time to helping out someone else. When in doubt, volunteer.

While I loved working with the kids at Sunday school, I also travel quite a bit for speaking and book tours. As a result, when I volunteer, I want to be assigned to one of my daughter's classes and requested this assignment to the head of the school.

However, the need is often for help with elementary school boys. Not wanting to be a bad volunteer or feel the guilt associated with it, I often would say "okay" and fill in for these slots. Then I would sadly say goodbye to my daughters as I dropped them off at their classes. While helping the boys is wonderful, it just isn't the same as leading my daughters' classes. I prefer spending time with my daughters.

This project had me examining every aspect of my life. At the top of this list was spending more time with family. As such, I sent another note to the head of the school:

Dear Kelly,

Thank you for the honor of allowing me to volunteer with the school children—my wife and I love it! Since I travel so much during the week, I'd like to spend as much time with my daughters on the weekend as possible, including Sunday mornings. So we can spend time with our daughters and help the other students, my wife and I are happy to volunteer anytime you need us for the following classes:

- *2nd Grade Girls*
- *3rd Grade Girls*

We were happy to receive the following response:

Of course, Erik. This makes complete sense. Thank you for the note, Erik, and for you and your wife always helping out!

The next week, I was assigned to my younger daughter's class. It was the highlight of my week.

The following week, I received this email:

Dear Erik,

Will you be willing to lead the 3rd-grade boys class this Sunday?

Upon receiving this note, I had the same initial reaction as always—reply with *"I'm happy to help."* Habits are hard to break. But, since I was in the middle of this project, it was the ideal time to experiment. If I behave the same as I have in the past, what is the point of the project? Further, I reminded myself of another maxim: If it's not an immediate "yes!" to the opportunity (i.e., would you be willing to lead the boys?) then it should be an immediate "no."

Most often a "hard/definitive note" is the best approach. In this instance, knowing the culture at the church, I decided this was one of the rare exceptions where a "hard no" would not be well received.

So here is my first response. I copied and pasted my previous note:

Hello Kelly,

Thank you for your note. Thank you for the honor of allowing me to volunteer with the school children—my wife and I love it! Since I travel so much during the week I want to spend as much time with my wife and daughters on the weekend as possible, including Sunday mornings. So that we can spend time with our daughters and help the other students my wife and I are happy to volunteer anytime you need us for the following classes:

- *2nd Grade Girls*
- *3rd Grade Girls*

Well, as much as I'd like to say this worked, it didn't. I soon received this note:

Hi Erik!

Thank you for your message and willingness to volunteer even at the last minute. Did you receive my note about volunteering for the boys 3rd grade class this Sunday?

What a great chess move on her part! Now I really had to dig deep to avoid "checkmate." Here's my reply:

Hi Kelly!

Thanks for the note! I'd be happy to volunteer this Sunday to take on the 3rd grade girls. So if one of the other teachers of the 3rd grade girls wants to lead the boys, then I'm happy to backfill them, and I'll lead the girls while they lead the boys' classroom. Please let me know if I can help!

Guilt and shame enveloped me. What kind of a church volunteer am I? A conditional volunteer? It was as if I were volunteering to be the parking attendant at the church and stating I'd be happy to do it but only on days when it's 75 degrees and sunny. Guilt and shame took turns ping-ponging within me.

I stuck my hand into the metaphorical mantra bag for this project and pulled out: *Real change is real hard.*

To help lessen the shame and guilt, I reminded myself that I was a much better teacher with the girls, and I looked forward to it. The boys would be better off having someone who was truly looking forward to the experience and was better equipped at dealing with and wrangling the limitless energy of elementary school boys.

Fortunately, it wasn't long before I received this email:

> *Hi Erik!*
>
> *One of the teachers is happy to lead the 3rd grade boys, so it will be great if you will lead the 3rd grade girls class.*

While some shame and guilt still lingered, it was more than offset by the joy of being able to spend time with my daughter and deepening the relationships with her and her friends. Also, it felt good to help the church fill all the volunteer slots in a creative way.

My daughter and I still laugh at some of the funny things she and the other kids said and did that day. Lifetime memories. Just think, before this project, this moment would've been missed. The cherry on top is that the leader of the boys found she enjoys leading boys better!

A win-win situation. It won't always end up being unicorns and rainbows, but you'll be surprised how often new pots of gold are discovered when everyone states their desires (we cover this next with the "Abilene Paradox").

The Abilene Paradox

The Abilene Paradox and other Meditations on Management, written by management expert Jerry B. Harvey, focuses on the well-known "Abilene Paradox," taught in classes around the world.

The basic plot and lesson are as follows:

On a hot afternoon in Coleman, Texas, a man, his wife, and his inlaws are comfortably playing dominoes. The father-in-law suggests that they take a trip to Abilene for dinner. The wife says, "Sounds like a great idea." The husband, despite having doubts about the long drive in the Texas heat, thinks his preference must be out-of-step with

A good marriage is where both people feel like they're getting the better end of the deal.

— Anne Lamott

the group, but instead of raising any concern, he says, "Sounds good to me. I just hope your mother wants to go." The mother-in-law responds, "Of course I want to go. I haven't been to Abilene in a long time."

The drive to Abilene is hot, dusty, and long. When they get into town, the family picks out a restaurant. The food, however, is as bad as the drive. After they finish eating, they head home, arriving exhausted and unsatisfied.

The mother-in-law dishonestly says, "It was a great trip, wasn't it?" Even though she would rather have stayed home, she went along because the other three seemed so enthusiastic. The man honestly complains, "I was delighted playing dominoes on the porch and would've been happy to continue doing so. I only went along to satisfy the rest of you."

His wife replies, "I just went along to keep you happy. I would've had to be crazy to want to go out in the heat like that." The father-in-law then says that he only originally suggested going to Abilene because he thought the others might be bored playing dominoes.

The group sits back, perplexed that they had collectively decided to take a trip which none of them wanted to actually go on. They each would've preferred sitting comfortably and happily enjoying the afternoon as they were, but none of them admitted it at the time.

The key takeaway for the purposes of this project is that we must make a decision and speak our minds, which is not always easy to do. Consider the mother-in-law's position: she's the last in the decision tree. How many of us would act as she did? Think about the many times you may have said to yourself, "Well, I don't want to be the only one to rock the boat."

Stating our opinions directly and honestly is imperative. Look at the multitude of potential decisions at our disposal each day. The possibilities are endless.

If the mother-in-law had to relive the situation, she would be better off with this statement: "The most important thing to me is that we are together, that is what makes me happy. I'm perfectly happy staying here. I believe that the drive will be long and hot and that we're better off given the weather today staying here. However, if I'm the only one that shares this opinion, then I'm happy to go with everyone."

Notice she didn't say, "That's a dumb idea," or "I don't agree with you." Instead, she merely stated her opinion, bracketing it by including what is most important to her ("being together"), while also making others feel good ("Being with you makes me happy"). She's taking an active leadership role.

Next time we find ourselves leading a meeting, at home or in the office, we must foster a level of openness so others follow by stating their true opinions. Alan Mulally, while CEO of Ford, told a story that maps directly to this idea. For update meetings with his top executives, he wanted the status of projects to be easily identifiable. Hence, he used the stoplight method. Similar to a street stoplight, projects are either red, yellow, or green.

All executives report on initiatives as either green (everything is fine), yellow (things appear OK for now but we need to keep an eye on them), and red (trouble spots). For the first few meetings, the status board was all green.

Mulally was a bit befuddled by this because one of the main reasons he was brought in as CEO was that Ford was struggling and needed to be turned around. Yet, his team was telling him the opposite—everything was perfectly fine.

Finally, at one meeting, someone apprehensively presented a few items in red. What did Mulally do? He started clapping. In the next meeting, almost everything was in red. Mulally indicated that from that time forward, they made significant progress because the employees felt safe stating what was going on—even if it was bad. As a leader, Mulally fostered this openness, allowing for more focused and rapid decisions for fixing the trouble spots.

You never hear someone say, "I really respect that guy, he agrees with everything I say and I therefore never know where I truly stand with him. What a great YES man!" But you do often hear, "I don't always like what she has to say, but I respect her because she always speaks her mind."

Focus on politely speaking your mind. If you do so, it will be the exception, rather than the rule, that you end up somewhere you don't want to be.

FOMO (Fear of Missing Out)

For many of us—especially those of us who identify with having tendencies of a squirrel—our issue is that every opportunity looks like the "must-do" opportunity. We are pulled away from completing our current project by the allure of the next big thing. Ironically, before the *next big thing* came along, there was the previous *next big thing*.

How do we cope with this without feeling we are missing out on a huge opportunity? One approach is understanding that being the first mover on something can often be a disadvantage.

This approach goes against the common perception in our entrepreneurial culture—that those first to market inherently win. In many instances, the exact opposite can occur. Gerald Tellis and Peter Golder discovered this in their well-known study comparing the success of pioneers (first movers) versus settlers (not first to market). The failure rate of pioneers was more than five times higher than settlers; 47%

versus 8% failure rate, to be exact. The conclusion is that there are several advantages to being patient enough to see how things play out. A prime example of this is the iPhone. There were several smartphone offerings before the iPhone launched, most notably the Handspring Treo 300. This was a smartphone, but it was still a flip phone, so it was about the size of a small brick.

I was fortunate to have access to a test pilot version of it. I well remember my friends making fun of me. "It looks like a dumb phone," they cackled, "It's so big!" as they flipped open their large paper notebooks, holding them up to their ears, saying, "Hello, yes, Houston, the eagle has landed." "Why," they questioned, "would I ever want email on my phone or to watch video on my phone?"

Timing it perfectly, Steve Jobs and Apple launched a much better and radically designed smartphone that forever changed the game.

Ironically, Steve Jobs was famous for vehemently stating that "Apple will never make a phone." As one executive recalls, "The exec team was trying to convince Steve that building a phone was a great idea for Apple. He didn't really see the path to success."

One of the failures of many organizations and founders is that they're on the bleeding edge instead of the cutting edge. They are too far in front of the market. The market just isn't ready for this type of product. On the other hand, settlers can wait and watch until the market is ready. It's important to be one year ahead of our competition, but never be a year ahead of our market.

There are certainly first-mover advantages, but the advantages of waiting, of being a settler—will perhaps help us avoid FOMO. This will help us avoid chasing the wind. Often, it's about playing the long game. It's about persistence in the short term and patience in the long term.

It's always darkest before the dawn.

CHAPTER SUMMARY

The One Big Thing

Memento Mori: Remembering that we will die helps us treat time as a gift. Death reminds us that life isn't pointless but purposeful.

Grade: *B+*

This month felt like a splash of ice water. I was unknowingly letting important relationships in my life take a back seat. This month was beyond rewarding. Every phone call, every lunch, and every connection lifted my spirits and reminded me that life is all about relationships.

Top Takeaways

1. Set up two lunches per week and call two people per week and thank them for something.

2. Draw a mind map for the next 12 months.

3. Always state your opinion (Abilene Paradox).

Learning

My daughter's birthday was approaching and it was a good "marker" for my progress in learning Spanish. My wife and her family are from Colombia, and the party with my Spanish speaking relatives would be a great opportunity for me to demonstrate my progress.

The party turned out to be a harsh reality check. I'd been learning Spanish for over a decade, yet it felt like I'd just started. Her birthday was a cruel reminder that my progress wasn't impressive. Had you asked me ten years ago if I would be fluent in Spanish after ten years of practicing, I would've replied emphatically—"Ten years? For sure! You will think I'm Shakira."

However, this is the slow boil, my friends. I'd been merely pecking away. Well, this month, I was going to go all-in on learning Spanish. It would be my top focus. It was a nice reminder of why I undertook this project in the first place. For many of us, a month of focus is better than ten years of nibbling at the edges.

Consider this old Cherokee parable:

An old Cherokee chief was teaching his grandson about life...

"A fight is going on inside me," he said to the boy. "It is a terrible fight and it is between two wolves. One is evil—he is anger, envy, sorrow, regret, greed, arrogance, self-pity, guilt, resentment, inferiority, lies, false pride, superiority, and ego. The other is good—he is joy, peace, love, serenity, hope, humility, kindness, empathy, generosity, truth, compassion, and faith. This same fight is going on inside you—and inside every other person, too."

The grandson thought about it for a minute and then asked his grandfather,

"Which wolf will win?"

The old chief simply replied, "The one we feed."

I wasn't feeding my Spanish enough.

My wife speaks Spanish exclusively to my daughters. I needed to "up my game" so the entire house was speaking Spanish. Ana Maria didn't have the patience to speak to me in Spanish, and I don't blame her!

Now, it would be ideal to spend a month in Colombia with family—it's baptism by fire. Spanish is often the only language spoken—it's full immersion.

The stars weren't aligning for a trip to Colombia. The next best thing? Spending a month in Miami with Ana Maria's parents! Not only are they amazing people and grandparents (abuelos), but Ana Maria's mom and friends speak only Spanish in the home. This would be semi-immersion for me and the kids.

I also realized that my online learning through the Spanish language learning app, Duolingo, was always solitary, making it difficult to find time to peel away to practice. Then one day, my daughters expressed interest in the app. While my daughters were much better than me at speaking Spanish, I was better at reading and writing it. We discovered that learning to use the app together was fun for the family.

I also realized that when Ana Maria was speaking Spanish with our kids or with her parents, I was involuntarily tuning it out. I wasn't capitalizing on the opportunity. It was as if I was a character in "Peanuts." Whenever an adult is speaking, all that Charlie Brown, Snoopy, Lucy, and the rest of the gang hear is "wa...wa...wa...wa...wa..." Now, when a Spanish conversation is occurring in our home, I'm "tuning in" versus "tuning out."

At first, I believed immersion meant I would simply be speaking in Spanish. But, I soon realized that to learn Spanish, all forms of my communication needed to be in, you guessed it, Spanish! Focusing on this change would really help increase my learning curve. My default habit was to text Ana Maria in English. I had to break this habit.

> *Anyone who stops learning is old, whether at twenty or eighty. Anyone who keeps learning stays young. The greatest thing in life is to keep your mind young.*
>
> — Henry Ford

Making this texting adjustment immediately started paying dividends with my learning— and it was fun! Rather than gloss over the family text messages in Spanish, I would read them and look up words and grammatical strings that were new to me.

Occasionally, I would get something wrong, and my error would become a source of humor for us. One time I was trying to type about a friend who always had the latest gossip. In Spanish, I thought I had texted "she gets the dirt." Instead, what I had erroneously texted in Spanish was "she's so very dirty." No bueno.

Mistakes aside, when everyone sees how seriously I'm trying to learn Spanish, they go out of their way to help me.

Whatever Works, Do It

My daughter arrived home from school—here is a paraphrase of our conversation:

> Me: I hope you had a great day. Let's get ready quickly so we can be one of the first ones at Chloe's birthday party.
>
> Sofia: It's going to be a great party! A unicorn and mermaid party with a giant water slide. But, Daddy, I need to practice my piano for 15 minutes first as Ms. Karen has me on a 100-day challenge. I'm on day 43 and don't want to break the streak.
>
> Me: Oh, yeah, of course. That's wonderful, let's make it 44! Go practice and then we'll head out to the party.

Reflecting on the conversation, I realized 1) Ms. Karen rocks—instilling responsibility and excitement in my daughter and, 2) Ms. Karen's challenge related to this project: people in motion tend to stay in motion.

The Spanish learning app I was using had gamification and streaks. If I missed a day practicing, my streak reset to zero.

You can pay money to repair a broken streak—yes, you can game the gamification. Many of my friends actually pay to repair their streaks. On principle, I couldn't allow myself to pay to repair the streak. It just didn't feel right, unless, of course, the streak was over ten days—well then, moral principles be damned!

We desire to maintain momentum. We need to use this to our advantage, whether that's keeping a Spanish streak alive on a learning app, giving up chocolate for 40 days, or my daughter trying to maintain her 100-day streak of playing the piano for fifteen minutes. Whatever works for you, do it.

For many of us, we must radically change our mindset. We need to change our wants into musts. For ten years I wanted to learn Spanish. Now I realize that I must learn Spanish. What if we were in South America and an emergency involving the girls occurred and everyone started shouting incoherent Spanish to me? I would be the reason that my girls were seriously injured or died.

I switched my mindset from:

I want to learn Spanish to improve my communication with my family.

to

I must learn Spanish to be the best Dad, husband, and family member possible.

This shift in mindset helped hyper-accelerate my learning.

A bonus this month was discovering that research shows bilingual speakers are better at maintaining focus and attention than those only mastering one language.[114]

> *I didn't have time to write you a short letter, so I wrote you a long one.*
> — Mark Twain

Keystones

I contemplated dedicating a month to playing golf every day to see how much I could improve. It didn't make the cut (no pun intended) for this particular project, but my hope is that it will make the next project.

A golf pro I know coaches the women's golf team at Wellesley. He mentioned that when he took over as coach, the average golfer recorded a score of 101 for 18 holes. After only a year, the average score dropped to 81! A remarkable improvement.

The secret? Of the six days the team practiced, five were dedicated to working on the short game (i.e., chipping and putting). When practicing golf, most people mindlessly start hitting balls as far as they can. It's fun to tee it up and watch the ball sail. Chipping and putting can be quite tedious and frustrating (ha—golf!).

The coach's focus for the team was the exact opposite: *Drive for show* and *putt for dough* (dough is slang for money/winning). Meaning five of the six practice days would be on putting and chipping.

How many of us are metaphorically mindlessly just hitting balls versus focusing on the keystone that will make us more successful at whatever we do?

Whether you want to learn how to chip better in golf or learn a language, first determine the keystone. In architecture the keystone is the most important stone; it provides the stability to any arched doorway. In this golf example, the short game is the keystone.

Keystone is figuratively used to mean the most important part of anything. Today, we should:

1. Determine our keystone
2. Maniacally focus on it

If you want to focus on saving money, the keystone might be getting rid of your credit card or no longer buying expensive shoes. If you want to increase your business network, the keystone might be setting up five business lunches per week.

The fun part of learning Spanish is learning all the new words. However, I realized that increasing my Spanish vocabulary isn't the keystone. This is analogous to hitting long drives on the golf practice range. Learning Spanish grammar is more tedious, but it is the keystone to hyper-accelerate my learning.

Cheating at Monopoly

Hasbro, the parent company of the iconic board game, Monopoly, was wrestling with how they could get more out of the brand. Over the years they had struggled with various editions of the original game with modest success, but turning their focus from inside the company to outside the company led to a major breakthrough.

After surveying their users, they were shocked by what they discovered. The discovery? Over half the world cheats at Monopoly. While this figure sounds crazy, I want you to pause and think about a particular person you know who cheats at Monopoly. You have a name, don't you?!

Based on this discovery, Hasbro launched a new edition of the game called *Monopoly Cheaters' Edition*. It was the most successful launch in over 100 years of the company.

Grab or visualize a t-shirt and turn it inside out. Most of us, and most organizations, fall into thinking inside-out versus outside-in. To help your outside-in thinking, ask a few friends or family members what they would do if they were you. Knowing you well, what would they recommend you focus on? Also since this is a month of learning, one of the greatest ways to learn is getting viewpoints from the outside.This is exactly what Hasbro did.

Even though you know a thousand things, ask the man who knows one.
—Turkish proverb

Why Steve Jobs Banned the iPad

From a very young age, Philo Taylor Farnsworth dreamed of a better world. At age 14, Philo aspired to trap light in an empty jar from where it could be transmitted. In 1927, at the age of 21, Philo succeeded in creating the first electronic television transmission. Philo evolved his first model into an all-electric television image, allowing the image of his wife, Pem, to become the first human image to be transmitted, voilá! Pem appeared on a television screen.

Philo loved television and all of its possibilities to better the world. He believed television could transform our educational system. According to his wife, Pem, "Phil saw television as a marvelous teaching tool. There would be no excuse for illiteracy. Parents could learn along with their children. News and sporting events could be seen as they were happening."

Philo was passionate and inspired by his new invention, "Symphonies would mean more when one could see the musicians as they played, and educational movies could now be viewed in our own living rooms." Philo said, "There will be a time when we will be able to see and learn about people in other lands. If everyone understood each other better, differences could be settled around conference tables instead of wars." In essence, television could help break down these cultural barriers.

As television evolved, Philo's attitude toward his invention changed. He disliked the commercial reality of television programming. Similar to Steve Jobs banning his kids from using the iPad, Philo forbade his son, Kent from watching TV. Kent recalls his father's perspective on television, stating, "I suppose you could say that he felt he had created a monster, a way for people to waste a lot of their lives. Originally, Philo saw television as a way to expand our horizons and live fuller lives, but as television evolved, he realized how limiting television really was. It prohibited people from going out and exploring the world around them. Instead, people could sit and watch from the comfort of their homes.[115]

Today, we have even more media outlets and gadgets to distract us. It's not that the tools are inherently bad; in fact, they can be amazing learning tools. The problem arises when we aren't intentional with our use and consumption. If we are mindlessly consuming media instead of being intentional, we can easily fall into the trap that Philo indicated.

Isn't it interesting that we are witnessing history repeat itself? Instead of TV, it's social media and video games. Keep in mind, as the author of *Socialnomics*, I love technology. Similar to Philo, I love technology for its educational capabilities and its ability to globally connect us. The more we understand each other's cultural differences, the less we will need to go to war to resolve these differences.

> *If you are not willing to learn, no one can help you. If you are determined to learn, no one can stop you.*
>
> —Zig Ziglar

Just like the TV, the way we use these tech tools can be either good or bad for us. Philo prevented his son from watching TV, and Steve Jobs prevented his kids from using the iPad. "We don't allow the iPad in the home. We think it's too dangerous for them in effect." Clearly, Jobs recognized how addictive the iPad can be.[116]

We must learn to use these incredible technological tools for better outcomes. A knife is an amazing tool—it can be used to chop up food to feed people, it can be used for protection, and it can be used during surgery (scalpel) to save a life. Yet, the knife can also be used to take someone's life. Does this mean we should ban knives from the world? Certainly not, but it also doesn't mean we should hand a razor-sharp knife to a toddler. Yet, this is what we do with technology. Our use of technology needs to be intentionally focused whether we are a toddler or a retiree.

CHAPTER SUMMARY

The One Big Thing

Full immersion is often the best path to learning; keeping in mind that this isn't always possible and our goal isn't perfection, our goal is progress.

Grade: *B-*

This was another great month. The reason it isn't an A is that a) I didn't go full immersion; b) it's obvious I'm not gifted with languages, so I will have to put in the extra work; and c) sometimes I still zone out in my home when Spanish conversations are occurring.

Top Takeaways

1. When we are hyper-focused on something, we can't help but see that almost everything around us relates to it. This is called selective attention. For example, if we focus on learning Spanish, it seems that everywhere we turn there is an opportunity to practice the language—putting subtitles on the movie we are watching or talking with a Spanish speaking barista.

2. We need to change our wants into musts.

Creativity

The purpose of this project is getting us to a place where we are focusing on activities that bring us joy. There are some things in life we just have to do (e.g., taxes) but otherwise if it doesn't bring us joy, why are we doing it?

Ironically, when we are doing what we enjoy, we start to focus. Some call it getting into the zone or "flow."

A fundamental concept of creativity—including building a company, forming a team, writing a screenplay, or engineering a car—is that we were raised with a falsehood. When we were younger most of us learned to play an instrument and/or practiced a sport. We all had one particular adage drilled into our heads since kindergarten: *practice makes perfect*. This adage, unfortunately, is 100% false. If we practice the wrong way, we develop the wrong habits. If I mindlessly shoot 50 basketball free throws without the same level of concentration I'll need in a game, then I'm potentially developing bad habits.

NFL Super Bowl-winning quarterback Drew Brees understood the concept of proper practice. One of his wide receivers, Marques Colston, provided insights:

> The biggest thing I remember is how OCD (obsessive-compulsive disorder) he was about everything. He's a repetition guy. They've got to be perfect reps. We would run these routes until he felt like they were good to go for the game...I can remember him keeping his routine very similar every day; and when he got out of that routine, it would noticeably throw him off.
>
> At first, you think it's funny, but then you realize and see how much success he's had. You see how those things play a part in that and it becomes something you admire. That's something I've learned from him—getting in that routine, sticking to it. Now I understand if you get off of that...how it affects my play. It's certainly something that rubbed off on me.

Too often we are going through the motions—not practicing properly—because we think it's something we should be doing, or it's something our parents think we should be doing, or our boss, or society... Here's the thing...everyone can see that we are just going through the motions. The only person you're fooling is yourself, and that's the worst person to fool.

Whether a school teacher or a CEO, we often fall into these traps.

Proper practice leads to progress and improper practice leads to problems.

Don't go through the motions this hour, during this day, in this life. Practice doesn't make perfect. Instead, in your creative endeavors, embrace the mantra: "Proper practice leads to progress while improper practice leads to problems." The main problem is that you're developing bad habits that can become permanent.

One of the easiest ways to practice properly is to do what brings us joy. Famous mythologist, Joseph Campbell, calls it "following your bliss."

Money can't buy joy and money can't buy time. A significant goal of this project is determining ways to better manage time, freeing up capacity for creative thinking. Bill Gates once wrote that one of the greatest things he learned from Warren Buffett is how to properly value time.

"I can buy anything I want, but I can't buy time," says Buffett.

"There are only 24 hours in everyone's day and Warren has a keen understanding of this constraint. He doesn't let his calendar get filled up with useless meetings. This frees up time for meetings that he does value—developing relationships. He *is* willing to use that time to work with people that matter most to him. He is very generous with his time for the people he trusts," says Gates.[117]

During a joint interview, Gates recalls seeing Buffett's little paper calendar and appointment book for the first time.

Buffett handed his little book to the reporter for examination.

"There's nothing in it," said the surprised reporter, flipping through the book.

"Absolutely," replied Buffett.

"It's very high tech, be careful, you might not understand it," Gates joked.

The reporter flipped to a week in April and mentioned there were only three entries listed for the entire month. "There will be four, maybe, by the time April arrives," indicated Buffett.

"You know, I had every minute packed and I thought that was the only way you could do things," said Gates. "But Warren taught me the importance of giving yourself time to think."

"You control your time," says Gates. "Sitting and thinking may be a much higher priority than a normal CEO, where there are all these demands and you feel like you need to go and see all these people. It's not a proxy of your seriousness that you fill every minute in your schedule."

This is yet another instance of *comparative trading*. Leaving most of his calendar blank allows Buffett to spend time with the people that matter most to him—like Gates. It also allows time for deep thinking.

Richard Branson agrees with Gates and Buffett. "Open your calendar and schedule time just to dream," recommends Branson. "Put it in your diary like you would a meeting. Far too many people get weighed down in doing, and never take the time to think and feel. Take five minutes, an hour, a day, or even a holiday. If you free up some time to think freely, you'll be able to see the bigger picture much easier."

Emma Seppälä, the science director of Stanford University's Center for Compassion and Altruism Research and Education, confirms what Buffett and Branson have discovered.

"From Vincent Van Gogh on through Kanye West, the figure of the broody, tortured artist looms large in the popular imagination. But research suggests that the key to creativity has little to do with angst. But, the biggest breakthrough ideas often come from relaxation," says Seppälä. "History shows that many famous inventors come up with novel ideas while letting their minds wander. Simply put, creativity happens when your mind is unfocused, daydreaming, or idle. This is why we have so many "eureka" moments in the shower."[118]

Scheduling "idle" time or time for "blue sky thinking" can be the most productive use of our schedule. I know first hand that it helps free my mind when writing a book or a script.

Comparative trading also works for my writing. If I'm on a 15-hour flight to Vietnam, I'll spend much more time writing than binge-watching episodes of the latest binge-worthy series. Don't get me wrong. I just mentioned how important downtime is, and I can binge with the best of them. It's just balance. For example, instead of binging on ten episodes, I'd watch two.

A eureka moment for me occurred when I realized that while we weren't wasting time, we were being wasteful with our time. This is a big distinction. We weren't being lazy, but we were ending up in the same place as someone being lazy. We weren't reaching our goals. Worse, we weren't doing what we enjoyed. We were falling into a trap. We were mistaking activity for progress.

> *There are decades where nothing happens; and there are weeks where decades happen.*
> —Vladimir Ilyich Lenin

Talking over Texting

We had a creative call scheduled with a big automotive client based on the east coast. I was in San Francisco scheduled to join Condoleezza Rice on stage mid-morning, so the call was early morning.

While at the hotel gym, my team texted that our client meeting canceled. Hallelujah! 45 minutes were given back to me.

The team began texting me about any direction we potentially lacked from the client as a result of not having the call. I read these while exercising on a spin-bicycle. Should we send a note to the client? What should the note say? Our team is young, amazing, and prefers texting over talking, which is effective for some items but not great when a phone call would solve the issue more quickly or an email would be a better tool. I looked at my watch and realized we'd been texting back and forth for 50 minutes. It would've been more efficient to have had the actual meeting!

Training my mouth and sometimes my thumbs to respond "no" was easier said than done. Every question doesn't warrant an immediate answer—or any answer for that matter. I need to pause and ask myself, "Does this require a response?" Often the answer is no. Or, if it does require a response, I'll now type: If my response requires more clarity, please give me a call.

Eureka moment: Be quick to listen, slow to speak.

From Bourbon to Instagram

Instagram Founder Kevin Systrom recalls a critical moment in Instagram's life cycle. Instagram was originally a check-in app called Burbn (pronounced *Bourbon*). Burbn was failing and was running out of cash. They were planning on laying off all their employees and shutting down. Users weren't interested in using any of the features the app provided, with the exception of one feature. Users enjoyed posting stylized photos of what they were doing. This was very similar to the concept of Twitter at the time, but instead of texted tweets, these were status updates via pictures only—after all, a picture speaks a thousand words.

When failing, we often default to an additive mindset—somewhat analogous to adding more chairs to the deck of the Titanic. When Burbn was sinking, the founders did the exact opposite. They started stripping everything away. Metaphorically, they started tossing chairs off the ship's deck.

It wasn't easy.

The founders struggled with destroying their "baby." They had spent considerable time, money, and emotion making Burbn. Stripping away these features was painful. However, they did it. They removed everything but the photos feature. People thought they were crazy, including people close to Systrom. One evening, he was walking on the beach with his wife, and he asked her if she was excited about the new app—they hadn't yet named it Instagram.

Wife: I probably won't use it.

Systrom: Why is that?

Wife: Well, my photos just don't look as nice as yours or your friends.

Systrom: Ours only look better because we use filters.

Wife: Well, maybe you should add filters to your new app, then I might use it.

That evening, Systrom coded the first Instagram filter (X-Pro II). Systrom explains, "If you're good at one thing, that's all that matters. Successful entrepreneurs fail at many things, then they focus on the one thing that works. Doing that one thing really, really well takes care of the rest. Be the best at one thing and forget the rest."

People loved the filters and Instagram's popularity exploded—so much so that their server was overwhelmed with the amount of traffic. They needed to get another server or two to handle the massive increase in data. There was simple coding available they could copy and paste to keep the data organized, but instead they went with a more powerful software solution.

This software was considered the best available to handle the traffic surges they were experiencing. However, it turns out, the software was extremely difficult to implement. After a few weeks, despite all the time they were pouring into it, it still wasn't functioning properly.

After a few days, Systrom's Co-Founder and top programmer took two hours to write a simple code to resolve the solution. Systrom realized he'd made his life complex for no reason. He should've done the simple code from the beginning and saved a lot of time, hassle, and money.

> *My works are like water. The works of the great masters are like wine. But everyone drinks water.*
>
> — Mark Twain

Despite this, Instagram continued its rapid growth. Systrom, along with only 13 employees, sold Instagram to Facebook for $1 billion dollars. Roughly $77 million dollars per employee.

Many years later, Systrom reflected on the key to their success, "People in general—tend to make life more complex than it needs to be."

Game of Thrones

One of the most commercially successful fiction writers of this century attributes much of his success to staying entrenched in the last century, especially regarding technology.

Graduating from Northwestern with a degree in journalism in 1971, George R.R. Martin didn't release his first novel until 13 years later. His fourth book was an absolute disaster, and the author knew it. He explains that the disaster "destroyed my career as a novelist at the time." From there he managed to scrape a living writing for television before revisiting fiction writing again in 1991. Millions of words later, he became famous. He penned the fantasy series *A Story of Fire and Ice*. The first book in the series is called *A Game of Thrones*, which later became one of the most popular shows of all time.

Martin is closing in on two million words and continues to write, using a program that is so antiquated that most of us have never heard of it. In fact, the program he uses, Wordstar 4.0, was invented in 1977 and was last updated in 1999—last century. Martin uses a DOS machine—yes, think green screen with no Internet capabilities and no distractions. The office he works in isn't even connected to the main house.

However, the simplicity of the program and approach allows Martin to focus, as he explains:

> So here's the thing. I am a dinosaur, as all my friends will tell you. A man of the 20th century, not the 21st. Yes, I have been using a computer for twenty years now, but while I cruise this interwebby thing with a PC and Windows, I still do all my writing on an old DOS machine running WordStar 4.0, the Duesenberg of word processing software (very old, but unsurpassed). I have my website, which someone else runs for me, and I have this LJ account, the blog that I vainly called my Not A Blog in hopes that might prevent me from blogging.[119]
>
> But that's it.
>
> I am not on Facebook.
>
> I am not on Twitter.
>
> I will not be on the next new thing to come along.
>
> I have neither the time, energy, or the inclination to get on any of these social media myself. There's WAY too much on my plate.

This type of focus helps Martin. The iconic map Martin created for the series helps establish and define the drama through spatial recognition and topography. Readers are able to embrace the fascinating geography of Westeros and the Free Cities. For such an involved and intricate world, mapping it out must have taken forever, right?

Through the proper focus, Martin drew the map in "about 30 minutes." [120]

This certainly doesn't mean that Martin doesn't struggle with focus. While fans clamored for the final two books in the series, Martin kept missing deadlines. The show producers had to finish the television series to the best of their ability. Martin gave insight into his struggle when, despite his best intentions, the rise in popularity of the show meant the time demands of the modern world started to close in on him.

"Writer's block isn't to blame here, it's distractions," he said. "In recent years, all of the work I've been doing creates problems because it creates distractions. Because the books and the show are so popular, I have interviews to do constantly. I have travel plans constantly. It's like suddenly I get invited to travel to South Africa or Dubai, and who's passing up a free trip to Dubai? I don't write when I travel. I don't write in hotel rooms. I don't write on airplanes. I really have to be in my own house undisturbed to write. Through most of my life, nobody bothered me, but now everyone bothers me every day."[121]

> *To raise new questions, new possibilities, to regard old problems from a new angle, requires creative imagination.*
>
> — Albert Einstein

Creative Visual Cues: Turning Paperclips into $200,000

Creativity doesn't just apply to fields like writing, music, and the arts. When we shift our focus we can infuse creativity into everything we do. This particular story, from James Clear in *Atomic Habits*, caught my attention.

Grabbing 120 paper clips could increase your salary by $200,000. Don't believe it? Someone proved it as far back as 1993. All it took was a little creativity.

In Abbotsford, Canada, stockbroker Trent Dyrsmid, 23, started his first day of work with no particular indication of a successful future.

Others around him had more experience and were located in affluent areas. But what Dyrsmid had was a plan.

In his first week, the young man casually placed a jar on his desk and filled it with 120 paperclips. He pulled out another empty jar and placed it next to the first jar. Both jars were within reach.

Every morning, Trent would greet his jars and begin making outbound sales calls. He wouldn't distract himself by checking the news or listening to the radio. Instead, his focus was on making sales calls.

For each call he made, whether successful or unsuccessful, he would move a paperclip from the full jar to the empty jar. By the end of each and every day, he took great pride in seeing the empty jar now filled with 120 paperclips representing his 120 calls made that day.

By focusing on this habit, he quickly saw his salary raised. Within eighteen months, Dyrsmid was bringing in millions of dollars to the firm. Shortly after, he parlayed this into another increase in his salary; he was now making three times his original salary.

What does moving paperclips mean for you? It's all about getting into the right habit of doing things. So, how can you utilize the paperclip method on a day-to-day model for what you do? Start with the large stack of pennies you have lying on the kitchen counter and use them as a visual reminder of what you're trying to accomplish.

If you want to do 100 sit-ups during the day, grab five pennies. Each time you do 20 push-ups, move one of those pennies. Or, if you want to write two thank-you notes per day, either use the penny method or just simply put those two unwritten thank-you notes on your desk so they remain sitting there, reminding you to write them. Visual clues are simple but powerful.

It might not even be a physical object—my daughters taught me this. They were in the kitchen, and I could hear my youngest, Katia, arguing with her older sister, Sofia. I could hear Katia exclaiming that it was "her turn." This wasn't anything new, as "my turn" accounted for 50% of all arguments in our household. However, what they were arguing about was new. Sofia was recovering from surgery and needed to take a certain medication 21 times over the course of the week. As such, they would tally each time Sofia took her medication. They were using an old piece of construction paper and a black marker to draw a vertical line each time. They would mark four vertical lines. When they got to five, they would do the diagonal line to complete the set of five. Not only was it Katia's turn, but she wanted to draw that cool diagonal line to complete the bunch.

Seeing how effective this seemed to be with Sofia diligently taking her medicine, the next day, I adopted the same ploy for writing. To be frank, while I was loving this project, I sometimes struggled with the writing aspect.

I wanted to write for two hours per day. So, just like Sofia and Katia were marking off their medicine intake, I started to mark off twenty minutes of writing. When I got to six sticks or marks, I fulfilled my day. What a difference this made! Get creative on what visual clues work for you—it can be as simple as a series of handwritten sticks or paperclips.

A timer is also helpful. If I'm unexpectedly interrupted, I'll stop the timer. Scheduling a specific time to write also helps. This varied depending on my travel and family schedule but, as much as possible, it was in the morning. My favorite days are those when I've already put in my two hours in the morning and I'm able to sneak in some bonus writing time in the afternoon.

You can't depend on your eyes when your imagination is out of focus.
—Mark Twain

Turn It Up!

"Turn your music down; you will never learn anything with all this racket!" yells a parent to her teenager. But perhaps the parent has it all wrong. What if some types of music, even pop, rap, and rock songs, actually improve your focus and boost your intelligence?

Findings show that listening to the same song repeatedly while working can help creativity and concentration.[122] Different types of music affect different parts of the brain and can benefit various areas of learning.

Every person has a unique sound that causes this effect, and once the sound is found, listening to it can maximize focus and learning. Classical music has commonly been attributed to boosting performance in math. Typically, 12% of students perform higher on exams after listening to Mozart and Beethoven. In contrast, pop songs are associated with an increased sense of creativity that pairs well with subjects like English, drama, and art.

But how do these songs affect the brain? "It is important that the music is in the range of 50-80 beats per minute, as this can help induce the alpha state of mind; calm but alert, imagination stimulated and concentration heightened, a state of mind that is thought to be the best for learning," says Gray.[123]

Gray states that listening to these types of songs while studying has a calming effect that induces concentration. Students think more logically and rationally. Gray explains that the number of beats per minute is the largest component in affecting brain responsiveness, "Concentration is not limitless, so it is important that the music does not divert the listener's attention away from the task but focuses towards it, so music without lyrics or familiar lyrics is always preferable. Music should always be played in the background. What diverts our attention is specific to the listener and depends on particular interests, likes, and dislikes."[124]

Gray advises that classical, ambient, and jazz are typically the most successful genres for keeping emotions steady and are a good study buddy for material requiring logical thought and problem-solving skills—subjects like math, science, and languages. Subjects like art, fashion, media, and drama pair better with punk, rock, pop, and dance genres.

I tested listening to music while writing this month. The results are mixed. Sometimes it is a nice pick-me-up; at other times it is distracting. Listening to music provides the most value when I'm doing editing versus creative writing. To Gray's point, the music that seems to work best for me are Disney songs, the non-lyrical piano and symphonic versions of them. It works best for me playing in the background versus via my headphones.

Fun in the Sun

Many of us bunker down at our desks thinking that creativity will find us. This is an easy trap to fall into. Americans, on average, spend about 90% of their time indoors. Yet, we should turn the outdoors into an office. Little by little, I began moving a meeting or two to a table outdoors, taking a phone call while on a quick walk instead of cooped up at my desk, writing under a tree, or taking my lunch break outside.

Turn your face toward the sun and the shadows fall behind you.
— Maori proverb

Plants use sunlight to convert its rays into energy, and the same holds true for us. These positive effects include the following.

Improved Quality of Sleep

The sun can help improve our quality of sleep. When our eyes are exposed to the sun's light, the pineal gland is notified to halt production of melatonin, the sleep-inducing hormone, until it gets dark outside and it is time for rest.[125] Once the sun goes down, our body notifies itself that melatonin production can begin again, and we will begin to feel tired. When we confine ourselves to being indoors all day, we are depriving our eyes of sunlight, resulting in an overproduction of melatonin during the day. In essence, our mind and body don't know it's time for bed, resulting in poor sleep quality. When we are well-rested, our brain allows us to think more creatively and strategically.

The Green Effect

Going out into nature and physically surrounding oneself with trees, leaves, and plants makes us more joyful and productive. In a German study by Dr. Stephanie Lichtenfeld,[126] subjects exposed to green rectangles outperformed those exposed to white, grey, blue, or red rectangles while performing creative tasks. Lichtenfeld coined this the "green effect." Exposure to greenery for as little as two seconds can benefit us. The reason? The brain associates green with growth. We crave exposure to nature.

Higher Level Brain Functioning

Increased exposure to sunlight improves brain function. While conducting a University of Cambridge study, neuroscientist David Llewellyn discovered reduced cognitive function in subjects with decreased levels of vitamin D.[127] The sun is our primary source of vitamin D. Absorbing the sun's rays positively impacts how our brains process information.

Exposure to Sunlight Lowers Blood Pressure

University of Edinburgh researchers discovered that nitric oxide, a blood pressure-reducing compound, is released into our bloodstream when sunlight hits the skin.[128] Lower blood pressure helps reduce the risk of heart attacks and strokes, and it can potentially increase our life span. Being exposed to more oxygen results in an increase in serotonin, which makes you feel calm, happy, and relaxed.[129]

No Wi-Fly

WiFi on planes can be unreliable, slow, and frustrating. Typing in a cramped position with a white-hot computer inches from your waistline is not a great experience. The fact that the passenger in front of you can flop his seat back and destroy your computer is no joy ride, either.

Throughout this project, if something isn't bringing me joy or happiness, I always ask, can this be flipped? Can I flip the game? Can I flip it in my favor?

This is exactly what I've done when it comes to flying. My new rule is zero WiFi on planes. I call it No WiFly (wouldn't this make a great t-shirt?). My airplane time is now dedicated to reading, writing, relaxation, and reflection.

Flights immediately became more enjoyable. Flights are a necessary evil for my job as a speaker, but I no longer dread them. Now, flights are a time of processing my thoughts.

Coming up with my No WiFly rule reminded me of a comment a mentor had when WiFi was first installed on planes. She said, "I love flying on planes, as it's the only time I'm not connected, that I can have some peace. I don't want them to start putting WiFi on planes. It would ruin this peace for me."

At the time, I thought she was crazy—having a WiFi connection made the flight go by so much faster. Expressing this to her, I saw the all-knowing twinkle in her eye, "Ah, young grasshopper, so much to learn."

I now fully grasp the wisdom of her words.

Set up these types of "time pockets" throughout your day. If you are at your child's piano lesson, don't mindlessly surf the Internet. Dedicate such time to reading, journaling, calling old friends, or whatever you want to do that you seem never to accomplish. For me, it's a time for writing, relaxing, reflecting, and resting. Look for these opportunities at doctor's office visits, commutes on the train, and other places.

Another flip-it moment for me relates to how much I enjoy writing fiction. Conversely, I have often struggled to write my business books. Identifying this challenge, I came up with a solution. Write my business books less technically and more personally, infusing them with creativity. Doing this, my joy soared, along with the readability of the book.

Logic will get you from A to B. Imagination will take you everywhere.

— Albert Einstein

CHAPTER SUMMARY

The One Big Thing

Creativity often occurs when your mind is unfocused; avoid being wasteful with your time so you can schedule blocks for white space. "Idle" time can be the most productive use of our time.

Grade: *B+*

Wow, did I enjoy this month! Fencing off time for deep thinking and writing. So, why not an A+? There were still a few times when I let the immediate items take precedence over the important items. As a result, I had to hit the "reset button" mid-month. Also, I didn't have as many zen coffee shop days as I'd hoped. But, all things considered, this was a wonderful month of creativity.

Top Takeaways

1. Find pockets of time you can turn into luxury time (e.g., No WiFly).

2. Combine a desired behavior (writing) with something you love (coffee).

3. Consider the outdoors an office.

Empathy

This month, the focus is to pour more empathy and love into the world by being intentional with every interaction—to leave a family member, friend, teammate, or stranger more energized. Connecting with others, we are either giving love or stealing love. On average, if we live to be 80 years old and we meet three new people per day, we have a lot of empathy to spread. Most of us can only remember people we meet after the age of five, so the simple math (factoring in leap year) is $(80-5) \times 3 \times 365.24 = 82,179$. We can positively influence over 80,000 people in our lifetime! If only 1% of them showed up at our funeral, we will have nearly 1,000 people in attendance.

You will see the words *love* and *empathy* throughout this chapter and I debated calling this chapter "Love." However, they are not the same thing. Love usually involves some level of empathy, but empathy doesn't always equal love. There are entire books dedicated to these subjects, which we will not cover here, rather this month is simply about focusing on adding more empathy and love to the world around us. The research shows that by doing so you will be happier and more successful both personally and professionally. Read Adam Grant's *Give and Take* for a deeper dive on this.

My goal this month is to engage in three hugs per day. Some of these hugs will be easy. Attempting to be the "World's Best Dad" for my daughters also meant being the "World's #1 Husband." Kids see everything, and they learn from observation. The best way to show how their future spouse should properly treat them is by showing them a living example.

A good way to showcase love is through signs of affection, not only with them, but with a spouse. When people hug or kiss a loved one, oxytocin levels increase; hence, oxytocin is often called "the cuddle hormone" or "the love hormone." In fact, the hormone plays a huge role in all pair-bonding. Oxytocin is the hormone that underlies individual and social trust. It is also an antidote to depressive feelings.[130]

Hugging my wife more and holding her hand is a good example for my daughters. Kids might not listen to us, but they certainly watch us. Most importantly, hugging is a great way to constantly reconnect with my wife.

Showing love or empathy also means being present. So often we are physically somewhere, but we aren't present because our minds are elsewhere. Often, we are engrossed in our phones instead of the moment. A good example of being present: You are boarding the plane and the gate agent says, "Have a safe flight," and you're mindful enough *not* to say, "You too," but rather say, "Have a great day!" After all, the personnel aren't flying anywhere. Essentially, we need to stop walking around like Zombies—being present is a present.

The Final Four

My dad had a big year. He was turning 75 *and* celebrating his 50th anniversary. Around this time, I was fortunate to share a beer with him and reflect on the years gone by.

Me: Dad, you really are doing some cool stuff right now. You're accomplishing a ton.

Dad: Well, Erik, that's because I'm calling it my final fifteen.

Me: What do you mean?

Dad: The Final Fifteen is my motto right now. I figure I have a good 15 years left where my mind and body will still be very sound, and I don't want to waste this opportunity. As such, I'm re-focusing on all the things I've wanted to do. I want to ensure I do these fifteen years the best I can. For example, I've lost 40 pounds and I'm in the best shape of my life. With my new waist size, it was a good excuse to get all new clothes, the best of the best. I can't take the money with me. We are redoing all the little things in the house that have been bothering me—all over the next six months, as I don't want it to drag on.

I loved "The Final Fifteen" approach. Inspired by this, I came up with my own tagline, "The Final Four." As a former college basketball player, I "got" the irony of The Final Four. We'd recently celebrated the 50th birthday of one of my best friends, Bill. We'd been friends for over 20 years. I couldn't believe we were celebrating his 50th birthday. Wasn't it yesterday that we'd met in the bathroom?

Yes, the bathroom.

I was in the bathroom changing into my dress shirt and sports jacket for class pictures. That morning, I'd scurried around to find my dress shirt—yep, only had one—balled up in a corner. The shirt had more wrinkles than a 100-year-old man sitting in a hot tub for 3 hours. I took only enough time to iron the small triangle area that would show in the photo. My suit coat would hide the rest of the wrinkled shirt.

Putting on my shirt, I heard some hearty laughter in a thick Boston accent, "Wow! That is some selective ironing! I respect it." We became fast friends.

My 50th birthday was also coming up...in four years. So, taking a page from my dad's book, I was doing my "Final Four" on the way to 50.

What do you have that will help you reset or refocus? Do you have a high school reunion? Is there a big beach trip coming up and you want to look good strutting your stuff in the sand? Are you a few years from retirement? From graduation? Do you want to write a book before you're 30? Do you want to scale El Capitan before you're 40?

Label these "tricks," but they are tricks that work.

Mr. Roger's Love Affair with 143

Due to text messaging, most of us have become familiar with the symbolic nature of 143. It's an abbreviation for "I Love You," derived from the number of letters in each word 1 (I) 4 (Love) 3 (You).

But when did it take on this meaning? The answer might surprise you.

The first recorded association of 143 with "I Love You" is from the year 1894. A new type of flashing lantern had just been installed in Minot's Ledge Light, a lighthouse located southeast of Boston Harbor. [131]

The National Lighthouse Board recommended all lighthouses have a unique numerical flash sequence. For this particular lighthouse, 1-4-3 was randomly chosen: one flash, then four flashes, then three.

Shortly thereafter, people began making a connection between "1-4-3" and "I love you." The lighthouse soon became known as "Lovers' Light." If you ever get the chance to visit Minot's Ledge, you will see that the lighthouse flashes this same pattern two centuries later.

Some of you who grew up watching Mister Rogers may have learned about 143.

As Tom Junod recounts from an interview with Mister Rogers:

Fred Rogers stepped on a scale and the scale read 143 pounds. For over thirty years Fred Rogers refused to do anything that would make his weight change. Every morning, often after swimming at the Pittsburgh Athletic Club, the scale told him that he weighed 143 pounds. This has happened so many times that Fred Rogers came to see that number as a gift, as a destiny fulfilled, because, as he says, "the number 143 means 'I love you.'"

To some, 143 is just a number. To Mister Rogers, and the lovers on Minot's Ledge, it has been a gift, a sign of love. Focusing on 143 gave Fred Rogers, the people near Minot's Ledge, and others something to rely on. In a sense, this focus helped keep them grounded. What numbers, phrases, routines or habits can you rely on to help keep you grounded?

Don't Widen the Plate

I was constantly reminded during this month that focusing will make achievements easier to accomplish, but focusing doesn't mean we hone in on the easy-to-achieve. In fact, the opposite is the case. We dismiss the easy, for example, answering emails so that we can focus on our big goals. And, our big goals aren't easy. They aren't supposed to be. If they were easy, they'd already be accomplished.

> *We need to receive empathy in order to give empathy.*
> — Marshall Rosenberg

In some ways, focusing is similar to how we treat and raise our kids. Loving our children, nieces, or nephews, we often think that making life easy on them is the best way to love them. Yet, such is often the worst thing we can do, depriving that child of the rewards of hard work. I'm reminded of a quote that hangs in my children's school: "You can prepare the road for the child, or you can prepare the child for the road."

The best way I've heard this explained was by a wise man imploring us not to widen the plate for future generations.

In Nashville, more than 4,000 baseball coaches convened for an annual convention, and 78-year-old John Scolinos, retired college baseball coach, took the stage.

He shuffled to the stage with a full-sized, stark-white baseball home plate hanging from his neck.

"You're probably wondering why I'm wearing home plate around my neck. I may be old, but I'm not crazy. The reason I stand before you today is to share with *you baseball people* what I've learned in my life, what I've learned about home plate in my 78 years."

"Do you know how wide home plate is in Little League?"

After a pause, someone offered, "Seventeen inches."

"That's right," said Scolinos.

"How wide is home plate in high school baseball?"

"Seventeen inches," they said, sounding more confident.

"You're right!" Scolinos barked. "And you college coaches, how wide is home plate in college?"

"Seventeen inches!" everyone said, in unison.

"Any Minor League coaches here? How wide is home plate in pro ball?"

"Seventeen inches!"

"RIGHT! And in the Major Leagues, how wide home plate is in the Major Leagues?"

"Seventeen inches!"

"SEV-EN-TEEN INCHES!" he confirmed, his voice bellowing off the walls. "And what do they do with a Big League pitcher who can't throw the ball over seventeen inches?" *Pause.* "They send him to *Pocatello!*" he hollered, drawing raucous laughter.

"What they *don't* do is this: They don't say, 'Ah, that's okay, Jimmy. You can't hit a seventeen-inch target? We'll make it eighteen inches, or nineteen inches. We'll make it twenty inches so you have a better chance of hitting it. If you can't hit that, let us know so we can make it wider still, say twenty-five inches.'"

Pause.

"Coaches..."

Pause.

"...what do we do when our best player shows up late to practice? What if he gets caught drinking? Do we hold him accountable? Or do we change the rules to fit him? Do we widen home plate?"

He turned the plate toward himself and, using a Sharpie, began to draw something. When he turned it toward the crowd, point-side up, they saw a house, complete with a freshly drawn door and two windows. "This is the problem in our homes today. With our marriages, with the way we parent our kids. With our discipline. We don't teach accountability to our kids, and there is no consequence for failing to meet standards. *We widen the plate!*"

"If I'm lucky," Coach Scolinos concluded, "you will remember one thing from this old coach today. It is this: If we fail to hold ourselves to a higher standard, a standard we know to be right; if we fail to hold our spouses and our children to the same standards, and if our schools and churches and our government fail to hold themselves accountable to those they serve, there is but one thing to look forward to..."

With that, he held home plate in front of his chest, turned it around, and revealed its dark black backside.

"...dark days."[132]

Coach Scolinos understood that the best way to focus on positively changing our lives is not by lowering our standards, but by raising them, and then settling for nothing less for ourselves and those around us. As Coach Scolinos implored, don't widen the plate in life. Being empathetic requires understanding someone's situation and sometimes delivering tough love. Tough love is often the best love.

Mind Games

Love also relates to our professions and hobbies—what we love to do—and how we reach our full potential in these endeavors. Success within these passions often relates to our internal and external focus.

For example, Andre Agassi hit a rough patch during the prime of his tennis career. His wrist hurt, he'd lost confidence, and his world ranking was plummeting because he wasn't winning.

At the urging of his wife at the time, Brook Shields, he reluctantly sat down with motivational coach Tony Robbins. Agassi was skeptical, but he'd run out of options.

Tony showed Agassi video from two different tennis matches. One was a match that Agassi had won. In the other match, Agassi was soundly defeated. These video clips didn't involve any footage of Agassi hitting a tennis ball. Instead, they only showed clips of Agassi entering the stadium and beginning his warm-up routine.

Robbins: Do you remember this match?

Agassi: Of course, that's when I first won Wimbledon.

Robbins: Look how you come out of the tunnel, bouncing on your feet with a confident smile and a sparkle in your eye. What were you thinking at this moment as you looked across at your opponent?

Agassi: I was thinking why did this guy (Goran Ivanišević) even bother to f*cking show up? I'm going to destroy him.

Robbins switched to the other video.

Robbins: Do you remember this match?

Agassi: Of course, it was one of my most humiliating losses.

Robbins: Now, look how you come out of the tunnel, look at your posture. Despite being in your prime, you have the posture of a ninety-year-old man. There is no bounce in your step. Do you remember what was going through your mind at this moment when you looked across at your opponent (Pete Sampras)?

Agassi: I was thinking of all the losses I've already suffered to this guy, and how painful it is every time and I really didn't want to go through it again.

Robbins: I know you came into my office today with the mindset of skepticism, that a lot of my work around psychological states impacting your physical performance is bullshit. But, you can clearly see this in the video clips we just watched. In both instances the outcome was determined before a single ball was hit. At Wimbledon, you had a bounce in your step. Your physical nature was positively impacting your psychological nature—you were going to destroy this guy. And, you went out and destroyed him. Conversely, in the losing match, you shuffled out there like an old man and your physical state negatively impacted your psychological state. You were already projecting upon yourself, and to the world, what losing this match would feel like.

In both instances, the subject of Agassi's focus prior to the match made the difference between winning and losing.

This type of mental focus, as it relates to achievement, was also the subject of a study involving basketball players. Dr. Blaslotto at the University of Chicago (1996) wanted to specifically test the powerful effect of visualization.

Blaslotto randomly selected a series of students and separated them into three groups. He measured their free throw shooting accuracy. Then, he asked each group to take a series of free throws. He recorded the percentage of free throws made.

The 3 Groups

Group 1: Didn't touch a basketball, no practicing or playing basketball whatsoever.

Group 2: Practiced free throw shooting for a half hour per day.

Group 3: Spent half an hour per day, at the gym, with their eyes closed, simply visualizing making every free-throw.

After the 30 days, all three groups came back to take the same number of free-throws.

The Results

Group 1 (didn't practice):	0% improvement
Group 2 (practiced):	24% improvement
Group 3 (visualized success):	23% improvement

The improvement in the group (3) that purely visualized making free throws was virtually the same as the group (2) who had physically practiced shooting free throws every day.

How we focus our physical state can impact our psychological state and vice versa. The mind and body work together. Focusing on desired outcomes is important. If we think negatively, most likely negative actions will occur. However, if we think positive thoughts, we are more likely to achieve great results. Just as in Agassi's case, our physical posture and state impact outcomes—positively or negatively.

Our physical posture also plays a key role in how others perceive us and how we feel about ourselves. A study by the *European Journal of Social Psychology* showed that having good posture positively affected an individual's perception of themselves in job interviews.[133] Even when we don't feel confident, we can influence our thoughts by simply sitting (or standing) tall, presenting a confident demeanor. The term "fake it till you make it" implies that even if we aren't feeling our best, standing tall and smiling can positively impact our mental state. In essence, we need to love ourselves more.

Standing Like Superheroes

Dana R. Carney, Amy Cuddy, and Andy Yap first introduced power posing in the journal *Psychological Science*. Their research suggests that our body language governs how we think and feel about ourselves, and thus, how we hold our bodies can impact our focus. The most popular example is standing like Superman or Wonder Woman before going in for a job interview. Cuddy found that those who sat in the high-power pose felt more powerful and performed better in mock interviews than those who had not. The second discovery was that power posing changes our body chemistry. Cuddy's study suggests that those who adopted high-power poses demonstrate an increase in testosterone and a decrease in cortisol—helping decrease stress.[134]

There is a superhero in all of us. We just need the courage to put on the cape.

— Superman

While the research on the specific hormonal impact is often debated, it doesn't hurt to try it out yourself. I've personally tested it with audiences in over 55 countries and discovered it's fun and positively uplifting to stand like superheroes! It positively works for 95% of those in my audience. For an extra jolt wear a Superman or Wonder Woman t-shirt while doing this.

You Are Not Normal

I was fortunate to share the stage with Astronaut Mark Kelly. One particular point from Kelly's message resonated. At NASA, they embrace the following mantra: "None of us is as dumb as all of us." Translation: Avoid groupthink. While this sounds simple, avoiding groupthink is difficult. By nature, we are inherently social animals. Groupthink is one reason so many scandals and scams keep happening, from Watergate to Enron to Bernie Madoff to Theranos.

By taking on a mindset of focus, you will be an outlier. Most people don't focus but instead, instinctively try to be like others. They mimic the unfocused behavior of others, much like a small planet being drawn to a larger one. In order to resist the pull of the unfocused behavior surrounding us, we must understand why we like to conform.

Keep in mind that not all conformity is negative. When you're speaking to someone who's talking in a lower, slower tone, it's comforting to that individual if you match their lower, slower tone. This natural inclination helps put the other person at ease. Great salespeople and politicians use this specific form of conformity, called *mirroring*. In prehistoric times, conforming into tribes helped provide protection from the wilderness and other aggressive tribes. Conforming helped you stay in the tribe—you fit in.

However, conforming to the norm of not focusing is *dis*advantageous. We need to resist this urge.

In the 1950's, renowned psychologist Solomon Asch set out to determine our conformity bias. He wanted to answer the question: How far would we go to ignore our own information and senses to conform with the majority?

Asch developed the figure below.

Compare the line on the left with the three lines on the right: A, B & C. Which of these lines is the same length as the singular line on the left?

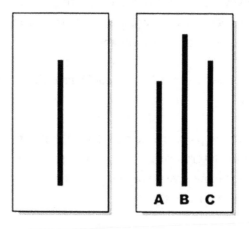

One can clearly see that C is the exact length. However, when Asch conducted the experiment, 76% of participants denied their own sense and selected A or B. What gives?

What is important to understand is that the precursor of Asch's experiment was based on a prior experiment conducted by Muzafer Sherif called *The Robbers Cave Experiment*. Sherif found that when faced with making a judgment on an ambiguous test, individuals will use other people's opinions as a reference point.

This makes perfect sense. If I'm not sure about something, I'll check with someone else. But this is only when I'm not sure, when I can't see it with my own senses (eyes, ears, touch, etc.).

But in this case, one can clearly see that two lines are the same length. How could 76% be going against their own eyes and judgment?

The Experiment

Asch brought one participant at a time into a room that already had 8 individuals seated. These individuals were "in" on the experiment. The proctor then asked those in the room which line was bigger. The "guinea pig," if you will, was always the sixth to be called on to answer. Prior to that, five other participants had given the wrong answer right before our guinea pig was to give his answer.

The results surprised Asch; 50% of people gave the same wrong answer—the crowd swayed them.

Intrigued about why participants had gone along with the majority, Asch subsequently interviewed them. We can probably relate to many of their answers. Below, I've juxtaposed answers from the 1950s with their modern-day equivalent.

    1950:   Many became self-conscious and anxious around disapproval from their peers.

    Today: If everyone around us is acting harried, hurried, and distracted, we will mirror their behavior.

    1950:   They trusted the group over their own senses.

    Today: Well, if everyone is checking social media every five minutes, maybe I should, too.

1950:   Some went along with the group to avoid standing out, although they knew the group was wrong.

Today: If everyone is "binging" this show—even though I think it's a waste of time—I should spend time watching it.

1950:   5% actually said they saw the lines in the same way as the group. That's just plain scary.

This study was considered so breakthrough that it resulted in other psychologists going deeper into it.

Historically, in Eastern societies, conformity has often been viewed as a positive—that by being like the others, you "fit in." One could argue that the reason so much innovation has historically occurred in Silicon Valley is that conformity is often frowned upon. It's more about being an outcast versus fitting in. Being original is applauded. Steve Jobs often referred to his small teams as the crazy ones or as pirates. He went so far as to fly a pirate flag on the office flag pole. He wanted to avoid conformity at all costs.

The "so what" is that if most people aren't focused—which they aren't—we will naturally try to conform to the norm. We follow the herd. This also makes sense from an anthropological standpoint. Thousands of years ago, forming tribes was essential for our safety and survival.

Being outcast from the tribe was a death sentence. Our brain is hardwired to protect us. Knowing these natural inclinations, pointed out by Asch in his study, is a key step for us in avoiding conformity traps. While everyone else around us may be swimming in a sea of chaos, we need to avoid conforming to the chorus of chaos.[135]

Social situations can influence us to extremes. We need to fight against this gravitational pull. Just because everyone else is going to the meeting doesn't mean we need to go. Or, when it seems that everyone else around you is posting social media videos, don't feel compelled to do the same. If three other families are getting a house on the beach for spring break, but you and your family prefer just to relax, unwind, and re-energize with a "staycation," then stay at home.

The best way to avoid conformity is by focusing on our best self. By trying to practice this more this month I've discovered it also allows me to better love those around me. I'm not having as much of an internal battle and I have more to give to my teammates, friends, and family.

Mirrors and Windows

I was chatting with a very successful entrepreneur about this book and he started laughing and said,

Owner:	Well, I'm thinking of compiling a book of my own on some of our team members that are focused, but on the wrong things.
Me (prodding):	What do you mean?
Owner:	Well, the other day our building had some issues with the water and there wasn't going to be coffee. I received a text message from a team member asking if they could work from home since there wasn't any coffee. They'd prefer to work from their apartment...You can't make this stuff up! But, you know what? Another employee got up a little earlier that morning and drove across town to a functioning coffee shop. She arrived early, with coffee, bagels, and donuts for the entire office. Guess who got promoted and guess who's no longer with our company?

Two people faced with the same situation took opposite approaches. Are we focusing on there being "no coffee" or are we focusing on controlling what we can control? Are we bemoaning our situation or are we going out of our way to pick up coffee for the entire team?

Are we being mirrors or windows? Are you a mirror looking only at yourself or are you a window looking at the world around you and how to make it better?

Turning Garbage into Gold

Mike Glickman, an eighteen-year-old living in a picturesque community in California, wanted to become a real estate agent. Being young and in a highly competitive market, Mike had trouble gaining credibility. None of his marketing materials were working. At around the same time, the city garbage collectors went on strike.

As the strike continued, the garbage piled up outside these beautiful homes. Seeing this happening to the community he loved worried Mike. He wanted to do something. A thought came to him. What if he started to haul off the garbage? He couldn't do it alone—way too many homes. He would have to hire a private company. This would be expensive; about $5,000 dollars at the time, which seemed like $5 million dollars to Mike. But, it was the right thing to do.

He did it, with one key twist. He didn't let anyone know he was doing it.

People were delighted to find that all the smelly, ugly garbage was gone. They had their beautiful community back. Assuming the strike must be over, when they turned on the local news that evening to hear that the strike was still alive and well, the homeowners were scratching their heads. If it wasn't the garbage collectors, who was it?

Within a few days, word leaked that Mike had removed the garbage. Mike's business was off to the races! He became one of the most prominent real estate agents in one of the hottest real estate markets in the country.[136]

When we adjust our focus to see a different perspective—particularly other people's perspectives—we can often turn garbage into gold.

Persistence & Patience

After one and a half years of failing at this project, a revelation hit me: Have patience with the process. Play the long game. I kept having false starts to this project. I would say *okay THIS is the month* I'm going to start and then I'd invariably fall back to my old habits. The key is to not get frustrated but instead say to yourself, "Well, this is interesting."

Failing to plan is planning to fail.

Patience doesn't naturally come to me. My mental state often borders on: *"Lord, please give me patience, but give it to me NOW!"* Focusing *requires* being persistent in the short term and patient for the long term. Eventually, I said, enough is enough and finally stuck to the project.

CHAPTER SUMMARY

The One Big Thing

Our success isn't what we take from the world, but what we leave behind.

Grade: *A*

Having victories each day made this month rewarding. Focusing on being empathetic and giving love in every interaction was more tangible than I believed possible. I could see the impact of my actions immediately—several times throughout each day. Conversely, when I wasn't in the best mood, I could feel the negative energy I was bringing to a room and either a) put a stop to it, or b) avoid interactions until the "storm" passed. I wasn't perfect at this, so no A+. But in total, it was a great month.

Top Takeaways

1. Avoid groupthink and don't conform to others' lack of focus.
2. We are like batteries—in every engagement, we are either positive (+) or negative (-) energy.
3. When you can afford to buy time, do it—you're buying time with your loved ones.

Mindfulness

For this *Month of Mindfulness,* serene spa images were floating in my head along with soothing music and water droplets. But mindfulness doesn't mean we need to sit in the lotus position in soundproof rooms burning incense. Our meditation might be playing the piano, walking on the beach in the morning, sewing a dress, jogging without headphones on, journaling without interruption, or playing at the park with our kids. The key isn't a specific place; the key is being mentally present in the particular place you find yourself.

For example, I often take my kids to the park. A parent will often announce, "We have to go!" This isn't surprising; I've done the same thing hundreds of times with our kids.

However, it isn't always the case that we have to go. Sometimes, sure, we have to get home for dinner or we have a birthday party or soccer practice. But, other times, I knew we didn't have to go. I wanted to go. I was dictating an order.

For the next couple of weeks I was going to wait until my girls requested to leave. I'm not going to lie, the first few times at the park were agonizing as we were there for hours. As a parent, pangs of guilt sprouted inside me at the thought of not enjoying every minute. "No, I can't push you on the swing for the thousandth time." Guilt.

I knew the day would soon arrive when they would be too big to want to play at the park, and then how would I feel that I couldn't be bothered to push the swing?

I struggled at first with waiting it out. But, over time, I started to realize the benefits of this new approach, enjoying this uninterrupted time with my daughters. What a blessing to be outside on a nice sunny day, breathing fresh air, being able to act like a kid again myself, and enjoying time with my daughters at such a precious age. I started to be mindful of the way they laughed or how their hair looked funny while hanging upside down on the monkey bars.

I also started noticing an improved focus in other areas of my life. This improved focus isn't unusual. As Harvard professor Joe DeGutis puts it, "Focusing on a single, complex task improves your ability to focus on other tasks. Making a habit of this can result in "attentional state training," where you are better able to get in a relaxed, focused state for other activities."[137] This month I was going to push the swing both physically and metaphorically.

Thousands of studies have documented the physical and mental health benefits of mindfulness, inspiring countless programs to embrace the concept for schools, prisons, hospitals, veterans centers, and beyond.[138]

Mindfulness means maintaining a moment-by-moment awareness of our thoughts, feelings, bodily sensations, and surrounding environment through a gentle, nurturing lens.

While we want to remain present, we don't always have to stay in the present. Ryan M. Niemiec, Psy.D., explains in *Psychology Today:*

A common misconception about mindfulness is that it means to stay in the present moment. People practice meditation and get quickly frustrated by their mind's disinterest in staying present. Many will exclaim: "I can't be mindful. I can't stay in the moment!" But the reality is no one's mind always stays in the moment. But, we have control over the return. We can always return our mind to the present moment, return it to our breath. Mindfulness is the self-regulation of attention with an attitude of curiosity, openness, and acceptance.[139]

This month, while it is impossible to be present all the time, I'm making an effort to be present more of the time.

Turning your Willpower into a Superpower

Most of us want to eat healthy foods, say the right words, and do the right things. But often we lack willpower. Are we doomed if our willpower is constantly failing us? No.

I'm too focused on my own grass to know if yours is greener.

While process and habits beat willpower, strengthening our willpower will help any of our established frameworks. Improving our willpower is similar to being able to ride a bike. If we stick with it, almost anyone can ride a bike.

We can mold and strengthen willpower. Stanford psychologist Kelly McGonigal, Ph.D., took a closer look and found that Willpower is our body's ability to send extra energy to the brain's prefrontal cortex, which keeps track of our goals and helps us override impulses and cravings.[140]

Our willpower can be depleted over the course of the day just like our muscles. This loss is called ego depletion. Hence, our self-control can be weaker at the end of the day—which may explain our opening the fridge at midnight for a snack. It also lends itself to something our parents drilled into us: "Nothing good ever happens after midnight."

Understanding ego depletion explains why it's advantageous to tackle important tasks first thing in the morning. But this doesn't mean that all night owls are out of luck.[141]

McGonigal explains it this way: "I prefer to talk about becoming a will-power athlete. If willpower is a muscle, even a metaphorical muscle, it should be possible to train it. As with physical exercise, using your self-control muscle may be tiring, but over time the workout increases your strength and stamina. So what starts out as difficult becomes easier over time. New behaviors become habits and temptations become less overwhelming."

If the brain can be trained like a muscle, that begs the question, can you see an actual physical change in the brain from our practice and efforts? A team of Harvard-affiliated researchers at Massachusetts General Hospital (MGH) set out to uncover the answer.

For the MGH study, researchers conducted magnetic resonance image (MRI) scans on the participants' brains two weeks prior to the study. They split the participants into two groups: a group that would practice meditation on their own (average of 27 minutes per day), and a group that would not practice meditation.

After just 8 weeks, the "meditators" showed increases in grey matter in the hippocampus. Grey matter naturally decreases with age, so the fact that meditation can help grow grey matter is a big deal. Grey matter is critical for learning, seeing, hearing, impulse control, speech, and memory. It has also been linked to improvements in self-awareness, compassion, and introspection. Grey matter helps us with processing and computation. White matter, on the other hand, is like highways connecting different parts of the central nervous system.

Participants reporting increases in stress correlated with decreased grey-matter density in the amygdala, which is known to play a significant role in anxiety and stress. High levels of cortisol can wear down the brain's ability to function properly. Stress can kill brain cells and even reduce the size of the brain. Chronic stress has a shrinking effect on the prefrontal cortex, the area of the brain responsible for memory and learning.[142]

Although the stress response begins in the brain, it is a full-body phenomenon. One of the best ways to counter stress is to pay attention to what is going on with you and around you. That may sound counterintuitive, but paying attention is the first step toward cultivating mindfulness—a therapeutic technique for a range of mental health problems (and physical ones).[143]

In sum, during the study, meditators were able to increase the grey matter where it positively helps us (hippocampus: learning, memory, self-awareness, compassion, introspection) and decrease it where it negatively affects us (amygdala: anxiety/stress).

Discovering that a little meditation can cause dramatic positive increases in our brains is literally mind-blowing. The study's senior author Sara Lazar sheds some light:

> Although the practice of meditation is associated with a sense of peacefulness and physical relaxation, practitioners have long claimed that meditation also provides cognitive and psychological benefits that persist throughout the day. This study demonstrates that changes in brain structure may underlie some of these reported improvements and that people are not just feeling better because they are spending time relaxing.

Britta Hölzel, one of the authors and a research fellow at MGH and Giessen University in Germany, states:

It is fascinating to see the brain's plasticity and that, by practicing meditation, we can play an active role in changing the brain and can increase our well-being and quality of life.[144]

Meditation is like floss for our brain. Similar benefits can be achieved via physical exercise, states Dr. McGonigal:

Physical exercise also leads to similar changes in the brain, especially the prefrontal cortex; however, it's not clear why. Regular exercise—both intense cardiovascular training and mindful exercise like yoga—also make the body and brain more resilient to stress, which is a great boost to willpower.

Numerous studies show there are two consistent ways to train your willpower: physical activity and meditation.

Related to physical activity and meditation, researchers Jason Chow and Shun Lau of The University of Hong Kong wanted to study the effect of physical surroundings. Specifically, do environments impact ego depletion and, correspondingly, willpower?

They conducted a series of tests showing participants a sequence of images. Some were shown hectic urban settings while others were shown nature scenes. They discovered that exposure to nature gives us strength and helps counteract ego-depletion.[145]

If we are able to meditate in a nice park during our lunch break, we will see more benefits than simply meditating inside.

This study helps explain why we always seem to feel a touch more elevated doing yoga on the beach versus in a studio, or why jogging in the woods seems to be more satisfying than trudging on a treadmill.

It's no surprise why leading companies build forests on their campuses for their employees to hold meetings, both sitting and walking.

So the next time we find ourselves being called by our screens...try these science-based ways to enhance willpower:

1. Set physical reminders—this might be a Post-It note or alarm to turn off your devices and start getting ready for bed at 9:30pm.

2. Meditate.

3. Eat a protein-rich diet—our willpower diminishes when we are hungry. Protein makes us feel full.

4. Commit to it! We need to set up structured milestones and plans to help our willpower. That's why Alcoholics Anonymous isn't just one step, but rather 12 steps.

5. Forgive yourself. Whitney Houston was right when she sang "The greatest love of all is learning to love yourself." Feelings of regret deplete our willpower. This may explain why, after refraining from eating Girl Scout cookies all week, we find that having just one Thin Mint late Friday night becomes virtually impossible. We tend to experience regret for our actions and the next thing we know we have eaten not just one Thin Mint, but (gasp) the entire box!

Diving deeper on forgiving ourselves, researchers conducted a series of studies on regret among participants.[146]

They discovered that the participants who felt regret performed worse on future tasks. Correspondingly, if they were able to find a benefit in the task they regretted, then they performed better on future tasks.

In the example of the Girl Scout cookies above, one may rationalize that you deserved a nice treat since you've been good all week. One's thinking might look something like this. Well, by eating these cookies I made the salesgirl happy and others happy since part of the revenue from the sale is going toward helping others, not just the girl I bought them from. Also, since there are no cookies in the house anymore, I no longer have that temptation or that voice in my head saying, "have a cookie."

In other words, learning to forgive yourself or finding benefits in the regret-inducing tasks result in positive benefits. Don't let one domino push a series of dominoes down the stairs. Instead, stop it in its tracks by letting go of regret.

The Harder We Squeeze Life, the Bigger the Mess

To make up for lost time, I start squeezing the gas pump handle as hard as possible. In my rush to get to the next thing, my thinking is, more squeezing equals more speed! However, this particular pump has a governor preventing it from going full throttle—it shuts off if I squeeze too hard. Hence, squeezing hard is actually slowing the process. The gas finally starts flowing. My mind wanders to the million things I need to do. By not paying attention, I accidentally fill my tank to the top. Without thinking, I quickly remove it while it is still flowing, drenching myself in gasoline. A chorus of delightful squeals come from my daughters inside the car. Aside from their laughter, this was an unmitigated disaster. Then it dawned on me: I'd slipped. I'd slipped back into my old ways. This gas station visit was a metaphor for my previous life—for so many of our lives. The harder we squeeze, the bigger the mess we create for ourselves. In this instance, I should have literally been "going with the flow."

Journaling

Daily journaling is beneficial on many levels including reducing stress, improving immune functions, keeping memory sharp, boosting your mood, and strengthening emotional health.[147] Trusting your mind alone is like walking a tightrope across the Grand Canyon. The world's cheapest pen is better than the world's best memory.

The challenge is that I never have time to journal. In the past, every time I have re-committed to journaling, instead of it being beneficial, it becomes a burden. The problem is, each time I approached it the same way; consequently, each time I failed.

I wasn't adhering to Einstein's wisdom, *"Insanity is doing the same thing over and over again but expecting different results."*

I needed to change my approach. This time I decided to approach journaling with two main differences:

1. Start with a sentence. If that's all I can do for that day, so be it, but at least write one sentence. This is a pragmatic approach. History has proven that on some days I will not have 15 minutes to journal.

2. Don't just chronicle the day but think back 5-10 years ago for a favorite memory or story and jot it down.

For example, write your elementary school teachers' names or quickly jot down your friends' names from little league or scouts. Draw your childhood home and sketch the neighboring homes, labeling them with the corresponding family name.

I find it helpful to have a theme for each week. One week I focused on high school memories and the next week around stories from my days working at Yahoo! Sometimes this sparked me to call someone for the first time in decades or send a nice note, like mailing a thank you card to my 5th grade teacher.

Brain Waves for the Ages

Around the age of 24, the processing speed of our brains starts to decline.[148] As processing declines, so does the ability to switch tasks and handle interruptions. For example, the older we get, the more we struggle with filtering out background noise in a crowded restaurant.

> *If you just sit and observe, you will see how restless your mind is. If you try to calm it, it only makes things worse, but over time it does calm, and when it does, there's room to hear more subtle things—that's when your intuition starts to blossom and you start to see things more clearly and be in the present more.*
> — Steve Jobs

This is why we often hear our fathers or grandfathers say, "I can't hear a damn thing in that restaurant. It's too noisy."

It's not simply the result of the physical decline of the ear itself. Older adults are 10 percent more likely to pay attention to the distracting information than younger adults who are able to block out these noises and distractions.[149] An older person's brain tends to function more like a 19-30-year-old early in the morning. This is another reason why earlier in the book we stressed the importance of winning the morning to win the day. Participants performed better on cognitive tasks when tested in the morning.[150]

Older people do, however, have other focus advantages. Specifically, Harvard professor Joe DeGutis, coauthor of a study on sustained attention, indicated that younger workers may have greater difficulty devoting their energy to tedious tasks. He goes on to say that older adults are often better at deeper focus and less likely to have their minds wander while performing difficult tasks.

Former Marine Bob McCann credits his ability to concentrate for his successful 26-year career in the Marines—where attention to detail is critical. "Younger kids can't focus because they're jumping between too many things. You can't be successful if your nose is stuck in your phone all day."

Diderot Effect

In 1765, French Philosopher Denis Diderot was 52 years old, and his daughter was to be married. Diderot is well known as the creator of Encyclopédie, one of the most read encyclopedias at the time. Despite his fame, Diderot wasn't rich; far from it. Diderot couldn't afford a dowry let alone an extravagant wedding for his daughter. Catherine the Great learned of his plight and bought Diderot's personal library.

Diderot suddenly found himself a wealthy man. To celebrate, he purchased a luxurious scarlet dressing gown. Diderot put his old robe into the trash. His new gown was so beautiful that it made all of Diderot's other clothes, possessions, and surroundings seem out of place in comparison. Diderot felt he must upgrade his sofas, chairs, and shoes to be of the same splendor as his robe.

This behavior eventually caused Diderot to fall into deeper debt than before his windfall of money. He replaced his old straw chair with an armchair covered in Moroccan leather; his old desk was replaced with an expensive new writing-table; his formerly beloved prints were replaced with more costly prints, and so on. "I was the absolute master of my old dressing gown," Diderot wrote, "but I have become a slave to my new one."[151]

New possessions often create a domino effect causing us to obtain additional items of similar quality in order for us to feel happy, whereas previously we never worried about such items and were content. Diderot initially loved his scarlet robe but eventually came to resent it.

You probably experience the same domino effect in your life:

- You paint your daughter's bedroom sparkling purple and now she wants everything in the room to sparkle.
- You buy a new bike and now you need a new bike pump, helmet, shoe clips, water bottle, lights, gloves, bike pants, riding shirt, bike rack for the car, bike glasses, odometer, tire gauge, and more things than you knew could ever exist for a bike.
- You buy a new blouse and now you need a new skirt, shoes, belt, and bracelet.
- You change the lights in your pool and now the deck chairs seem to need replacing, as well as the table and grill.
- You get the latest iPhone and now you feel you need a new cover, MacBook, and iPad.

In life, there is a gravitational pull for us to want more things, more out of life, and we believe the way to go about doing this is to add more, to build.

Bestselling author James Clear, an expert in behavioral psychology and minimalism, gives great advice on how to combat the Diderot Effect:[152]

1. Buy items that fit your current system. When you purchase new clothes, look for items that work well with your current wardrobe. When you upgrade to new electronics, get things that play nicely with your current pieces so you can avoid buying new chargers, adapters, or cables.

2. Don't buy anything for a month.

3. Buy One, Give One. Each time you make a new purchase, give something away. Get a new TV? Give your old one away rather than moving it to another room. The idea is to prevent your number of items from growing. Always be curating your life to include only the things that bring you joy and happiness.

4. Let go of wanting things. There will never be a level where you will be done wanting things. There is always something to upgrade to. Get a new Honda? You can upgrade to a Mercedes. Get a new Mercedes? You can upgrade to a Bentley. Get a new Bentley? You can upgrade to a Ferrari. Get a new Ferrari? Have you thought about buying a private plane? Realize that wanting is just an option your mind provides, not an order you have to follow.

We should always be looking for items to remove from our lives, but that's not to say we shouldn't have beautiful items in our lives. The key lies in adding items that create fulfillment and removing those that don't.

Aside from understanding the negative implications of the Diderot Effect, the same type of domino effect can play out in a positive manner. For example, if you start focusing on exercising and take on the mindset of an athlete, then when looking at the options on a menu, you're more likely to select the grilled chicken versus the hot dog. The hot dog doesn't match your new framework. As you contemplate your food order you think, "A healthy person wouldn't order a hot dog, and since I'm now a healthy person, that means I will not order a hot dog." For vacation, instead of booking a trip to Las Vegas, you go on a Mountain Biking trip to New Mexico. Or, joining a CrossFit club enables you to finally quit smoking—smoking simply doesn't match your new framework or support group. In this sense, you're manufacturing positive momentum. Whether we derive positive momentum organically or we manufacture it, the key is understanding that a moving bicycle is easier to steer, and one turn can help start us down a better path.

Fika

No matter where we live, we can learn mindfulness from other countries and cultures. A simple Swedish concept is "fika." **Fika** is a laid-back chat over coffee. It's so imperative and embedded in the culture that fika is protected by Swedish law. The working day and even the school day may be interrupted twice for a "coffee diversion."

The best part of fika is the seven types of cookies served.

Forget grabbing a coffee from the Starbucks drive-thru and drinking it on the go. Fika is all about taking it slow—intentionally pausing for downtime. Sweden isn't alone. Other cultures embrace rituals surrounding coffee and tea breaks.

Gemütlich is the German concept of sitting in a cosy chair surrounded by close friends and a hot cup of tea, while soft music plays in the background.

The art of **hygge**—a Danish word hard to explain and even harder to pronounce ("hooga")—is so much more than the concept of coziness. Hygge is the concept describing something we want all the time but seldom have. Roughly translated, it means the "complete absence of anything annoying, irritating, or overwhelming, with the presence of and pleasure from comforting, gentle, and soothing things." It means creating a warm atmosphere and enjoying the good things in life. It's no wonder that Denmark is considered one of the happiest places in the world. When Danes gather in groups of two or more, hygge refers to that sense of friendly companionship when conversation is flowing and toasts are raised. The high season of hygge is Christmas, when gløgg (mulled wine) is shared with friends.

Friluftsliv is a Norwegian concept that directly translates to "free air life." It describes the feeling of being outside, exploring, and appreciating nature. It can include anything from meditating, taking photographs, sleeping outdoors, or even dancing.

Practicing friluftsliv doesn't require money, equipment, or a particular setting, and can be as simple as taking a walk outside.

Testing all four concepts (fika, gemütlich, hygge, friluftsliv), each improved my mood. My favorite is friluftsliv because it requires the least amount of planning, is free, and is healthy, although, admittedly, the seven cookies of fika are always a nice option![153]

3 Ways to Stop Your Mind from Wandering

Harvard researchers Matthew Killingsworth and Daniel Gilbert found that a wandering mind is an unhappy one.[154] This is alarming since our minds wander 50% of the time.[155]

The gap between what we are thinking about and what we are actually doing varies greatly throughout the day. The results show that our minds wander most when we are at work.

While this is helpful to know, knowing how to prevent it, when we desire to, is more helpful.

Here are three suggestions from the author of *Emotional Intelligence*, Daniel Goleman:

Manage: Manage the items that tempt or distract you. Most items hunkering for our attention are digital.

Mindful: Every few minutes check in both with your brain and with what you're doing. "Wait, how did I get in this rat hole when I was supposed to be writing my report?"

Meditate: This can be as simple as listening to yourself breathe in and out. Goleman indicates that practicing this daily is similar to lifting weights—it's similar to muscle memory. Mindfulness strengthens the brain's circuits for noticing when your mind has wandered, letting go, and returning to your chosen focus.[156]

Kick These 8 Time-Wasting Habits

A majority of these were inspired by bestselling author Tim Ferriss.[157]

1. Don't answer unrecognized phone numbers.

2. Track your time and eliminate the #1 time-waster—this could be a needy client that you have to set stricter parameters around or it can be a bad habit such as getting lost in social media.

3. Every meeting needs to have an agenda, goal, and end time.

4. Cut down on small talk without being rude. An easy phrase is, "I'm in the middle of something."

5. Batch your email—I prefer twice per day. If you're constantly checking email, then you're letting others prioritize your time. Don't check your email first thing in the morning.

6. Set time limitations around social media.

7. Make restaurant reservations—a stitch in time saves nine.

Change it Up

You're way too busy to read this chapter right now. You have too many fires that need to be put out. You have 25 browser tabs open filled with tasks that need tasking. When life gets overwhelming, your default is to double-down and work harder. To power through it. You tell yourself to get up an hour earlier, to skip lunch, and slosh down another coffee when you start feeling tired. You believe that once you get ahead of this particular mountain of stress, it will be smooth sailing. The problem is, it's fool's gold. As soon as you scale the mountain, an even bigger mountain presents itself. So the next time life gets overwhelming, instead of doubling down and simply doing more of what you've been doing, do the exact opposite. Change it up.

Our brain is constantly working to stay attentive. One study found that when we are listening to a boring professor or speaker, our brain is working on our behalf, rewording the lecture, making it more exciting. Our brain is trying to stimulate us into paying attention, but doing so takes energy.[158]

Our brain likes it when we change things up. When can you do more pull-ups? At the beginning of your workout or after lifting weights for two hours? Likely, at the beginning. Our brain works the same way. Focus doesn't require staring at the latest report for three hours if it isn't getting you anywhere. Rather, it's time to switch it up. According to the study, "prolonged attention to a single task actually hinders performance." We need to take strategic breaks from the same thing. It's similar to not doing push-ups for thirty minutes straight.[159]

The trouble with simple living is that, though it can be joyful, rich, and creative, it isn't simple.

— Doris Janzen Longacre

Here are some ways that we can change it up while also helping to promote healthy habits.

236

The 20-20-20 Rule

We don't know the long-term ramifications of looking at our devices all day, but we do know the short term impact. The average eye blink rate is 18 times per minute (tpm), and goes down to 4 tpm when working off a digital device. This represents a decrease of 70%. The blue light we are constantly staring into causes eye strain, and the main concern with eye strain is that it often causes our entire body to feel tired.

To help combat eye strain and increase productivity, I began testing the 20-20-20 rule:

1. Every 20 minutes, take a strategic break for 1-2 minutes.

2. Physically move—usually, this is as simple as standing up or walking to the drinking fountain.

3. Look at a fixed object at least 20 feet in the distance for 20 seconds (e.g, tree, sign).

The 20-20-20 rule was popularized by Dr. Jeff Anshel, a specialist in "vision ergonomics." Dr. Anshel came up with the idea after seeing many patients coming into the office with "strange" vision concerns. The only common thread he found were patients using computers for extended hours.

The basis behind the 20-20-20 rule, according to Dr. Anshel, comes from studies that found the benefits of shorter, more frequent breaks for musculoskeletal disorders. He adapted the information to the visual system.[160]

While twenty minutes works for most people, it isn't for everyone. You will need to test what works best for you. Some of you might work best in 30- or 40-minute segments. While the 20-20-20 rule works best for me, here are some other popular power break techniques.

Pomodoro Technique

The technique's name is derived from the Pomodoro tomato-shaped kitchen timer. In this method, you work for 25 minutes without interruption, then take a five-minute break. Stretch your legs, grab a glass of water, go to the bathroom. When the timer goes off again, you're back to it. The good news is that after your fourth period, you can take a longer break, 15 minutes or more.[161] I was first introduced to this technique in college when my parents purchased a learning guide for me called *Where There is a Will There is an A*. One point that has always stuck with me from that guide stressed that studying in small segments would help increase my retention and allow me to study longer. It dramatically helped improve my grades. While studying at the library, I would always take a break every twenty minutes and walk to the drinking fountain. If I needed a longer break, I'd walk to the nearby co-ed tables. Occasionally I would power nap using my textbook as a pillow—don't judge—we have all been there.

52/17

A study conducted by time-management app DeskTime finds that the most productive people work for 52 minutes, then take a 17-minute break.[162]

The secret to this method's success is the "100% dedication theory." In other words, whatever you're doing, give it your complete attention.

As DeskTime says, "During the 52 minutes of work, you're dedicated to accomplishing tasks, getting things done, making progress. Then, during the 17-minute break, you're completely removed from the work you're doing—you're entirely resting."

Pulse and Pause

This is the method endorsed by Tony Schwartz of The Energy Project. Similar to the previous techniques, it recommends alternating periods of focused work ("pulse") and rest ("pause").[163]

Each work period in the pulse and pause method is roughly 90 minutes long. Tony's research shows that "humans naturally move from full focus and energy to physiological fatigue every 90 minutes. Our body sends us signals to rest and renew, but we override them with coffee, energy drinks, and sugar...or just by tapping our own reserves until they're depleted."[164]

My recommendation, as it is throughout this book, is to test these methods to determine what works for you. The common thread is that strategic brain breaks are helpful. For me, the 20-20-20 rule works best, but for you, it might be something else.

Alcoholics Anonymous' 12 Steps

If you have ever gone through a 12-step program, you may know that it is based on overcoming alcohol addiction. As a result of its longevity and success, the 12 Steps of Alcoholics Anonymous has been used as the basis for many other programs.

We can utilize particular techniques from these programs to help us better focus. One such approach helps us determine what *not* to do; it helps us decide what makes our "not to do" list.

Several studies have proven that it's possible to formulate an addiction to our smartphones and social media. If you get anxious when your phone isn't nearby, that behavior is an addiction—there is no other word for it. While in most cases it's not as severe as an addiction to drugs, alcohol, or pornography, it is still an addiction that must be addressed.

Original 12 Steps of AA:

1. We admitted we were powerless over alcohol—that our lives had become unmanageable.

2. We came to believe that a Power greater than ourselves could restore us to sanity.

3. We made a decision to turn our will and our lives over to the care of God as we understood Him.

4. We made a searching and fearless moral inventory of ourselves.

5. We admitted to God, to ourselves, and to another human being the exact nature of our wrongs.

6. We are entirely ready to have God remove all these defects of character.

7. We humbly asked Him to remove our shortcomings.

8. We made a list of all persons we had harmed and became willing to make amends to them all.

9. Made direct amends to such people wherever possible, except when to do so would injure them or others.

10. We continued to take personal inventory, and when we were wrong, promptly admitted it.

11. We sought through prayer and meditation to improve our conscious contact with God as we understood Him, praying only for knowledge of His will for us and the power to carry that out.

12. We had a spiritual awakening as the result of these steps, we tried to carry this message to alcoholics, and we practice these principles in all our affairs.[165]

In their original format, relating these 12 steps to the addiction of the ping, bling, and buzz of our phones may be difficult. However, if you look at the summary of the components of the 12 steps as defined by the American Psychological Association, it's easier to see the application to our struggle:[166]

- Admitting that one cannot control one's addiction or compulsion;

- Recognizing a higher power that can give strength;

- Examining past errors with the help of a sponsor (experienced member);

- Making amends for these errors;

- Learning to live a new life with a new code of behavior;

- Helping others who suffer from the same addictions or compulsions.

If your or a loved one's lack of focus is primarily the result of addiction to something constantly, including your phone, social media, substances, etc., a 12-step program and group can help.

> *It takes as much energy to wish as it does to plan.*
> — Eleanor Roosevelt

Does Your Personality Change as You Age?

For many of us, our newfound focus is creating a "new me."

As we do this, many of us ponder the question: Are we stuck with the personality we are born with, or does it change and grow over time?

For centuries, personality was viewed as something we were born with and stuck with. It led to widely accepted maxims like *a leopard can't change its spots.*

Over the past few decades, this belief has been challenged. Many now believe that individuals have the power to become better people by consciously and purposefully altering one's personality traits.

As a glass 100% full kind of person—it's half-filled with oxygen and half-filled with water—I strongly believe positive changes are always possible. However, does science prove this transformation can occur?

Over 50 years of data have helped provide insights to the question: Are we stuck with the personality we are born with, or does it change as we grow?

The studies show that while some components of a person's personality remain concrete over the years, others can change in significant ways. One study specifically focuses on people's personalities between high school and retirement—a 50-year span of time.

For the most part, these changes are positive. "On average, everyone becomes more conscientious, more emotionally stable, and more agreeable," said lead study author Rodica Damian, assistant professor of psychology at the University of Houston. Traits such as consideration, congeniality, and emotional stability are also traits that last over the years.[167]

According to a study published in the *Journal of Psychology and Aging*, one's personality changes with age. Participants with an average age of 77, were tasked with filling out a personality assessment measuring the characteristics they rated themselves on as teens. Personality changes are often gradual but over the long haul, these changes are much easier to see.[168]

These researchers found virtually no major similarities other than the stability of mood and conscientiousness. It almost seemed as if the participants were two different people at the two different stages of their lives. There was the teenage self and the 77-year-old self. "The longer the interval between two assessments of personality, the weaker the relationship between the two tends to be. Our results suggest that when the interval is increased to as much as 63 years, there is hardly any relationship at all."[169]

Hence, several studies indicate that personalities do, in fact, change with age. Sometimes, these changes can be minuscule, but other times, especially between longer time spans, changes can be quite remarkable.

Car Crash Experiment

In their 1974 Car Crash Experiment, Loftus and Palmer aimed to reveal how our memories can often deceive us. The two were especially interested in how questions to an eyewitness could affect how the witness remembered the event. By simply changing how a question is phrased, could a witness's recall be changed?

In the first experiment, the participants were presented with video clips of traffic accidents. Following exposure to the video, the participants were asked to describe the collision.

Specific questions followed, including, "About how fast were the cars going when they (smashed/collided/bumped/hit/contacted) each other?" Based on the verb used (smashed, collided, bumped, hit, and contacted) the participants' answers varied.

More aggressive verbs like "smashed" led the participants to believe that the car was going faster. Lighter terms like "hit" led the participants to recall the car's speed to be slower.

The findings of the experiment indicate that different words used in questioning affect participants' perceptions and recall.

As it relates to our mission of focus, this experiment sheds light on the old adage that words matter— the words we say to others as well as the words in our "self-talk" really matter. What words are we focused on in our self-talk? Slightly modifying these words to be more positive can drive dramatic results. What you want to avoid is becoming a black belt at beating yourself up with your self-talk.[170,171]

CHAPTER SUMMARY

The One Big Thing

The mind is a terrible thing to waste. While we are often militant about carving out time to improve our bodies, we rarely carve out time for our minds.

Grade: *C*+

My grade for this month was a C+, but a vast improvement over my general lack of mindfulness. While I needed to dedicate more time and practice around mindfulness, I was now headed (pun) in the right direction.

Top Takeaways

1. Purposefully doing nothing is sometimes the best thing to be doing.

2. Be present.

3. Change it up and your mind will perk up.

Giving

Studies show we feel better when we volunteer to help others. I don't need research to tell me this. Volunteering always fills my cup. Yet, with a hectic schedule, finding time is a challenge. Starting this month, I'm going to stop *finding* time and start *making* time for volunteering. I will begin by volunteering every Sunday at our church. Not a huge commitment compared to many of you, but a giant step in the right direction for me.

Before I undertook this project, when life got hectic, (which, frankly, was all the time), the first item I stole time from was volunteering. This wasn't right then and is not right now. I need to turn *"wanting to volunteer"* into *"I must volunteer."*

The following stories and modules might seem to be "off topic" when it comes to being charitable, but a eureka moment for me this month was understanding that the better I was able to focus during non-charitable or non-volunteering activities, the more time I would have to donate to charitable contributions later that same day or week. Many of the studies and stories we cover in this chapter are around how we can be more productive with, and protective of, our time which results in a better ability to give of our time, treasures, and talents to those that need them.

Fill Someone's Bucket

My 7-year-old daughter's New Year's Resolution was to fill someone's bucket each day. The idea stemmed from the book *Have You Filled a Bucket Today? A Guide to Daily Happiness for Kids* by Carol McCloud.

> *If you want happiness for an hour—take a nap.*
> *If you want happiness for a day—go fishing.*
> *If you want happiness for a year—inherit a fortune.*
> *If you want happiness for a lifetime—help someone else.*
>
> — Chinese Proverb

The theme of the book is that all of us have invisible buckets, and they need to be filled. We can fill other people's buckets through acts of kindness. Conversely, bullying or saying snide remarks about someone might trick us into feeling good in the moment, but such behavior steals from another person's bucket. The joy you steal from that person's bucket can't be placed into your bucket. In fact, bullying, berating, or other negative activities depletes not only the other person's bucket, but your bucket as well.

Instead of asking my daughters what they did that day, the response to which every parent knows is, "nothing," I began asking, "Whose bucket did you fill today? Whose day did you make better? Who made you smile today? Asking these questions—and expecting their answers—helped me begin looking for buckets to fill, and I was grateful when someone filled mine as well.

It's also helping me avoid becoming upset about little things, and they're all little. *"I told the waiter three times no cheese on my kid's hamburger. How hard is it to do your job!"* While it's easier said than done, when I'm feeling upset this month, I'm pausing, breathing, and trying to flip the situation by asking "whose bucket can I fill?"

Say My Name

Knowing people's names is a great way of showing gratitude. Unfortunately, remembering names isn't my strength. To give myself a fighting chance, I put notes in my phone on where I'm most likely to bump into that person (e.g., school, restaurant, basketball game, work). That way, when I pick up my dry cleaning, I know it is Kirstin not Kristine.

Another good practice whenever you're introduced to someone, is to say, "It's great to *see* you," versus "It's great to *meet* you," helping you avoid embarrassment in case you have already met them a few times.

Remember the kid that gave up? Neither do I.

Saying No to the Number 7

During the process of editing this book, I used a trick a school superintendent gave me. She said that I should never use the number seven on a rating scale.

$$ \text{—} 1 \cdot 2 \cdot 3 \cdot 4 \cdot 5 \cdot 6 \cdot \cancel{7} \cdot 8 \cdot 9 \cdot 10 \text{ —} $$

I had my family, friends, fans, and team read through this book and rate each section on a scale of 1-10. The one twist was that they couldn't use the number 7 when assigning their ratings. They could give a section any number, say, 3, 5, or 9, but they could never give it a 7.

We only wanted the "cream of the crop" to be included in the book. As such, we made the rule that any section below an 8 would automatically be cut from the book.

The process of "No 7s" is very practical for evaluating much of what we do. Removing the number 7 changes everything. You either have to give the person an 8 or 6. An 8 is a pretty great score, but a 6 is barely a passing grade. So, by removing the safety of the 7, the whole dynamic alters. Most of us naturally default to a safe place when faced with difficult questions; hence, most of us use 7 out of 10 as a crutch. No 7s removes the crutch.

This method was particularly useful when checking in with my family or members of my team.

How often do you find yourself asking someone how they're doing? Often they robotically answer "good" or "great." Many of us will even say we are "great" when we are actually down in the dumps. It's similar to the answer we give a waiter who asks us how our meal is. Unless the food is toxic, we usually just chirp, "good"—even when it's utter garbage.

In working with teams throughout my career, I find it strange that companies only have annual employee reviews. This is insanity. Stemming from the belief that it's imperative to check-in in with teammates on a daily, not annual basis, I started the practice of asking my teammates and family members, "On a scale of 1-10, how are you doing?"

With these check-ins, I started to give two parameters—remember that focusing the question will help focus the response. The two guiding lights:

1. You can't say 7.
2. You can't say 10—nobody is perfect—9.99 is an acceptable answer; 10 is not.

Now here is the key to properly doing this—most people will make a common mistake, which is exactly what I did at first, and I want to help you avoid this mistake. Let's take a look.

I'd ask my teammates how they were on a scale of 1-10 with work, and that's it. In theory, it makes sense. We are at work, so let's talk about work. Especially if I'm the team lead, I need to be careful not to get too personal or make anyone feel uncomfortable. However, the key I discovered is to ask our teammates how they're doing in totality—family, health, work, spiritually, and beyond. Asking this broader question is not only being a good human being, but it also provides context.

Here's the initial conversation—before I learned to ask about life:

> Me: Sarah, how are you on a scale of 1-10?
>
> Sarah: I'd say probably an 8 or 9.

Woohoo! She's one happy teammate. Then, the next day or week I would ask her the same question.

> Me: Sarah, how are you on a scale of 1-10?
>
> Sarah: I'm around a 3 [sigh].

Holy smokes! Sound the alarms, what did we do this week to upset Sarah? If she's a 3, she might be leaving the company! She's so valuable to our team and we love her positive attitude. What have we been doing to make her feel so bad? I start freaking out in my head with various doomsday scenarios because, wait for it...I have no context.

I have no idea if Sarah's dog is sick, if she has recently lost money in the stock market, if her parents have decided to divorce, or if she's going through a bad break-up with her partner. I have no context. To help get context I now ask for a 1-10 rating for life and then for work.

> Me: Sarah, on a scale of 1-10 how are all things with life?
>
> Sarah: I'm around a 3 [sigh].
>
> Me: What about work, the team?
>
> Sarah: An 8.

Now I have context. Now, I understand that work is a positive influence in her life. If Sarah feels comfortable, we can chat about what's troubling her and if I can help her.

Work-life harmony is imperative. If Sarah isn't her best self at work, she's not going to be her best self at home and vice versa. Both impact the other. Some might think it's crazy for companies to have work events that invite the employee's entire family. Personally, I think it makes all the sense in the world. Why not include the entire circle of people playing a role? It also dawned on me that being charitable isn't simply just donating money or time to the local soup kitchen, but it's also about being charitable with your loved ones and those at work. Taking time to show that you genuinely care.

Remember that people don't care what you know until they know that you care.

The Ben Franklin Effect:
Asking for Favors Makes People Like You More

It's normal to feel anxious or uncomfortable when asking others for favors. Human nature makes us apprehensive of burdening others with our problems. We fear that asking others for help may cause them to dislike us.

Benjamin Franklin didn't think this way; he practiced the exact opposite. At one point in Franklin's political career, he was tasked with winning over another statesman, a statesman who adamantly opposed Franklin's policies.

This particular politician owned a very rare copy of a book. Franklin, who loved to read, wrote the politician a letter asking to borrow the book. The man said yes, and within a few days of reading, Franklin kindly returned the book with a note thanking him. After this exchange, the politician was noticeably kinder and more accommodating to Franklin. The two men eventually became lifelong friends.

Franklin strongly believed that asking someone for a favor made people like him more.[172] But, is this really true? Can asking someone for something actually make a person like us more?

In 1969, almost two centuries after Franklin, two psychologists, Jon Jecker and David Landy, set out to test this theory. They separated participants into three groups. A secretary told one group of the participants that the psychology department had paid for the study and that funds were almost gone and asked if they could please return the money. The experimenter told the second group of participants that he had personally paid for the study and that funds were running low, then asked if he could have the money back. The third group was given their money to keep. The study found that volunteers who were approached by the experimenter himself to return the money preferred the experimenter the most. Those who were allowed to keep the money liked the experimenter the least. This shows that Franklin's theory holds some truth—people like you more when you personally ask them for a favor.

Psychologist Yu Niiya of Hosei University in Tokyo, conducted a similar study in the U.S. and Japan. The study found that participants liked other participants better when they asked for help. Yet, they didn't like a participant more when asked by the experimenter to help that participant. In other words, when a "middleman" was asking for the favor on behalf of someone else. Most people enjoy being charitable and prefer that the person needing the favor ask them directly rather than asking someone else on his or her behalf.

While we are all about being charitable this month, *part of giving is actually asking*. By asking for help, you're allowing that person to give some of herself, to be charitable—to experience all the positive feelings that come along with it.[173]

Also, when someone else proactively asks to help you don't deny them the opportunity of doing you the favor. It actually makes them feel better about themselves and they accomplish something for you, so it's a win-win. This is often difficult for many of us to embrace. We are often stubborn and simply say, "I got it," or we don't accept the helping hand. We don't want to burden others. Flip your mindset and understand that when you allow someone to do you a favor you're helping make that person feel good too!

So do yourself a favor this month, allow someone to help you. Ask for a favor, and give the concept of No 7 a try!

Financially Focused

For most of you embarking on your own focus projects, finances will be high on the list. Whether getting out of debt or diversifying a portfolio, aligning your finances and having a plan for the future requires focus.

The reason finances weren't on my list for this particular project was that a few months prior to this project I'd done a deep dive on getting our finances in order. From reading numerous financial books and listening to and interviewing some of the world's top financial minds, here is the broad summary on financial focus:

1.   Start saving today—try to set aside 10% of your income.
2.   Don't take on credit card debt—or if you do—get out of it ASAP.
3.   Having your money in the stock market is less dangerous than having it on the sidelines waiting for the right moment to invest. Nobody can time the market.
4.   Invest in Index funds, not individual stocks—the best pros in the world over the long term can't beat index funds.
5.   Diversify (real estate, stocks, index funds from different verticals, countries, bonds, CDs, etc.).
6.   Invest in items that have recurring payouts (rental properties, index funds with dividends, etc.).

7. Don't pay hidden management fees—these add up over time.

8. Be disciplined and play the long game—time is your friend and compound interest is your best friend.

9. Don't forget rule #8.

If we can save more, then we can give more to others. A great formula.

Anticipating & Avoiding Distractions

In order to be charitable with our time, we need to learn to not be wasteful with our time. Especially when it comes to work.

In the office, nearly 50% of employees work for only 15 minutes before becoming distracted[174] and it takes us up to 25 minutes to return to task, if we return to the original task at all.[175] Microsoft Research Labs found that following interruptions, such as an email, participants moved to a different task 40% of the time.

> *It is not the man who has too little, but the man who craves more, that is poor.*
> — Seneca

Over half of us report wasting an hour or more a day because of disruptions. Unrelenting email inboxes, the chatty office janitor, feelings of fatigue or stress, almost anything can cause us to lose focus.[176]

To uncover the consequences of constant interruptions, *The New York Times,* in conjunction with Carnegie Mellon, designed an experiment to determine the extent of brain loss in the moment of interruption. For the test, participants were separated into three different groups and asked to complete a task. During the task, the participants experienced various levels of interruption.

For ease, we will call the groups:

1. Group 1:   Zen (at peace, no interruption)

2. Group 2:   Interrupted

3. Group 3:   High Alert (waiting for an interruption)

You would expect the Zen group to perform better and for both the Interrupted and High Alert groups to struggle. This was, in fact, the case, which isn't surprising. The surprise was how much they struggled. The interrupted groups both had 20% more errors than the Zen group. How significant is this? That is the equivalent of turning a B-student into a failing student (62 percent). Interruptions, even when we get back to our task, contribute to an increase in brain loss and error rate.

The second part of the test got really interesting, as the High Alert group actually wasn't interrupted this time. Without the expected interruption, they ended up improving their performance by 44% and outperformed the control group! Training ourselves to anticipate distractions can dramatically help us, even when no interruption takes place.

Also, many of us excel when there is a deadline. In fact, many of us can't function if we aren't given a deadline. Another reason to block a specific time for our most important task is that this hard stop can potentially improve our decision-making and productivity. We should always give ourselves a deadline for anything we want to tackle. It's difficult for us to give ourselves deadlines because then it becomes "real," but that is exactly the point.[177]

Due to the high costs of distractions some organizations implement systems that limit them or ban them entirely (e.g., internal emails). Jamey Jacobs, a vice president at Abbott Vascular, uncovered that 200 of his employees expressed anxiety over juggling projects while also having to respond to emails.

To combat this, Jacobs promoted the use of phone calls. This resulted in projects being completed more quickly and more efficiently.[178] Jacobs's actions helped his team break the habit of defaulting to emailing or texting when a simple phone call would suffice.

If you're constantly being interrupted by fellow employees, instant messages, or phone calls, reserve a small conference room for a block of time, grab your laptop, and crank away. If you're at your home, go to a local coffee house or a park to avoid interruptions. Another trick is to wear your phone's earbuds even when you aren't on a call. People will be less likely to interrupt you.

Writers have known for years the importance of focus to churn out their best work. Often they seek solitude in a remote location void of distractions. We don't all have to become David Thoreau, who spent two years in the woods writing *Walden* (1854), but moving our lifestyles a little in that direction during certain seasons is a positive step.

Just like writers, teams from the National Football League and Major League Baseball go to remote locations for their training camps. The NFL teams go to small towns outside their respective cities for a few weeks, while MLB has spring training in small, warm-weather towns. Companies often hold offsite meetings or retreats, in remote or naturally beautiful locations. Anything we can do to help simplify our lives is a win. Consider the following story about Alan Mullaly, the former CEO of Ford.

There are two types of distractions—external and internal. External are the annoying laugh in the office, the loud train outside your window, co-worker stopping by to chat, or the flight attendant babbling on the intercom. We often consider these sensory items to be our main distractions, but our main distractions are actually internal.

The internal distractions are the constant chatter we have in our minds, which are often emotional. If we are having a tiff with our significant other, we find concentrating on anything else to be challenging. Hence, we have the adage, "never go to bed angry." To ensure proper rest, it's best to resolve any arguments; otherwise, we will be in for a long, sleepless night. The reason? Both our attention span and emotions are housed in the same part of our brains—the prefrontal cortex.[179]

Our brain is designed to resolve issues of stress so that we can put them away. But, until they're resolved, our brain will keep wrestling with them.

When David Thoreau escaped to Walden Pond, he realized he could leave the external distractions behind, but that he was still there and his mind couldn't be left behind in Boston. Having no external distractions allowed him to allocate more energy to resolving his internal conflict—who he was and wanted to become.

According to Jonathan Schooler of UC Santa Barbara, your mind is wandering at least 30% of the time when you're doing your normal day-to-day tasks, and in some cases—for example, when driving on an open highway, it might be as high as 70%.[180]

Perhaps you've experienced this on a recent drive, where you snap to attention and are scared because you don't really remember driving for the last thirty minutes.

There are some benefits when our mind wanders. It sometimes increases our creativity and problem solving ability. Our brain should not be 100% focused all the time, nor can it be. The goal isn't completely stopping the mind from wandering, the goal is being able to avoid distractions and interruptions and focusing when we need to.

Texting While Driving is More Dangerous than Drinking While Driving

Information about texting while driving exposes the dark side of multitasking. If you have been imploring your teenager, husband, or wife to avoid texting or tweeting when they're behind the wheel, but they haven't changed their habits, please show them these sobering results from a test conducted by *Car & Driver Magazine* in which two drivers' reaction times were observed.

Specifically, *Car & Driver* found that compared to a baseline of attentive driving, drunk drivers traveling at 70 MPH (103 feet/second) took 8 feet longer to react to danger and begin braking their vehicle. By contrast,

test results showed that texting drivers took 40 feet longer to react and begin braking. Importantly, the texting drivers reacted five (5) times *slower* than the drunk drivers. Multi-tasking can crash your car, your business, your health...your life.

Ford's Focus

During Alan Mulally's tenure at Ford, I was fortunate to share the speaking stage with him. I was transfixed by his story. Coming to Ford from Boeing, Mulally found several issues within the company culture surprising. One surprise occurred when he pulled into the executive parking lot—not a single Ford was in sight! Land Rovers, Jaguars, and Aston Martins—brands Ford had acquired over the years—were being washed, waxed, and buffed. Right there, Mulally knew change was coming. Ford had zero chance of turning around its brand if the executives were focusing on numerous luxury brands, cars that the average person couldn't afford.

Moreover, the number of brands under Ford was causing confusion in the marketplace. As Mulally states, "Nobody buys a 'house of brands.'" Thereafter, the teams concentrated on shining and buffing the Ford brand.

Deciding what not to do is just as important as deciding what to do. This central idea is what focusing is all about. As mentioned earlier in the book, your not-to-do list—Your *Not Yet List*—determines your to-do list.

Mulally focused over 200,000 employees across the globe on growing the Ford brand. The concept was called One Ford. The One Ford Innovation Plan was as simple as 1-2-3:

1.   Bring all Ford employees together as a global team.

2.   Leverage Ford's unique automotive knowledge and assets.

3.   Build cars and trucks that people want and value.

To remind everyone at the company of the One Ford strategy, Mulally had credit-card-sized plastic plates distributed to all employees. One side read, "One Ford" while the other side read, "One Team. One Plan. One Goal." Mulally carried spares of these One Ford cards in his pockets in case employees couldn't produce theirs when prompted. Despite living in a digital era, we still find physical items to be effective, helpful reminders (recall the red paper clips from earlier in this book). Mulally believed that, "The more each of us knows what we're really contributing to, the more motivated and excited and inspired we are."

Training/Practice

As explained throughout this project, a key to focusing is to inhibit whatever causes us not to focus, both internally and externally.

> *Information is gushing at our brains like a fire hose pointed at a tea cup.*
> —Scott Adams

Neuroscientists administer a popular test called the "stroop" test, involving a series of the words for various colors. These words are printed either in the color grey or black. Volunteers are asked to read aloud the *color* of the word (grey or black), not the *word* itself. It's much easier for our brain to read a word than to identify a color. Hence, in the example listed below, our brains have a strong desire to read answer d as "Grey" (the text of the word) versus the actual color itself (which is obviously black).

a. Black

b. Grey

c. Black

d. Grey

Not to read answer d as "Grey" requires us to suppress an automatic response. Advances in technology have allowed scientists to use sophisticated scanners to determine that our brains are actively working to override our natural responses. This activity occurs the most in the left ventrolateral prefrontal cortex (VLPFC)—sitting behind the right and left temple. In a sense we simply can't help ourselves from saying that it's the color grey, even though we can clearly see that grey is black!

David Rock, author of *Your Brain at Work*, discusses the brain in the way that one would a car. Using this metaphor, Rock explains that the brain has many different "accelerators/gas pedals" with different parts of the brain involved in language, emotions, movement, and memories. Yet there is only one central braking system used for all types of braking. Hence our brain has many gas pedals, but only one brake.

> If you were a car company and were building a new type of on-road vehicle you would make sure the braking system was made out of the most robust materials possible because brake failure is not a happy thing. Well, in the case of human brains, the opposite has happened. Our braking system is part of the most fragile, temperamental, and energy-hungry region of the brain, the prefrontal cortex. Because of this, your braking system only works at its best every now and then. If cars were built like this you'd never survive your first drive down to the store. All this makes sense when you consider it: stopping yourself from acting on an urge is something you can do sometimes, but is often not that easy. Not thinking about an annoying, intrusive thought at times can be very difficult. And staying focused, well sometimes that appears downright impossible.[181]

Taking Rock's analogy one step further, the key to braking properly is understanding problematic conditions. Are the roads icy? Is it getting dark? The key to driving a car with bad breaks is to avoid these difficult conditions.

Similarly, we need to be mindful of what we are doing. Like a car's ABS (automatic braking system) we should constantly pause to ask ourselves: Am I working on what I was ten minutes ago or did I get distracted? Is what I'm working on what I should be working on? In short, make sure to pump the breaks periodically in your life to ensure you're headed in the right direction.

Treat Time Like Tomato Farmers

Part of a tomato farmer's success is built on how many tomatoes he can pick in an hour. The more productive and efficient he is at picking tomatoes, the more tomatoes he can sell.

In a study of tomato pickers across 820 fields, Paul Green, a doctoral candidate at Harvard Business School, tested the impact of unexpected interruptions on the farmers.

Farmers were periodically interrupted for two reasons:

1.   the truck broke down and they would need to help repair it,

or

2.   they had to wait on an empty truck to arrive.

Would you be surprised that the two scenarios above had dramatically different results on their productivity following interruption? Do you think these breaks made them more or less productive?

It turns out that after fixing the truck and returning to the tomato picking, the farmers became less productive. Green credits this change in productivity with a cost of refocusing, "When you have an unexpected work-related task come up, it means you're changing your mental focus to another activity. Changing it back to your regular job isn't easy. This involves a re-start cost, when you have to get back into the flow of things, and that takes a little while."

The second group did not pay the same kind of "restart cost" from their unexpected wait for an empty truck. Instead, they became more productive after their break. They didn't know how long the wait would be, so they didn't start additional activities. These breaks lasted an average of ten minutes and their average productivity gain was 12.81% right after the break. Green considers these quick breaks as "opportunities to recharge without losing focus."

The majority of us aren't picking tomatoes; rather, we are most likely staring at a screen most of the day. So, what does this have to do with us? The same researchers performed a similar test on office workers, and their findings were similar. The workers who were randomly interrupted, this time by their computers freezing up (equivalent to the tomato truck not showing up), reported more accuracy and productivity—15% to 20%—right after they returned from the break. As Green indicates, the key to this success was that the office workers and tomato farmers "didn't change their focus...they kept their minds on standby. Your mind and body get the benefit of mindless rest."[182]

Don't Let Bad Days or Losses Pile Up

Michael Parrish Dudell is the author of the bestselling *Shark Tank* books. These books give readers insights into the personalities of the entrepreneurs appearing on the award-winning television show. For both books, Dudell was given seemingly impossible timelines to complete the task—in one instance he was only allowed three months to put the entire book together.

I asked him to share the secrets that allowed him to produce great content in such a short amount of time. His response, "Well first, when I'm writing, I'm writing. I try to make that my sole focus as much as possible, whether that is bunkering down in a coffee shop or going to a remote place in Florida to get away from it all. The second thing is that when I've had a day when I didn't write or writing was just simply a struggle, I don't let those days get me down, but I also don't let them pile up, either. I need to make certain I keep the momentum going. If my plan was to write 2,000 words one day, but I only knocked out 100 words, then the next day it's essential I get back on track. The next day I write 3,901 words—meaning I doubled it up plus one additional word."

This attitude is common to numerous top performers like Dudell. Whatever our goals are, we will have days when we simply miss the mark. The key is that the next day we wrestle back that control. If your goal is to do 10 pull-ups per day but then your daughter unexpectedly needs to go to the doctor, shrug it off and the next day try to do 2 sets of 10 pull-ups. The key is not to let the losses pile up. If you miss a day or two, no big deal. Give yourself a break. However, if you were to go six weeks without working out, it's probably not realistic to do 140 pull-ups in a day or write 28,000 words in a day. That's not how it works.

Treat Your Body and Mind Like an iPhone

We've touched on the relationship between willpower and ego depletion. Thinking about your mind and body like a smartphone can help us better navigate the day. At night, we always charge our smartphone. We also do this for our bodies by sleeping. When we wake up, we are at full battery. Then we think about every decision facing us. Just the thought of these decisions drains our batteries, both mentally and physically.

Although the brain amounts to less than 2% of our body weight, the average person burns about 320 calories a day just by thinking.[183] These numbers mean that roughly 20% of our energy consumption per day is from thinking.[184] Whether it be as mundane as washing the dishes or as complex as learning to speak another language, when we are thinking and acting, the brain is consuming a substantial amount of energy and draining our batteries. Recall the ways to recharge during the day—taking a quick twenty-minute power nap, getting into nature, grabbing some fresh air, meditating, exercising, etc. While these recharging exercises should be performed, equally important is to avoid unnecessarily draining our batteries in the first place. Avoid draining your brain's batteries over little daily decisions such as figuring out what to wear, what to eat for breakfast, where to park, and other such concerns. Put systems in place to make them automatic.

Negative thoughts are also strong brain-drains, decreasing the capacity to think, reason, and form memories.[185] Thinking positively and avoiding negative thoughts like jealousy, pessimism, stress, and worry are all beneficial ways to prolong your brain's battery life.

Keeping goals on our 'to-do list' that we aren't actively working on can still play a role in draining our batteries. Again, we need to think about our brains in the way that we use our phones. When we aren't engaging with or using a particular app, we should close it out. Remember the last time you drove somewhere and then an hour later you grabbed your phone out of your purse and your battery was dead? What happened? You had accidentally left the mapping app open long after you had arrived. You weren't even using it, and it depleted your battery.

Our brains are like our phones. We need either to engage with an issue or close the damn thing out. We cannot let important but unaddressed details run in the background draining our batteries.

Mile-High Friendship

I settled into my seat for my flight to San Francisco. Our animation studio was working on a piece for Disney, and I was engrossed in my phone sending some last-minute creative direction. With the plane taking off, I put my phone away and felt someone grab my arm. Across the aisle was one of my best friends.

We'd been trying to get together for lunch for several weeks, but both our hectic travel schedules wouldn't allow for it. We laughed at how long it took us to notice each other.

While we both had plenty of work to do on the plane, we spent two hours chatting on the flight and then shared a ride into the city. It was the highlight of my week. Nothing work-related was more important than this friendship.

What a shame it would've been had we never noticed we were sitting by one another.

Reduce Stress by Attacking It

For items we deem worthy of our time, Amazon founder Jeff Bezos says we need to attack the associated stress of these projects head on. Stress is often caused by the projects or items that we aren't doing but we know that we should be doing. According to Bezos, hard work doesn't cause stress; in fact, working hard on the issue causing you stress can often resolve the item causing your stress.

Also, let's remember that the word *stress* is an adult term for *fear*. Let's embrace what some SCUBA instructors pass onto their students. FEAR is simply False Evidence Appearing Real.

You Deserve a Focus Break

When the McDonald brothers started their first restaurant, they had 27 items in their old fashioned drive-in. They had speaker boxes with waitresses on roller skates taking orders from customers seated comfortably in their cars. However, they soon recognized that 87% of the orders were for hamburgers, fries, and soft drinks.

> *The trick isn't adding stuff, it's taking away.*
> — Mark Zuckerberg

They decided to shut down a good business to reinvent a simpler one. They would focus their efforts by dramatically reducing the menu to just hamburgers, fries, and soft drinks. To brainstorm, they went to some empty tennis courts to map out a radically redesigned kitchen and had their staff practice mock-making hamburgers and fries. They used chalk to draw and modify the kitchen until they got the process flow just right. All orders would now be walk-up orders instead of having waitresses on roller skates delivering to customers in cars.

This reinvented business would all be based around simplification and speed.

The brothers had a grand re-opening, but instead of a bunch of customers, a torrent of flies showed up. The flies finally subsided. After a disappointing day, they were ready to close when a kid walked up to order a hamburger and then another person showed up, then another, then another, and the rest is history. It's estimated McDonald's has now served over 300 billion hamburgers.

One Key

My 96-year-old grandfather graduated from Princeton, served in the Navy during WWII, and, as a chemist, wrote the formula for Stroh's Signature Beer. He also surrounded himself with other interesting people. During one particular conversation with my grandfather, a man I didn't recognize joined us. I asked the men what they thought the key to a happy life was. "You've already said the word, young man, *key*," he said as he pulled out a single house key, "I've worked very hard during my life to get to this one key. You see, the more keys you have the more things that can weigh you down, that can own you. You might think that success looks like a lot of keys to houses, boats, cars, art studios...Well, I'm here to tell you it's the exact opposite. It's one of the hardest things in the world, but if you can get to one key, there is no doubt in my mind that you will be happy."

This type of simplicity is also powerful in business. When I was the Head of Marketing for a very successful Internet company, Travelzoo, we had a new employee come in to give us ideas about our email newsletter—an email that had amassed over 30 million subscribers. In a meeting, this new employee brashly piped that we should make the newsletter more robust and snazzy by adding more images and video to it.

The room went silent as we all pondered the suggestion when our founder and CEO replied,

> Why, might I ask, would we want to throw away the many years of hard work and sweat that went into creating the newsletter in the simple state we have today? I would never want to burden our readers with the complexity you suggest.

Stepping into Discomfort

Whether it's helping a stranger, re-inventing our company, or re-inventing ourselves, we need to learn to step into discomfort.

Marcus Porcius Cato the Younger, better known simply as *Cato,* was a Roman senator credited with bringing Stoicism into the mainstream. He emphasized that because "virtue is sufficient for happiness," a sage would be emotionally resilient to misfortune. Because of this, Julius Caesar wanted him dead. Yet, over the years, his list of admirers came to include George Washington, Dante, Benjamin Franklin, and emperor Marcus Aurelius. The Founding Fathers viewed him as a symbol of resistance to dictatorship.

One stoic method that Cato practiced can be particularly helpful in our desire to focus. Cato donned unpopular colors like black instead of the popular purples of the day. He often left his home without sandals— considered extremely taboo at the time. He'd even strut around town without his tunic. These actions would turn heads. Was he a narcissist seeking attention? Not at all. He was training himself. At first he would feel ashamed by wearing such unpopular apparel. Over time this taught him to be ashamed only of what deserves shame, and to despise all other sorts of disgrace. In other words, he had learned to focus only on what truly matters and not to worry about insignificant matters.

I've been wearing bright green classes for years. Oh, the stares I receive. Some people think they look foolish, while others love them. Like Cato, at first, I felt embarrassed, ridiculous, and ashamed. However, as the days stretched into months, I started to realize the genius behind what Cato had learned centuries ago. Learning to walk in discomfort made everything else seem more comfortable. Wearing green glasses also taught me to focus on what was important and what was not. Who cares if someone I don't know at the airport thinks I look silly wearing green glasses? It doesn't matter. These little things just don't matter. The glasses taught me only to focus on the significant areas of my life.

Go ahead and try it yourself. The next time you get up to the register at your local coffee shop, but before you order, ask if you can have a 10% discount before you order, or ask if you can have a large cup for the cost of a medium.

Similar to what the ancient philosophers discovered, actions that force us out of our comfort zones often lead us to enlightened moments. We can train ourselves not to sweat the small stuff.

Stop Lying to Yourself

Imagine it's 1959 and you're a student at Stanford participating in a research project. You're instructed to move empty thread spools around in a box, and then move pegs around on a board. Watching grass grow would be more exciting.

You finish, and the experimenter thanks you, mentioning that many other participants before you found it very interesting and stimulating. You wonder how anyone could find this interesting, but you let the comment pass.

Focus is deciding what to be bad at.

The experimenter looks baffled and quickly explains that he's sorry, but his colleague hasn't arrived, and asks if you can help with the next group. Can you stay a few minutes to explain how exciting the task is that they will be performing?

This next group will also be moving spools and pegs around. As compensation for your time, you will be paid $1—enough for a nice lunch at the time. You will also be considered for future paid experiment opportunities. You think to yourself, wow, this is great!

A student walks into the room, and you tell her about the exciting tasks she will be performing. As she leaves to perform the experiment, you feel a little guilty about the expectations you have given her. You don't have much time to reflect as they usher you into another room for your "exit interview."

In the next room you're questioned about the tasks you performed. One of the questions is about how interesting it was. Instead of blurting out "I'd rather watch grass grow," upon reflection, you think perhaps it wasn't so bad. The motion of the spools was pretty cool and having to arrange the pegs in different orders was a little stimulating. Plus, this was to benefit science and the human race. While you wouldn't rate it as super exciting, you decide to rate it as moderately interesting.

Afterwards, you go talk to a friend who did the same experiment. Interestingly enough, her experience matched yours. Yet, instead of being paid $1, she was compensated $20! You're shocked, so you ask her about her task, only to find that it was exactly the same as yours, and she remarks, "Oh, that was soooo boring."

And you surprise yourself by saying it wasn't so bad, that there were parts that were interesting.

What's going on here? What's happening is the mental conflict called cognitive dissonance. This cognitive dissonance study focused on learning how we deal with two opposing thoughts—items that contradict each other.

In this instance, when you're given $1 to tell the next student the experiment is interesting, your mind is in a jam. The money, while nice, isn't enough to justify lying, but you aren't the type of person to lie, especially to a fellow student. Therefore, your mind resolves this conflict by determining that the experiment actually wasn't that boring after all.

Your fellow student who's paid $20 doesn't have to wrestle with her thoughts very much. She was given $20 to lie, a large sum of money for a student in 1959. She justifies that lying is worth the money as well as her contribution to research and experimentation. The task to her remains boring regardless of what the researcher tells her.[186]

Since 1959 similar studies of cognitive dissonance have been helpful in understanding psychological stress when presented with contradictory ideas, beliefs, or values. Here are a few conclusions from Morton Hunt's *The Story of Psychology*:

1. The harder it is to join a group, the more you will value the membership. Once we get in, even if the club is average at best, we will convince ourselves the club is amazing.

2. We have selective attention. We look for items that support our current beliefs. This explains the difficulty of persuading folks who aren't "in the middle" during political elections. Politicians spend all their money on the middle because these people might be open to ideas, whereas those on the "edges" are not.

3. We will adjust our value system if our behavior goes against it, even when our behavior is immoral. If you're working in a movie theater and you eat the candy or popcorn when no one is looking, you justify it by saying that all employees here do it, or I'm underpaid, so this is just part of my compensation, or this popcorn will go stale and it will have to be thrown out if I don't eat it. I certainly did this when I worked at a movie theater in high school!

When focusing on our wishes and goals, we must ensure that we don't start believing our own lies.

We need to be aware of the daily cognitive dissonance we cycle through. The most prominent form is:

- ❑ "I'll start tomorrow."
- ❑ "I was too tired this morning for the gym, but I'll be sure to go tomorrow."
- ❑ "So many unexpected things happened today, tomorrow will be easier."
- ❑ "I was supposed to write 200 words for my screen play today, but I wasn't inspired. Tomorrow when I'm in the right frame of mind I will easily be able to write 400 words."

We are often lying to ourselves when we say these things. Let's face it, sleeping in and eating chocolate is fun. Focusing on what we should be doing sometimes is a grind, so we lie to ourselves.

Of course, we all experience bad days. A loved one dies, a pandemic forces us to quarantine, a child wakes up sick and needs to go to the hospital, an accident backs up traffic—life happens. However, when we focus, the days we are able to dedicate zero time to our main focus should be few and far between. Remember that focusing is often just prioritization. Many that I interviewed for this book indicated the easiest way for them to focus is simply to dedicate thirty minutes to their focus area when they first get up—before anything else can distract them.

One young woman said, "I needed to give myself permission that it is okay to still focus on my goals while I handled a certain personal situation. It sounds silly, but sometimes we simply need to give ourselves permission to continue toward a goal in the face of adversity, in the face of life."

Are You Focusing on the Right Things?

It's one thing to be focused and another to be properly focused. It's similar to being twice as fast as your grandma, but running in the wrong direction. Who do you think will win that race?

There is a story of two brothers. One drank too much and quickly became addicted to drugs. When intoxicated, he often physically abused his family.

If you help people get what they want, I've found that you will get what you want.

The other brother was a successful businessman who was respected in society and had a wonderful family.

How could two brothers from the same parents, brought up in the same environment, be so different? The first brother was asked, "How come you do what you do? You're a drug addict, a drunk, and you beat your family. What motivates you?" He responded, "My father. He was a drug addict, a drunk, and he beat his family. What do you expect me to be? That is what I am."

The same questions were asked of the other brother, "How come you're doing everything right? What is your source of motivation?" His response was the same, "My father."

"When I was a little boy, I used to see my dad drunk and doing all the wrong things. I made up my mind that is not who I am. I'm going to be the exact opposite of my father."

Both were deriving strength and motivation from the same source, but one was focused on using it positively and the other negatively. Which way are you focused? Are there others around us that we can help focus on the positive things?

Avoiding Chocolate Fondue Sushi

I'm blessed to own a small animation studio specializing in 3D and 4D stories and films for companies like Chase, Cartier, Disney, and others. We're fortunate to have wonderful relationships with our partners, but this wasn't always the case. We are in a good spot today because of our failures early in our existence.

I recall that one of our first clients wanted a two-minute film to help their salesforce generate leads. They loved the first iteration we gave them and wanted a few "minor" changes. These changes led to more changes which led to more changes.

Choosing everything is the same as choosing nothing.

Along the way, they kept taking what they liked best from each subsequent version and started cobbling them together like Frankenstein. We kept warning them that this isn't a good process for producing a great film. Specifically, if we take a little from here and add a little from there, the end result will be disjointed. It's similar to being in the kitchen and saying, "Well, I like chocolate fondue and I like sushi, so let's make chocolate fondue sushi!" Not a good idea.

We were just starting out and they were one of our first clients so we wanted to make sure they were happy. We argued internally about what to do, finally deciding, "Hey, it's their money, so if this is what they want, let's give it to them. While we might disagree with this approach, and will continually voice our concerns, let's make sure that we please them by doing specifically what they're requesting." In hindsight, by doing every request asked of us, we were doing a very poor job of guiding their focus. We weren't doing our job.

You're probably already guessing the end result. Neither party was happy. It reminds me of the Henry Ford quote, "If I asked a man what he wanted, he would have told me he wanted a faster horse."

Learning from this experience, our contracts now allow for only one revision—which is unique in the industry. This strict allowance gets all of the key decision-makers to focus from the beginning, it limits groupthink, and avoids us making films resembling chocolate fondue sushi. Having everyone focus from the start produces the best work in animation films and in life.

CHAPTER SUMMARY

Grade: *B+*

This month reminded me of the maxim: to live is to give. Give to others, give of yourself, and give yourself a break from blame and blaming. Also, much of this month related to focusing on not being wasteful with time. This allows us to have more time to give to others.

Top Takeaways

1. Move the time allocation for volunteering from the "should" column to the "must" column.

$$-1\cdot2\cdot3\cdot4\cdot5\cdot6\cdot\cancel{7}\cdot8\cdot9\cdot10-$$

2. No 7s: Using a rating scale of 1-10 while removing the number 7 is a powerful tool.

3. Asking others for favors makes them like you more—the Ben Franklin Effect.

4. Step into discomfort—every day.

Gratitude

U.S. citizens celebrate Thanksgiving on the third Thursday in November. What better month than November to focus on gratitude? Owing a debt of gratitude to many people, I was giddy at the prospect of spending blocks of time calling, writing, and texting folks to thank them.

When doing this, I planned on mixing up how I said "thanks." Studies show that as recipients, we have become accustomed to "thank you" and "thanks" as throwaway words. To mix it up this month, instead of simply saying "thanks" at my local breakfast taco joint, I'm saying, "That's cool that you remember my order when I walk in. I really appreciate you!"

> *Don't ruin an apology with an excuse.*
> — Benjamin Franklin

Setting Ourselves Up for Success

Researchers in Australia discovered that laughing makes us more persistent. People who watched a boring video before performing a difficult task were less likely to stick with it than those who watched a comedy prior to performing the same task. Those watching humorous videos had more sustaining power. Being in a better frame of mind will make one want to push harder and stay on task longer.[187]

This intuitively makes street sense. We've all had those days where we hear ourselves say, "I'm just not in the right mood to deal with this." The next time you're about to tackle a difficult task, engage in humor prior to starting. Even if the task doesn't work out well, at least you will get a good laugh.

With our minds in the right place, our results will improve. The same holds true for our stomachs. A study at Cornell University determined that what we fill our stomachs with prior to grocery shopping also matters. Those who ate an apple slice before grocery shopping bought 13 percent more fruits and vegetables than those who ate a cookie prior to hitting the aisles. "Eating the apple puts shoppers into a health-focused mindset," says study author Brain Wansink, Ph.D., Director of the Cornell University Food and Brand Lab.

Putting ourselves in the right frame of mind—whether through humor or food choice—is a step toward helping us forge an iron will.[188]

Tim Ferris in *4 ½ Hour Work Week* stresses the importance of being effective over being efficient. Instead of succumbing to every ping and treating each buzz as urgent, we become more effective if we focus on our most important personal goals.

> *Happiness does not lead to gratitude. Gratitude leads to happiness.*
> — David Steindl-Rast

Most Important Items (MIT) first is an important concept from Leo Babauta, the author of *The Power of Less*. Babauta suggests that at the end of each day you should write down the most important item that you need to accomplish or attack before you do anything else the following day. Accomplishing this task should take under one hour. The more we can relate this task to our intention and gratitude for the day, the more likely we are to accomplish it.

Happy Awake Day

An amazing wife, mother, and personal friend, Celeste Steinhelper-Wood, found herself in the fight of her life against an aggressive cancer. She posted this to the world as she entered her 11th round of chemo:

Well, as usual, on my first night of at-home chemo, I'm now wide awake at 3:00 am. Not exactly a side effect, but I think it's because I slept for 8 hours of the infusion, and my body is out of whack.

So I share with you some early day insight. I happen to really like this country song called "Happy Birthday" sung by an up and coming young female artist whose name escapes me. So, this Birthday song gets stuck in my mind often. While at the dentist this week my hygienist, whom I have known my whole life, reminded me to celebrate the days that "we are on the right side of the dirt." This got me thinking that each day is a mini-bday, more of an "awake-day." A day that needs to be celebrated on a different level.

So when you wake today don't get bogged down with the millions of things on your list. Don't worry about the guilt you feel when you don't check them all off in one day—most motherly lists would make that humanly impossible. Then you add on a worklist, family list, grocery list, back to school list, and your head spins off.

Instead, find some time to celebrate your "awake-day." Even if that just means getting coffee with a friend, a phone call, sending a card to someone, extra hugs, a jog/walk to look at nature, a cat nap, reading in the sun, helping out in your child's classroom, an out of the norm adventure with the family, ice cream, dinner dates, a movie, a family game night, dessert after dinner for no reason, French fries and ranch, your favorite glass of wine, or watching the sunset—anything to make each day a worthy "awake-day."

You got this Warriors, I know you do.

Be thankful for what you have; you'll end up having more. If you concentrate on what you don't have, you will never, ever have enough.
— Oprah Winfrey

Have a great "awake-day" on this hump day.
Love, Celeste

Celeste passed a few months after posting this. While she's now an angel in heaven, her memory and advice live on within us. In honor of our beautiful Celeste, *Happy Awake Day* to all of us.

Trading Expectations for Appreciation

Any time Ana Maria empties the dishwasher, I invariably find myself becoming upset. While she puts the knives back in the knife block, she doesn't return each knife to its specific slot. I have OCD on this. Actually I'm probably CDO—that's having OCD in alphabetical order.

All the knife handles look exactly the same in the block, and each specific knife—from a paring knife to a spreader—has its proper place. When they're in the right slot, this saves time.

A eureka-moment or practice for this month was to trade *expectations* for *appreciation*. So, instead of getting upset that the spreader was in the bread knife slot, I started being grateful and appreciative that my amazing wife is emptying the dishwasher, saving me from doing it. This led me to be appreciative of her also sorting out the kids' tiny Tupperware—my kryptonite!

My realization that, yes, the spreader is in the wrong place, but I'm coming out way ahead on all the stuff my wife does selflessly each day. This realization made me start to pitch in on cleaning the Tupperware. The more I helped with the Tupperware, the more I started to see that my wife also began to improve at putting the knives in the right slot. My eureka moment came when instead of expecting her to put away the knives correctly, I'm now appreciating all of her help and counting my lucky stars.

The same mindset holds true for complaining. Or, as Will Bowen, founder of A Complaint Free World, suggests, "Complaining is like bad breath—you notice it when it comes out of someone else's mouth, but not when it's out of your own." Over 11 million people have taken Bowne's complaint-free challenge. The challenge? Can you go 21 days without complaining? Here's how it works. Simply put a bracelet or rubber band on your wrist and every time you complain switch it to the other wrist as you are now starting over. The average person takes 4 – 8 months to complete the 21-Day challenge. But stick with it! Remember, you can't complain your way to health, happiness, or success.

The easiest way to live a happier life is to turn your expectations into appreciation.

Things Happen for You, Not to You

One day, an old farmer's horse ran away. Upon hearing the news, his neighbors came to visit. "Such bad luck," they consoled.

"Perhaps," the farmer replied.

The next morning, the horse returned, bringing with it three other wild horses. "What great luck!" the neighbors exclaimed.

"Perhaps," replied the old man.

The following day, his son tried to ride one of the untamed horses, was thrown, and broke his leg. The neighbors again came to offer their sympathy on his misfortune. "Such bad luck."

"Perhaps," answered the farmer.

The day after, military officials came to the village to draft young men into the army. Seeing that the son's leg was broken, they passed him by. The neighbors congratulated the farmer on how well things had turned out.

"Perhaps," said the farmer...[189]

The wise farmer understood that life events often happen *for* you, not *to* you. That when something bad happens, something good will probably come of it, but your eyes need to be open to see it. As Forrest Gump famously quipped, "Life is like a box of chocolates. You never know what you're going to get." But we can control our thinking into believing it will all work out for us. When we do this, it usually does have a strange way of working out. When we have a chance to be grateful, be grateful.

> *When I started counting my blessings, my whole life turned around.*
> — Willie Nelson

A Broken Smile

My daughter started inspecting my smile and a quizzical look came over her face. "Daddy, why are three of your bottom teeth more yellow than the others?"

"That's because these teeth are fake. The real ones were knocked out," I explained.

"Oh, I'm sorry, Daddy!"

"Don't be sorry, honey. They remind me of one of the best things that ever happened *for* me, not *to* me."

"What was it?"

I explained that growing up there was nothing I wanted to do more than to play college basketball. After I was cut from the high school team, I realized my dream was most likely not going to become a reality. However, I kept at it, and I loved basketball so much that when I arrived at Michigan State University, I became a manager for the basketball team—a waterboy. I loved being a manager, but I'd still lie awake at night dreaming of making the team as a player.

Seeing firsthand what it takes to be one of the 13 players on the country's number one ranked team, I started not only to dream, but I started to play before and after practice, as well as lift weights and run. Looking back, by my junior year I was good enough to be on the team, but unfortunately I didn't realize it at the time. I didn't have the confidence. I wasn't willing to walk into discomfort. I wasn't willing to step into my story. I didn't try out. In my mind I was constantly questioning myself, "How could I, a kid cut from his high school basketball team, play for one of the top ten programs in the country?"

Later that year, in the same week, many of the players got sick and injured. Not having enough players forced me into practice. This was my time to show the coaches—and myself—that I was more than good enough to be on the team. While I was nervous, I was performing extremely well.

Then misfortune struck.

Going up for a rebound, an elbow hit me in just the right spot to knock out three of my teeth. I already had one fake tooth. That fake tooth was the point of impact. The tooth I spat into my hand was a fake one. I did *not* realize that two real teeth had been knocked out and lay on the floor near the player's bench. I felt that this was my moment, and I was doing well, so I kept playing through the pain. I figured I could get the fake tooth replaced in the weeks ahead—this was my chance and nothing was going to stop me! Or, so I thought.

About ten minutes later, the trainer discovered the real teeth by the bench and noticed that I was still bleeding. They stopped practice and rushed me to the dentist. The entire way there I couldn't believe my rotten luck—my one chance and I'm being rushed to the dentist. The next day, Coach Izzo addressed the team, "Well Qualman, I don't know if you're the dumbest kid I know or the toughest kid I know. Probably a little of both."

At that moment, and when I made the basketball team the next year, I didn't realize that getting my teeth knocked out and continuing to play through the pain was the best thing to happen for me. Coach Izzo has built the Michigan State program on grit and grind. He saw this grit and grind in me that day, turning one of my worst days into one of my best days. The next season I made the team and eventually earned a scholarship.

Things happen *for* us, not *to* us. Even getting your teeth knocked out.

4U not 2U

Let It Go

During a lunch discussion the topic turned to how stressed we all were. My friend chimed in, "Let me show you what I just learned recently that relates to stress, and it all starts with this glass of water."

She picked up the glass of water and continued:

> The absolute weight of this (glass) doesn't matter. In fact, this glass is relatively light. But, the fact it's light or heavy doesn't matter. What matters is how long I hold it. If I hold it for a minute, that's not a problem. It's pretty light. If I hold it for an hour, my arm will start to ache.

> If I hold it for a day, you'll probably have to call an ambulance to come get me. In each case it's the same weight, but the longer I hold it, the heavier it becomes...and that's the way it is with stress. If we carry all of our burdens all of the time, they become heavier and heavier. Sooner or later we won't be able to carry on. As with the glass of water, you have to put it down for a while and rest before holding it again. When we're refreshed, we can carry on with the burden, holding stress longer and better each time.

So, as early in the evening as we can, we need to put all our burdens down. We shouldn't carry them through the evening and into the night. If we must, and only if we must, we can pick them up again tomorrow.

Joie de vivre: not only the enjoyment of life but an enthusiastic, exuberant joy of living.

Cherry on Top

In 1965 a ten-year-old boy walked up to the counter of a soda shop and climbed onto a stool. He caught the eye of the waitress and asked, "How much is an ice cream sundae?"

"Fifty cents," the waitress replied. The boy reached into his pockets, pulled out a handful of change, and began counting. The waitress frowned impatiently. After all, she had other customers to wait on.

The boy squinted up at the waitress. "How much is a dish of plain ice cream?" he asked. The busy waitress sighed and rolled her eyes. "Thirty-five cents," she said with a note of irritation.

Again, the boy counted his coins. At last, he said, "I'll have the plain ice cream, please." He put a quarter and two nickels on the counter. The waitress took the coins, brought the ice cream, and walked away.

About ten minutes later, she returned to find the ice cream dish empty. The boy was gone. She picked up the empty dish—then swallowed hard.

There on the counter were two nickels and five pennies. The boy had had enough for a sundae, but he had ordered plain ice cream so he could leave her a tip.

How much better would the world be if we put others ahead of ourselves? If we were willing to eat the ice cream without all the sprinkles, or perhaps have no ice cream at all so others could have more? Many studies speak to the fact that the more we give the more we receive, and I was finding it out firsthand this month.[190]

When you are good to others, you are best to yourself.
— Benjamin Franklin

CHAPTER SUMMARY

The One Big Thing

You can never go wrong with an attitude of gratitude.

Grade: *B*

This was one of my favorite months. The reason I'm not giving myself an A is that I realize how much I need to be grateful for each day, from the most profound (amazing wife and daughters) to the often overlooked (someone smiling at me or a sunny day). If we allow ourselves to see it, it's truly eye-opening how blessed we are just to be alive.

Top Takeaways

1. Trade expectations for appreciation.

expectations 🤝 *appreciation*

2. Be a bucket filler.

3. Things happen *for* us, not *to* us.

4U not 2U

Your Story

This is a one-sentence chapter because this month is about consistently practicing the focus habits that work for you—to begin focusing on what matters most. It's time to step fully into your story.

THE FOCUS PROJECT

[This blank page is to remind you to have
the courage and audacity to do less, but better]

> *Beware of
> the bareness
> of a busy life.*
> — Socrates

Focusing for Life

How are you? A simple question that requires a simple response. However, I realized before starting this project, my response was anything but simple. My answer was always some form of "busy" to "crazy busy." Being crazy busy is not good. "Crazy Busy" is a synonym for "I don't have control of my life." Perhaps you can relate?

While many of us walk around with a "busy badge of honor," we should be striving for the exact opposite. We should be waking up every morning with the knowledge that it will be impossible to get everything done. Acknowledging this helps relieve the burden and stress of this go-go world. And, knowing we can't possibly get everything done, we should turn our focus to what we must get done.

The cliche "life is short," like most clichés, holds some truth. We need to think of eternity as a long shoelace and our life on earth as the plastic end of it, or if you prefer the technical term, the aglet of the shoelace. The words "age" and "let" are contained in aglet. At what age will we stop letting life simply happen to us?

At what point in your life will you be intentional with every moment? This doesn't mean that every moment needs to be filled. Living every moment with intention doesn't increase the number of breaths we take; rather, doing so increases the number of moments that will take our breath away. If we live life unfocused, we will be doomed to wake up one day and realize we have wasted our gift. Our lives are determined by what we focus on every day. How we spend our days is how we spend our lives. Here's to us beginning to live intentionally right here, right now. As legendary UCLA basketball coach John Wooden always stressed, "Make every day your masterpiece."

Focusing in this unfocused world is hard. Really, really hard. But, it can be learned. It can become a habit. Fulfillment comes from growth. We all want to grow mentally, physically, and spiritually. If we live day after day without growing, the culprit is that we didn't focus on the one thing that matters most.

This problem can be fixed.

We can fix it because we control it. Taking back control rather than being at the whim of emails, interruptions, requests, and other distractions is imperative. The reason we are *crazy busy* is that we consciously and subconsciously make decisions to put too much on our plates.

If we are the ones piling stuff on our plates, we are also the ones who can stop it. The buffet of life will always be there, and we need to realize we can always go back for more. In other words, we need to break the habit of taking one item off and putting two items on. We need to do the exact opposite.

My wish is that this book helps guide you to a more focused life, your best life. While we can't do it all, we can have it all. Godspeed.

Acknowledgments

It takes a village to raise a book. This one is no exception. Ana Maria, Sofia, and Katia were willing participants in my experiment—thanks for the patience and the laughter. Our parents on both sides are always lending editorial enhancements and words of encouragement, thank you. Emily Welter's positive attitude and contributions to the book helped keep me going when I felt like stopping. The beautiful illustrations are from the talented Sahiti Rudravajhala with help from Kelsey Gomez. Kelsey also pitched in wherever needed. The book cover is the result of the tireless work of Anthony Ortiz. Round after round of edits were completed by Yvonne Harreld—she helped supply the final push to get this bird from its nest. Emily Crawford-Margison and Renee Skiles provided additional editorial support and Lorie DeWorken masterfully crafted the interior layout.

Last, but certainly not least, a heartfelt thanks to all of you—my readers and supporters. Your love and encouragement make this all possible.

Books that inspired this project and that you might enjoy:

Give and Take by Adam Grant

The 4 ½ Hour Work Week by Tim Ferriss

The Happiness Project by Gretchen Reuben

The One Thing by Gary Keller and Jay Papasan

Essentialism by Greg McKeown

Stillness is the Key by Ryan Holiday

Stop Worrying and Start Living by Dale Carnegie

Atomic Habits by James Clear

Made to Stick by Chip and Dan Heath

Purple Cow by Seth Godin

The Bible

Endnotes

In an effort to save paper, please find all endnotes for *The Focus Project* at equalman.com/endnotes

About the Author

#1 Bestselling Author and Keynote Speaker Erik Qualman has performed in over 55 countries and reached 40 million people. He was voted the 2nd Most Likeable Author in the World behind Harry Potter's J.K. Rowling.

His *Socialnomics* work has been on *60 Minutes* to the *Wall Street Journal* and used by the National Guard to NASA. Over 500 universities around the world use his materials. Qualman's animation studio wrote and produced the world's most-watched social media video "Social Media Revolution."

Qualman was Academic All-Big Ten in basketball at Michigan State University and has been previously honored as the *Alum of the Year*. A scholarship bears his name at MSU. His MBA is from the University of Texas. He is a former sitting professor at MIT and Harvard's edX. He received an honorary doctorate for his groundbreaking work. Most importantly, he's still trying to live up to the "World's Greatest Dad" coffee mug he received from his wife and two daughters.

The Focus Calendar is available for sale at equalman.com/calendar.
Get one for your unfocused friend or loved one today.

*You get what you focus on,
so focus on what you want.*

Additional Books & Resources from Erik Qualman

A must-read for the teen in your life